max maths primary

A SINGAPORE APPROACH

Workbook 5

ALICE HANSEN DANIEL COLE
TONY COTTON DR BERINDERJEET KAUR

macmillan education
INTERNATIONAL CURRICULUM

Macmillan Education
4 Crinan Street
London, N1 9XW
A division of Macmillan Publishers Limited

Companies and representatives throughout the world

www.macmillanic.com

ISBN 978-1-380-01790-1

First published 2018

Page layout, illustrations and picture research by Star Publishing Pte Ltd
Cover design by Macmillan Education
Cover illustration by Daniel Limon/Beehive Illustration Ltd

Printed and bound in Brazil

2022
20

The authors and publishers would like to thank the following for permission to reproduce their images.

Bananastock/p120(tr), 151(container)
Brand X/p152(t), 173(vanilla)
Comstock Images/p173(lemon and chocolate)
Corbis/p189(tl)
Creatas/p31(t)
Getty/p83(tr), 189(cr)
Getty Images/adventtr p151(handheld console), Getty Images/iStockphoto Thinkstock Images/Irina Drazowa-Fischer p103(r), Getty Images/iStockphoto Thinkstock Images/egal p103(l), Getty Images/Blend Images - JGI/Jamie Grill p31(c), Getty Images/Hemera/Thinkstock/Simon Krzic p102(r), Getty Images/iStockphoto Thinkstock Images/Anzor Mizaushev p189(br), Getty Images/iStockphoto/Thinkstock/Oleksiy Mark p189(cl), Getty Images/iStockphoto/Thinkstock/Alexander Shirokov p132(tr)
Image Source/Image Source/Frazer Cunningham p151(teddy), Image Source/Image Source/Bjarte Rettedal p31(b), 189(tr)
Macmillan Publishers Limited/Paul Bricknell p151(doll, teddy), Macmillan Publishers Limited/Haddon Davies p189(bl)
Macmillan South Africa/p119(b)
Photodisc/p121(tr), 152(b), Photodisc/Creative Crop p151(toy car)
Stockbyte/p55
Stockdisc/p173(strawberry)

Contents

Preface vi

1 **Numbers up to 1 000 000** 2

Practice 1: Numbers up to 1 000 000 2
Practice 2: Comparing and ordering numbers within 1 000 000 8
Practice 3: Multiplying numbers by 10 or 100 15
Practice 4: Positive and negative numbers 17
Practice 5: Number patterns 21

2 **Addition and subtraction** 22

Practice 1: Addition of more than 2 numbers 22
Practice 2: Subtraction of more than 2 numbers 30
Practice 3: Adding and subtracting near multiples of 10 and 100 34
Practice 4: Calculating the difference between two near multiples of 1 000 38
Practice 5: Written methods 40

3 **Geometry** 44

Practice 1: Angles review 44
Practice 2: Angles on a straight line 49
Practice 3: Triangles review 53
Practice 4: Parallel lines 57
Practice 5: Perpendicular lines 60
Practice 6: Creating patterns with 2 lines of symmetry 63
Practice 7: Reflective and rotational symmetry 66
Practice 8: Review of 3D shapes 68
Practice 9: Review of nets of solids 69

4 **Multiplication** 70

Practice 1: Multiplication review 70
Practice 2: Multiplying multiples of 10 to 90 and multiples of 100 to 900 by a single-digit number 74
Practice 3: Multiplying by 19 or 21 mentally 75
Practice 4: Multiplying by 25 mentally 77
Practice 5: Using factors to multiply 79
Practice 6: Multiplying by a 2-digit number 81
Practice 7: Word problems 90
Practice 8: Mixed operations with a pair of brackets 94

5 **Division** 99
Practice 1: Dividing 3-digit numbers by 1-digit numbers 99
Practice 2: Division word problems 102
Practice 3: Dividing with a remainder 106
Practice 4: Expressing a remainder as a fraction 108
Practice 5: Rounding up or down after division depending on the context 109

6 **Area and perimeter** 110
Practice 1: Perimeter of shapes 110
Practice 2: Area 113
Practice 3: Word problems 119

7 **Time** 122
Practice 1: Time review 122
Practice 2: The 24-hour clock 125
Practice 3: Word problems 131

8 **Fractions** 134
Practice 1: Review of equivalent fractions 134
Practice 2: Review of decimal and fractional equivalence 136
Practice 3: Improper fractions and mixed numbers 138
Practice 4: Ordering numbers on a number line 141
Practice 5: Review of fractions of shapes 142
Practice 6: Review of finding fractions of numbers 146
Practice 7: Fractions as division 149
Practice 8: Proportion 151
Practice 9: Ratio 153

9 **Decimals** 155
Practice 1: Review of decimals 155
Practice 2: Deriving pairs of decimals with a total of 10 157
Practice 3: Doubling and halving decimal numbers 159
Practice 4: Ordering decimals 160
Practice 5: Rounding off decimals 163
Practice 6: Written calculations using decimals 164
Practice 7: Word problems 170

10 **Percentages** 173

Practice 1: Percentages 173

11 **Length, mass and volume** 179

Practice 1: Review of units of length, mass and volume 179

Practice 2: Length, mass and volume in decimal form 183

Practice 3: Ordering measurements in mixed units 187

Practice 4: Review of measuring length, mass and volume 189

Practice 5: Interpreting a reading that lies between two divisions on a scale 190

Practice 6: Measuring lines to the nearest centimetre and millimetre 193

12 **Data handling** 198

Practice 1: Reading and constructing graphs 198

Practice 2: Describing the occurrence of familiar events 208

13 **Position and movement** 211

Practice 1: Reading and plotting coordinates 211

Practice 2: Reflection 214

Practice 3: Translation 216

Preface

max maths Primary – **A Singapore Approach** is a mathematics course specially designed to meet the needs of learners following the **Cambridge Primary** curriculum framework in Stages 1 to 6.

The **Max Maths Primary** workbooks guide learners through key mathematical concepts, addressing the learning objectives in the **Cambridge Primary** curriculum framework. With plenty of scaffolded practice, the workbooks support the learning process at home and will help to further develop learners' enthusiasm towards learning.

Workbook features

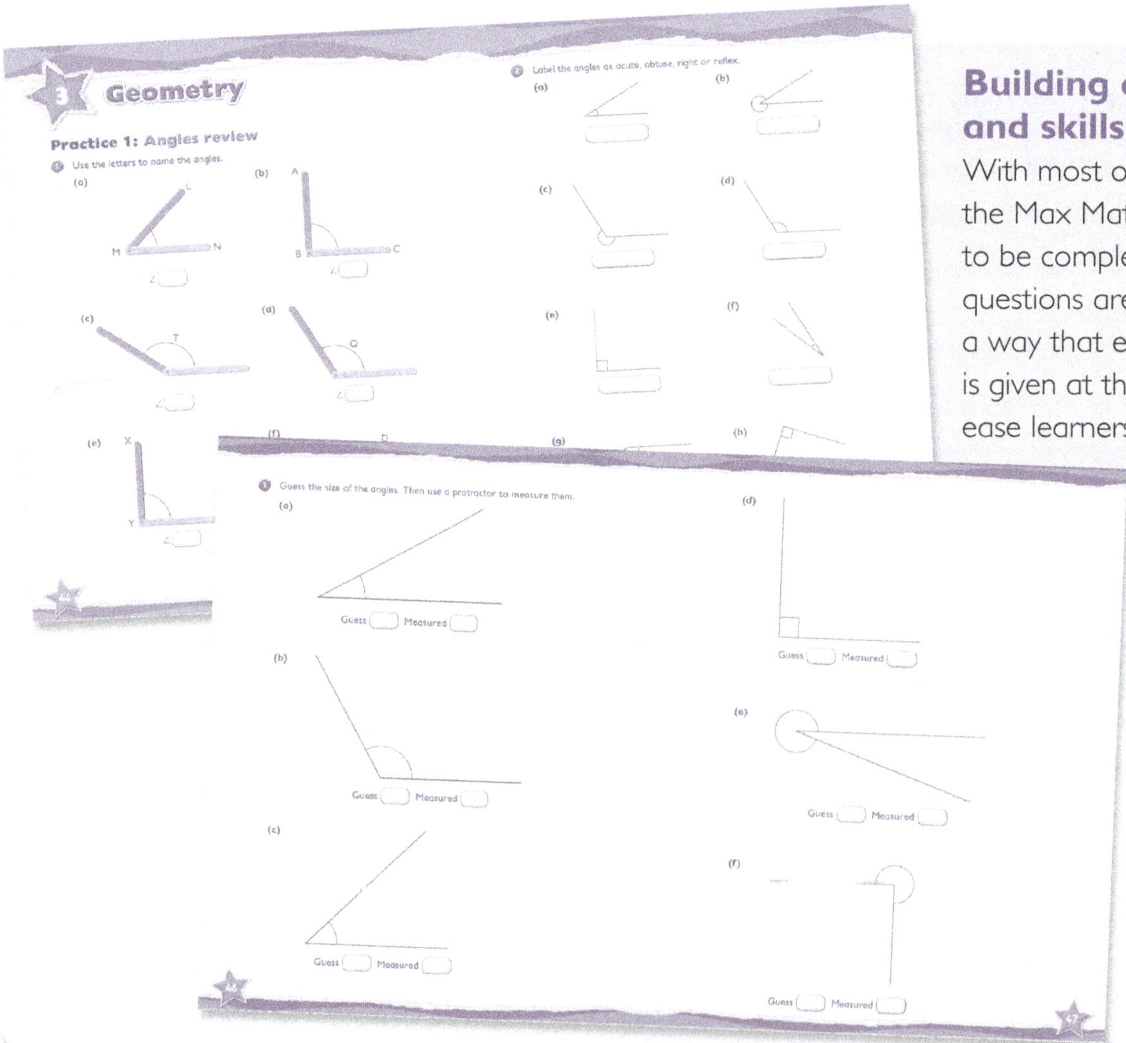

Building on concepts and skills

With most of the activities in the Max Maths workbooks to be completed at home, questions are scaffolded in a way that extra support is given at the beginning to ease learners into the task.

Engaging photographs and illustrations

Rich illustrations and photographs help to engage learners and encourage an enthusiastic approach to learning mathematics.

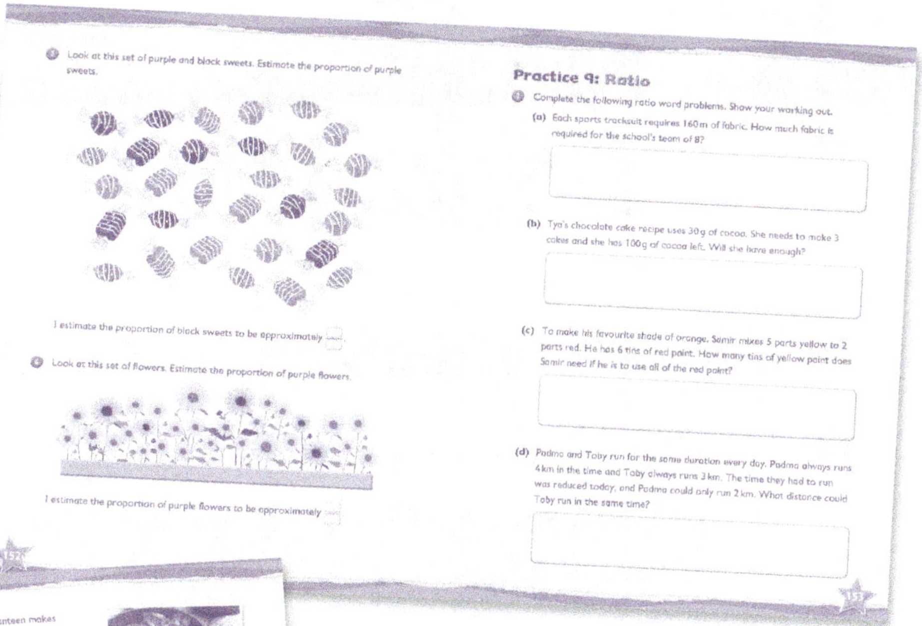

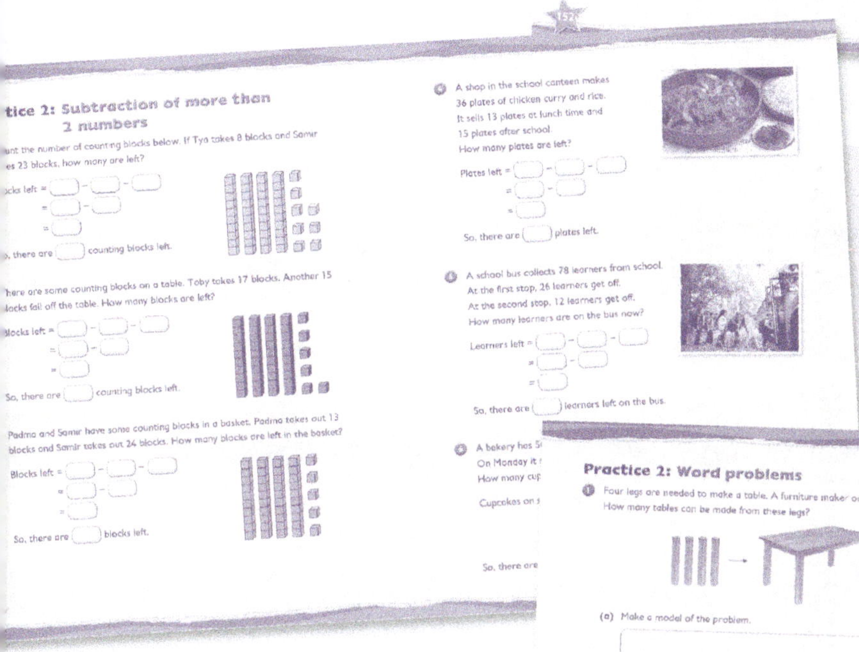

Concrete, pictorial to abstract

Questions are graduated in a way that guides learners through the sequence from concrete, pictorial and abstract understanding of concepts.

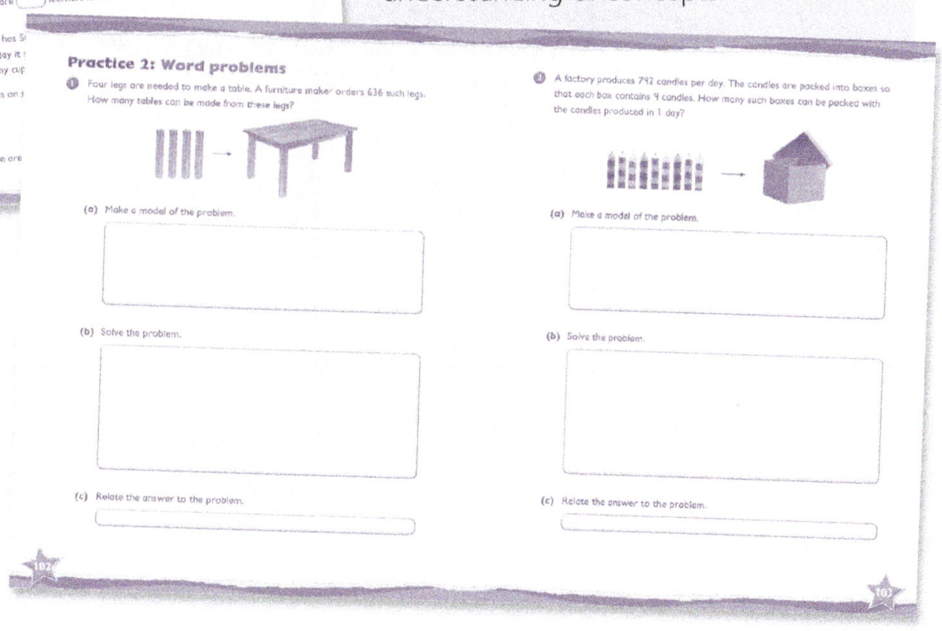

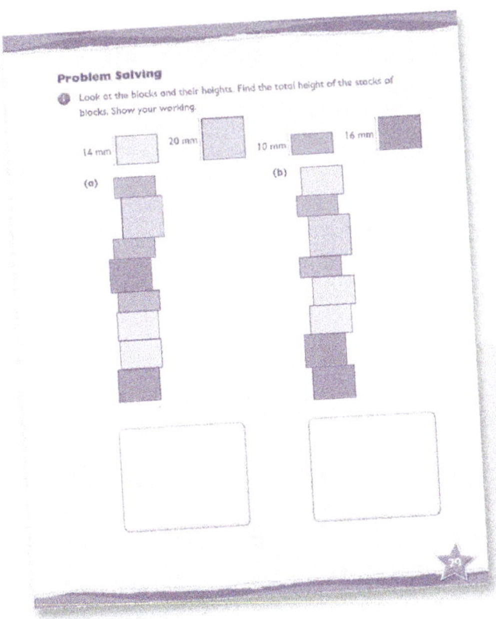

Self-guided problem solving

Problem-solving activities are embedded within practises for learners to combine knowledge of mathematics content and problem-solving skills.

1 Numbers up to 1 000 000

Practice 1: Numbers up to 1 000 000

1. Complete the following.

(a)

Millions	Hundred Thousands	Ten Thousands	Thousands	Hundreds	Tens	Ones
	2	1	7	7	4	3

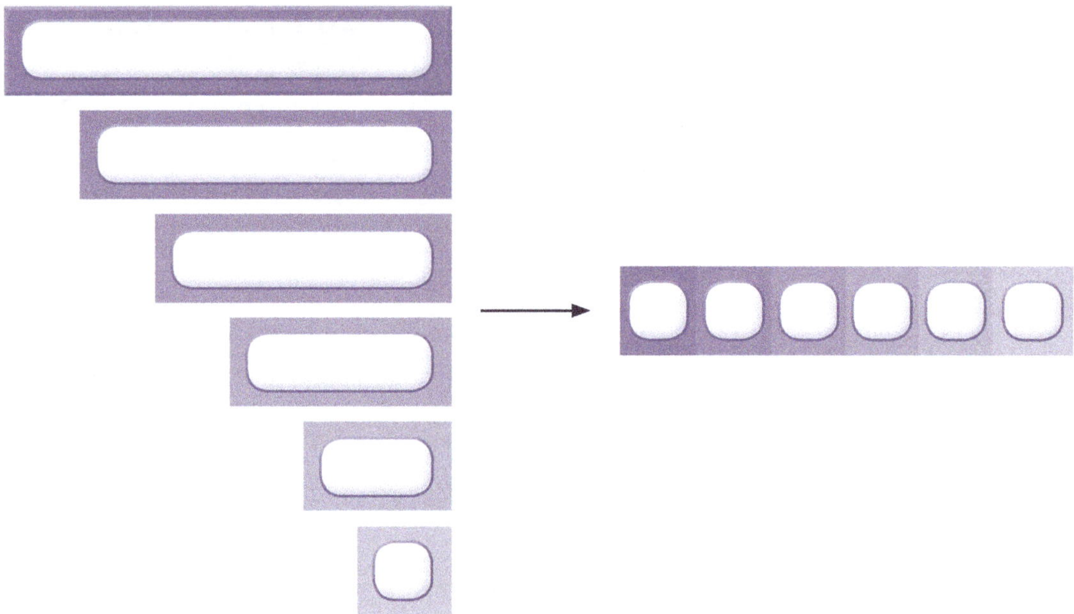

(b)

Millions	Hundred Thousands	Ten Thousands	Thousands	Hundreds	Tens	Ones
	9	4	5	1	6	3

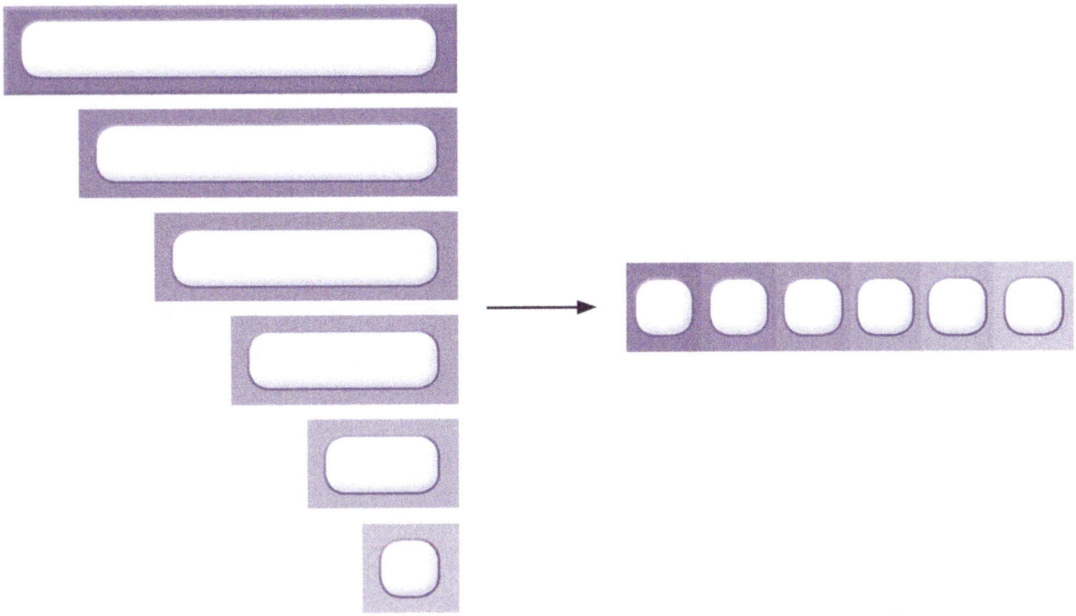

(c)

Millions	Hundred Thousands	Ten Thousands	Thousands	Hundreds	Tens	Ones
	4	0	6	7	1	4

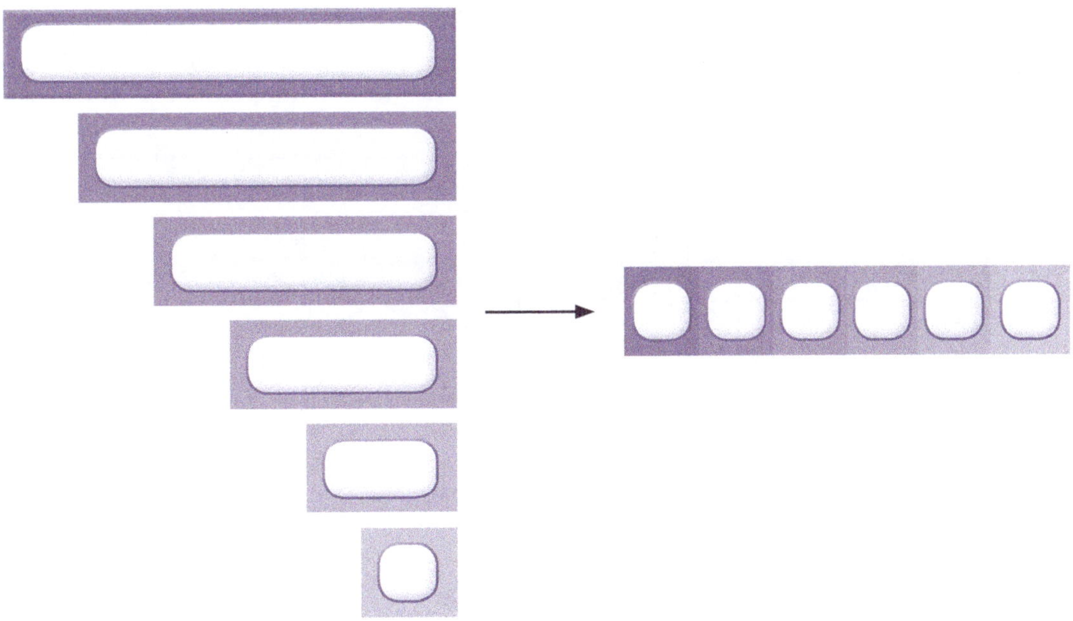

2 Write the number as numerals and words.

(a)

Millions	Hundred Thousands	Ten Thousands	Thousands	Hundreds	Tens	Ones
	7	3	4	5	3	0

Numerals:

Words:

(b)

Millions	Hundred Thousands	Ten Thousands	Thousands	Hundreds	Tens	Ones
	7	5	1	7	1	4

Numerals:

Words:

(c)

Millions	Hundred Thousands	Ten Thousands	Thousands	Hundreds	Tens	Ones
	2	8	2	4	1	6

Numerals:

Words:

(d)

Millions	Hundred Thousands	Ten Thousands	Thousands	Hundreds	Tens	Ones
	7	5	1	7	1	4

Numerals:

Words:

(e)

Millions	Hundred Thousands	Ten Thousands	Thousands	Hundreds	Tens	Ones
	5	2	0	1	0	1

Numerals:

Words:

(f)

Millions	Hundred Thousands	Ten Thousands	Thousands	Hundreds	Tens	Ones
	8	2	5	0	1	3

Numerals:

Words:

(g)

Millions	Hundred Thousands	Ten Thousands	Thousands	Hundreds	Tens	Ones
1	5	2	0	7	3	8

Numerals:

Words:

(h)

Millions	Hundred Thousands	Ten Thousands	Thousands	Hundreds	Tens	Ones
6	0	2	4	8	0	9

Numerals:

Words:

3. Write the numbers represented by the tables.

(a) 43 187

Hundred Thousands	Ten Thousands	Thousands	Hundreds	Tens	Ones

(b) 21 304

Hundred Thousands	Ten Thousands	Thousands	Hundreds	Tens	Ones

(c) 70 948

Hundred Thousands	Ten Thousands	Thousands	Hundreds	Tens	Ones

(d) 38 363

Hundred Thousands	Ten Thousands	Thousands	Hundreds	Tens	Ones

(e) 76 109

Hundred Thousands	Ten Thousands	Thousands	Hundreds	Tens	Ones

(f) 91 073

Hundred Thousands	Ten Thousands	Thousands	Hundreds	Tens	Ones

(g) 836 018

Hundred Thousands	Ten Thousands	Thousands	Hundreds	Tens	Ones

(h) 672 901

Hundred Thousands	Ten Thousands	Thousands	Hundreds	Tens	Ones

(i) 900 253

Hundred Thousands	Ten Thousands	Thousands	Hundreds	Tens	Ones

(j) 835 224

Hundred Thousands	Ten Thousands	Thousands	Hundreds	Tens	Ones

(k) 402 738

Hundred Thousands	Ten Thousands	Thousands	Hundreds	Tens	Ones

(l) 299 125

Hundred Thousands	Ten Thousands	Thousands	Hundreds	Tens	Ones

Practice 2: Comparing and ordering numbers within 1 000 000

1. Look at the numbers in each table and complete the following.

Table A

Hundred Thousands	Ten Thousands	Thousands	Hundreds	Tens	Ones
2	3	1	7	4	2

Table B

Hundred Thousands	Ten Thousands	Thousands	Hundreds	Tens	Ones
2	5	2	3	6	0

(a) What number does Table A represent? ☐

(b) What number does Table B represent? ☐

(c) Which table has more hundred thousands?

☐ Table A ☐ Table B ☐ They are the same

(d) Which table has more ten thousands?

☐ Table A ☐ Table B

(e) Which table is greater?

☐ Table A ☐ Table B ☐ They are the same

2 Look at the numbers in the place-value chart and complete the following.

Hundred Thousands	Ten Thousands	Thousands	Hundreds	Tens	Ones
6	7	7	0	1	9
8	7	4	5	5	2
3	0	9	1	8	6

(a) Which number has the greatest number of hundred thousands?

[ ]

(b) Which number has the smallest number of hundred thousands?

[ ]

(c) Arrange the numbers from smallest to greatest.

Write the correct < or > symbol.

[ ] □ [ ] □ [ ]

(d) Arrange the numbers from greatest to smallest.

Write the correct < or > symbol.

[ ] □ [ ] □ [ ]

3 Complete the following.

(a) Use the numbers below to make three 6-digit numbers.

5 3 6 2 1 7

Hundred Thousands	Ten Thousands	Thousands	Hundreds	Tens	Ones

(b) Arrange the numbers from smallest to greatest.
Write the correct < or > symbol.

(c) Arrange the numbers from greatest to smallest.
Write the correct < or > symbol.

4 Complete the following.

(a) Use the numbers below to make four 6-digit numbers.

2 5 1 0 6 9

Hundred Thousands	Ten Thousands	Thousands	Hundreds	Tens	Ones

(b) Arrange the numbers from smallest to greatest.
Write the correct < or > symbol.

(c) Arrange the numbers from greatest to smallest.
Write the correct < or > symbol.

5 Arrange the numbers from the greatest to the smallest. Then arrange them from the smallest to the greatest. Write the correct < or > symbol.

(a) 25 656 618 010 161 009 99 512

greatest → smallest

smallest → greatest

(b) 37 310 272 314 116 189 314 156

greatest → smallest

smallest → greatest

(c)

464 276

467 220

470 033

54 920

greatest → smallest

smallest → greatest

(d)

118 462

120 314

118 154

118 291

greatest → smallest

smallest → greatest

Problem Solving

Samir and Tya are given a set of numbers each. Find out who has the greatest number. Write the correct < or > symbol.

Samir's set

876 340

367 966

336 521

Tya's set

834 904

879 232

685 399

(a) Arrange Samir's numbers from the greatest to the smallest.

______ ☐ ______ ☐ ______

greatest → smallest

(b) Arrange Tya's numbers from the greatest to the smallest.

______ ☐ ______ ☐ ______

greatest → smallest

(c) Compare the greatest numbers from each set.

	Hundred Thousands	Ten Thousands	Thousands	Hundreds	Tens	Ones
Samir						
Tya						

So, ______ has the greatest number.

Practice 3: Multiplying numbers by 10 or 100

1. Draw a line from each number to the one that shows the number multiplied by 10.

6 000 250

25 110

300

8 720

872

11

600 30

2. Put a tick by the sentences that are true.

When a number is multiplied by 10 all the digits become ten times bigger. ☐

When a number is multiplied by 100 you add two zeros at the end. ☐

When a number is multiplied by 10 you just need to put a zero on the end of the number. ☐

When a number is multiplied by 100 you move the digits two places to the right. ☐

3. Complete the table.

Original number	× 10	× 100
32	320	3200
254		
836		
	7630	
		67200
250		

4. Write your answers to each multiplication below.

(a) 240 × 10 = ☐

(b) 557 × 100 = ☐

(c) ☐ × 10 = 3890

(d) 34 022 × ☐ = 3 402 200

(e) ☐ × 100 = 7 802 000

(f) 63 300 × ☐ = 633 000

(g) ☐ × 100 = 3 787 900

(h) 3 798 820 × 10 = ☐

5. Put a tick by the correct solutions and a cross by the incorrect solutions.

(a) 478 × 10 = 4 780 ☐

(b) 6 833 × 100 = 683 300 ☐

(c) 7 020 × 10 = 7 020 ☐

(d) 56 798 × 100 = 5 679 800 ☐

(e) 3 000 × 100 = 30 000 ☐

(f) 7 982 × 10 = 79 820 ☐

(g) 8 920 300 × 100 = 8 920 300 ☐

(h) 9 274 × 10 = 927 400 ☐

Practice 4: Positive and negative numbers

1. Draw an arrow from the number to its correct place on the thermometer.

5°

18°

−9°

0°

−13°

−5°

19°

−2°

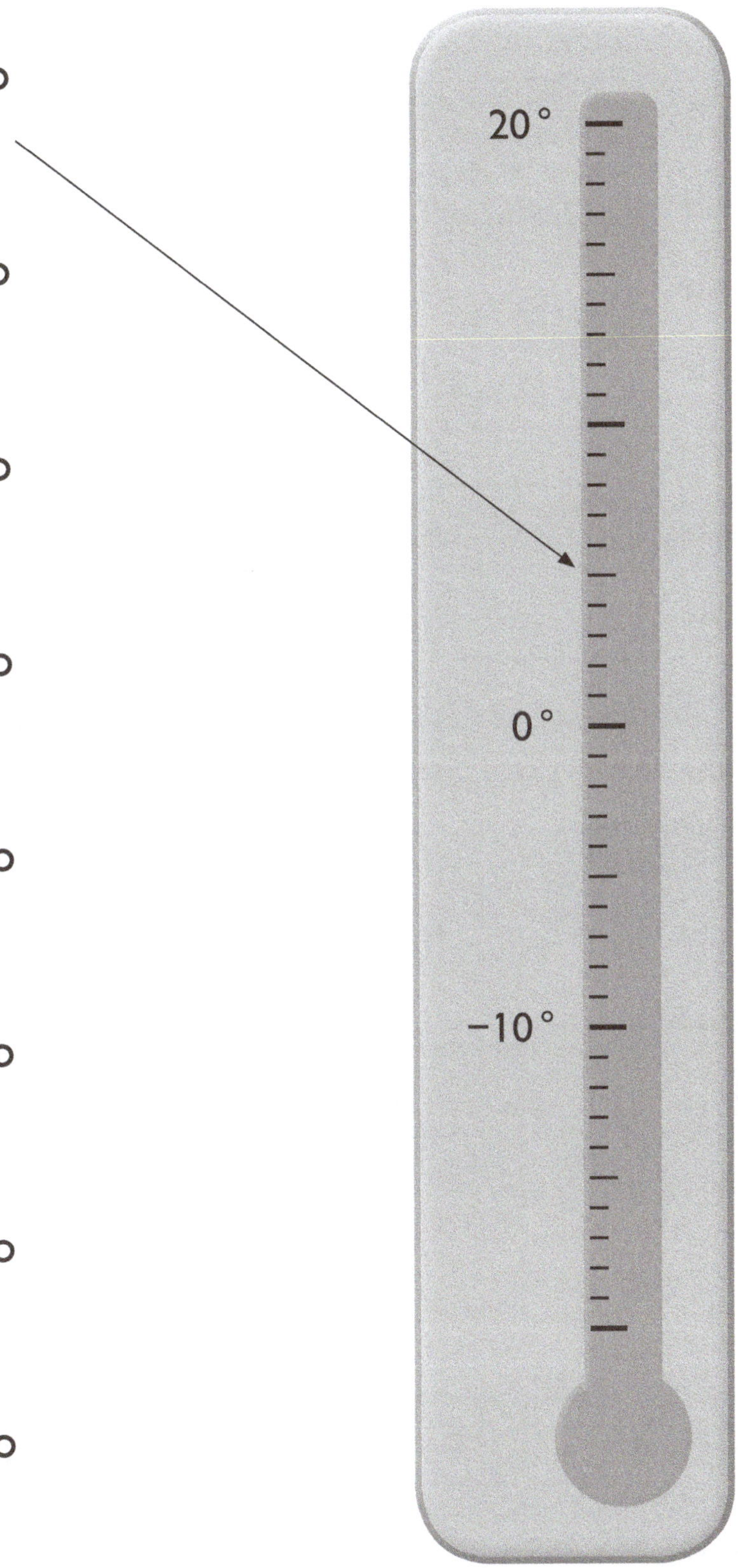

2. Write the correct word in each sentence.

warmer **cooler**

(a) 13 °C is [ ] than 16 °C.

(b) 23 °C is [ ] than −23 °C.

(c) −5 °C is [ ] than −2 °C.

(d) −3 °C is [ ] than 6 °C.

(e) 18 °C is [ ] than 15 °C.

(f) −18 °C is [ ] than −4 °C.

(g) −22 °C is [ ] than 22 °C.

(h) −11 °C is [ ] than −2 °C.

3. Calculate the answers and complete the sentences. The first one is done for you.

fall **rise**

(a) 14 °C to 7 °C is a [fall] of [7] degrees.

(b) 2 °C to 5 °C is a [ ] of [ ] degrees.

(c) −2 °C to −11 °C is a [ ] of [ ] degrees.

(d) −12 °C to 0 °C is a [ ] of [ ] degrees.

(e) 7 °C to −12 °C is a [ ] of [ ] degrees.

(f) 17 °C to 11 °C is a [ ] of [ ] degrees.

(g) −13 °C to 2 °C is a [ ] of [ ] degrees.

(h) 15 °C to −5 °C is a [ ] of [ ] degrees.

4 Write the numbers on the correct place on the number line.

(a) −4

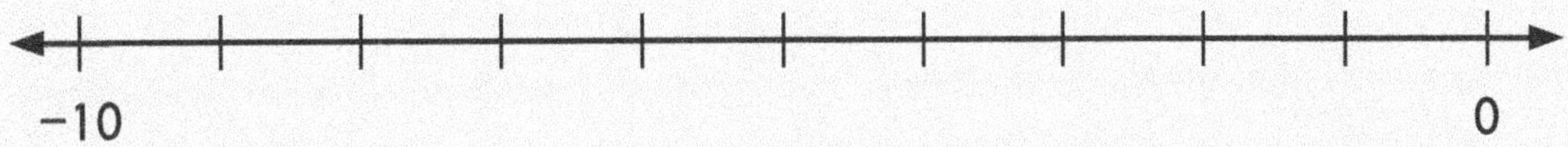

(b) 40

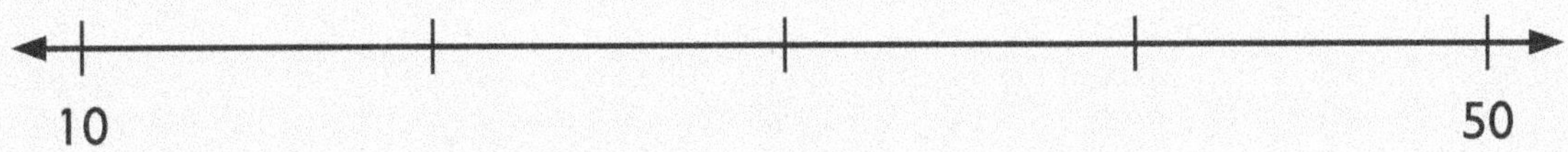

(c) −22

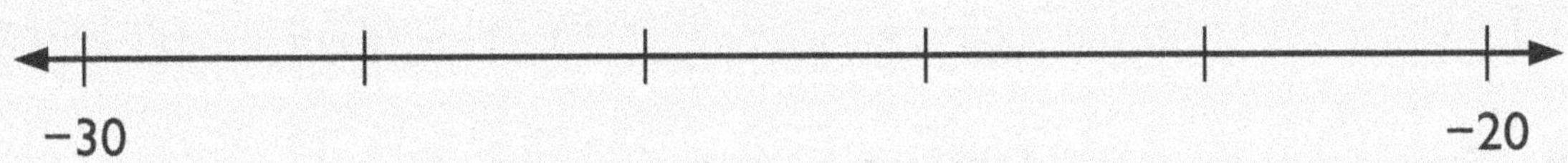

(d) −45

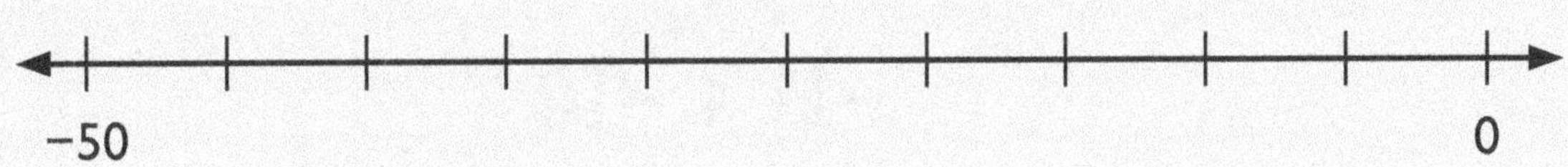

(e) 12

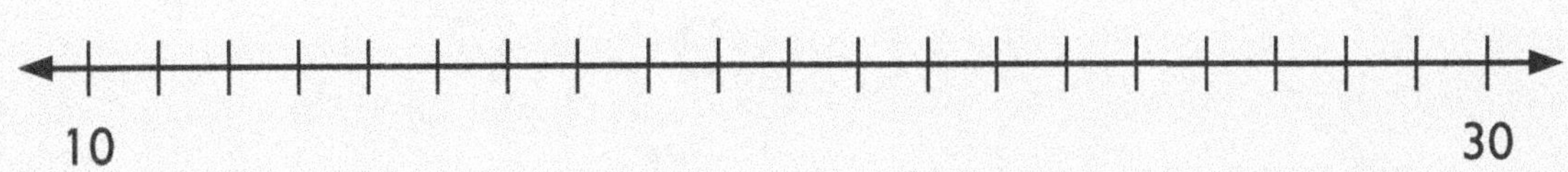

(f) 0

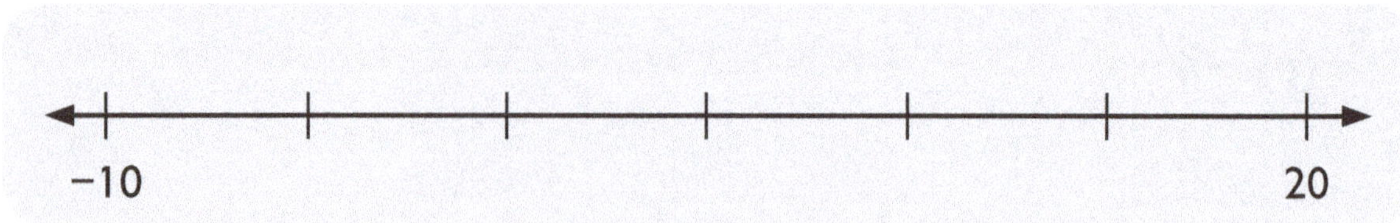

(g) −12

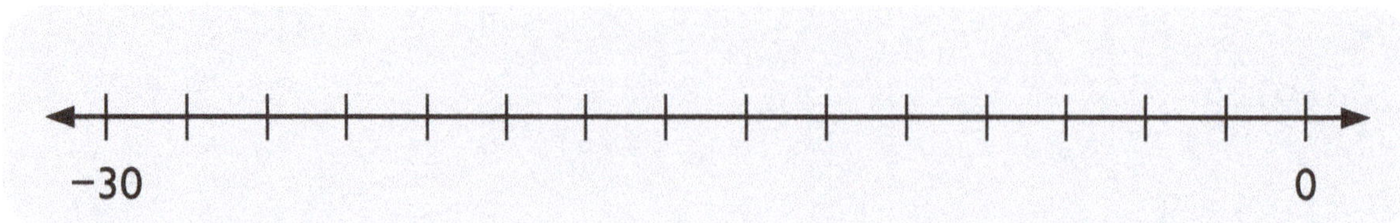

(h) 99

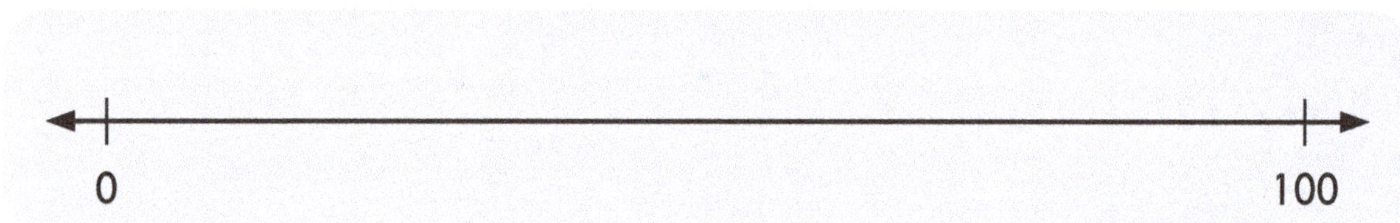

5 Draw a circle around the statements that are correct.

$23 < 34$

$42 > 13$

$-11 < -14$

$-23 < 50$

$23 < -52$

$-3 > -17$

$11 < -34$

$14 > -18$

Practice 5: Number patterns

1 Complete these number patterns then write the number that the steps are taking each time.

(a) 35, 30, 25, 20, [ ], [ ], [ ]

The pattern is counting back in steps of [ ].

(b) 45 320, 44 320, 43 320, 42 320, [ ], [ ], [ ]

The pattern is counting back in steps of [ ].

(c) −23, −21, −19, −17, [ ], [ ], [ ]

The pattern is counting up in steps of [ ].

(d) −7, −2, [ ], 8, [ ], 18, 23, 28, [ ]

The pattern is counting back in steps of [ ].

(e) 1 823, 823, −177, −1 177, [ ], −3 177, [ ], [ ]

The pattern is counting up in steps of [ ].

(f) −100, −75, −50, [ ], [ ], 25, 50, [ ]

The pattern is counting up in steps of [ ].

2 Cross out all of the numbers that do not belong in each pattern.

(a) −560, −555, −560, −550, −545, −540, −535

(b) 23, 18, 13, 8, 3, −2, −3, −7, −12, −13, 17

(c) 62 478, 62 428, 62 328, 62 178, 62 028, 61 878, 61 728, 61 628

(d) −241, −231, −213, −221, −211, −201, −200, −191, −181

2 Addition and subtraction

Practice 1: Addition of more than 2 numbers

1 Add the counting blocks.

Example

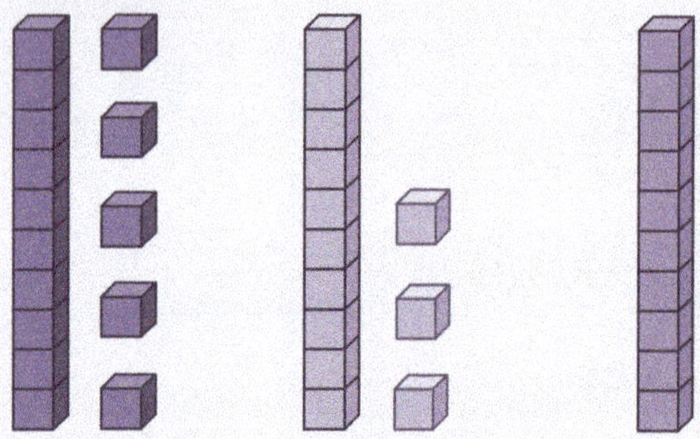

15 13 10

total = 15 + 13 + 10
= 28 + 10
= 38

(a)

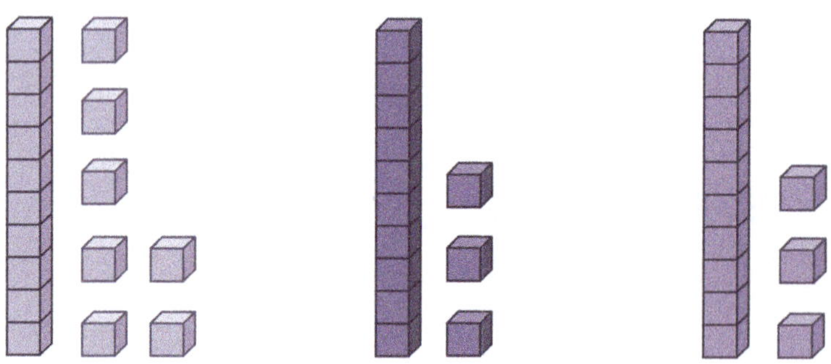

total = ☐ + ☐ + ☐
= ☐ + ☐
= ☐

(b)

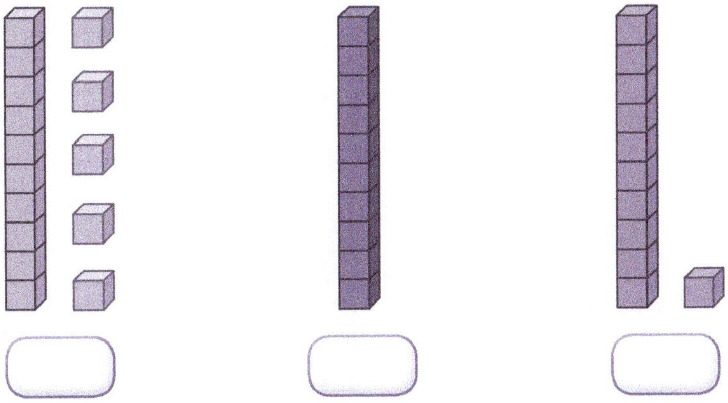

total = ___ + ___ + ___

= ___ + ___

= ___

(c)

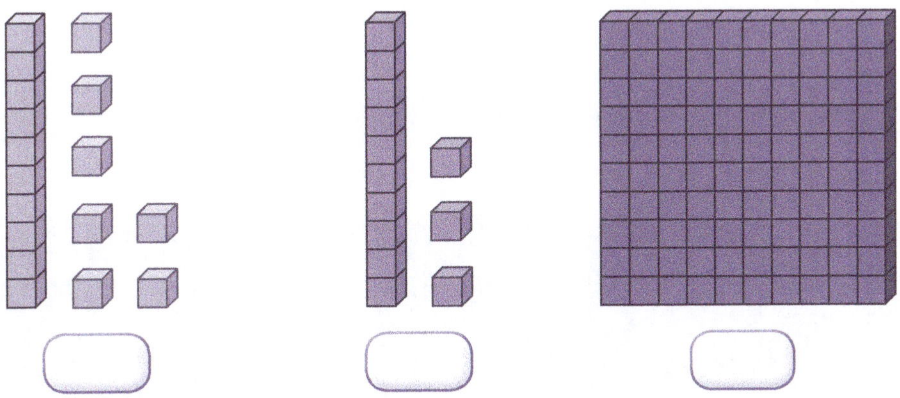

total = ___ + ___ + ___

= ___ + ___

= ___

2 Add the counting blocks.

(a)

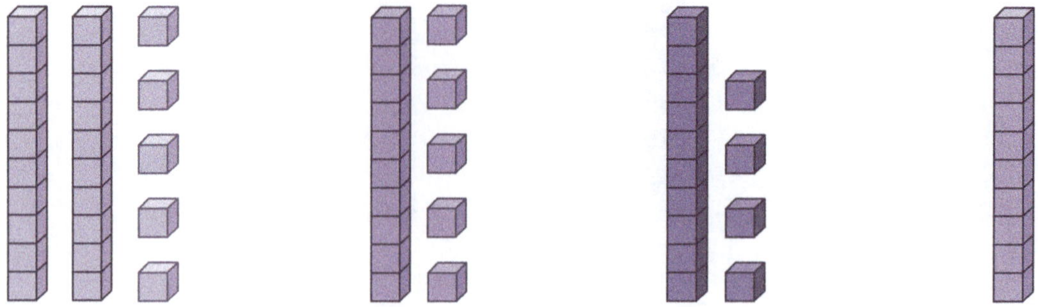

total = ___ + ___ + ___ + ___

= ___ + ___ + ___

= ___ + ___

= ___

(b)

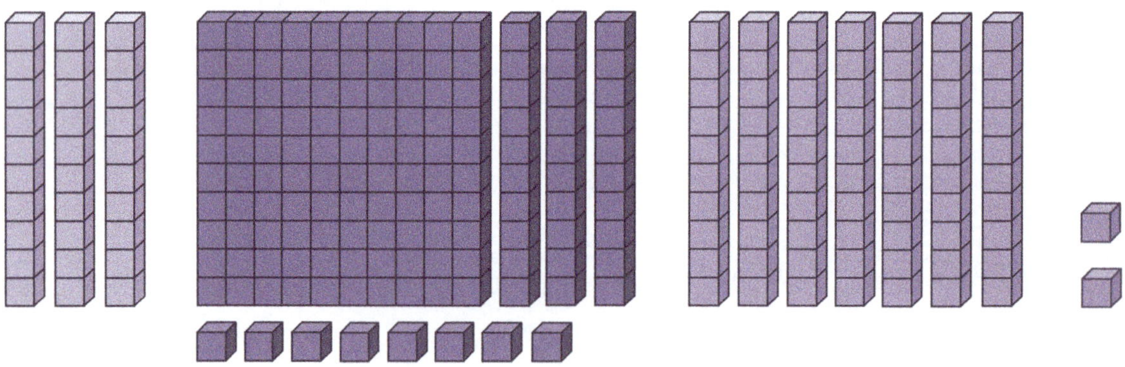

total = ___ + ___ + ___ + ___

= ___ + ___ + ___

= ___ + ___

= ___

3 Add the numbers mentally. Start by finding pairs of numbers that make 10.

Example

$2 + \bigcirc\!\!\!\!\!\;4 + 3 + \bigcirc\!\!\!\!\!\;6 = \bigcirc\!\!\!\!\!\!\!\;10 + 2 + 3$

$= 12 + 3$

$= 15$

(a) $4 + 8 + 1 + 2 =$ ☐

$=$ ☐

$=$ ☐

(b) $3 + 3 + 7 + 5 =$ ☐

$=$ ☐

$=$ ☐

(c) $8 + 9 + 1 + 5 =$ ☐

$=$ ☐

$=$ ☐

(d) $6 + 4 + 2 + 7 =$ ☐

$=$ ☐

$=$ ☐

4 Add the numbers shown on the tiles.

(a) 20 6 14 10

total = ☐ + ☐ + ☐ + ☐

= ☐ + ☐ + ☐

= ☐ + ☐

= ☐

(b) 35 12 31 25

total = ☐ + ☐ + ☐ + ☐

= ☐ + ☐ + ☐

= ☐ + ☐

= ☐

(c) 23 7 22 8

total = ☐ + ☐ + ☐ + ☐

= ☐ + ☐ + ☐

= ☐ + ☐

= ☐

(d) 25 8 25 14

total = ☐ + ☐ + ☐ + ☐

= ☐ + ☐ + ☐

= ☐ + ☐

= ☐

5 Add the following numbers and show your working.

(a) 21 + 18 + 9 = ☐

(b) 35 + 16 + 5 = ☐

(c) 4 + 28 + 16 = ☐

(d) 1 + 25 + 19 = ☐

(e) 7 + 33 + 13 = ☐

(f) 42 + 18 + 37 = ☐

6 Add the following numbers and show your working.

(a) 11 + 18 + 9 + 11 = ☐

(b) 15 + 16 + 25 + 4 = ☐

(c) 14 + 12 + 15 + 6 = ☐

(d) 27 + 13 + 19 + 11 = ☐

(e) 24 + 10 + 26 + 13 = ☐

(f) 19 + 9 + 21 + 8 = ☐

Problem Solving

Look at the blocks and their heights. Find the total height of the stacks of blocks.

Show your working.

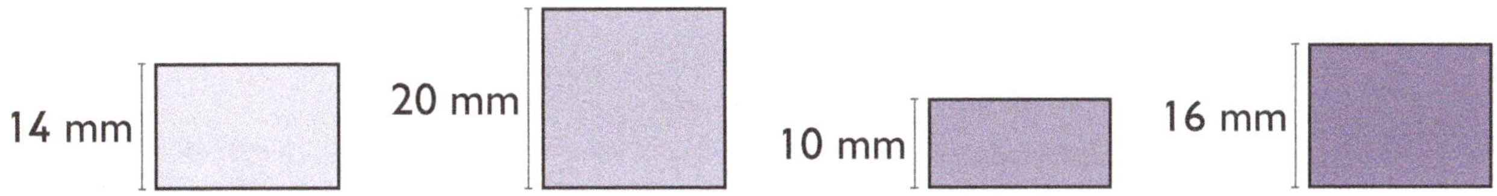

(a)

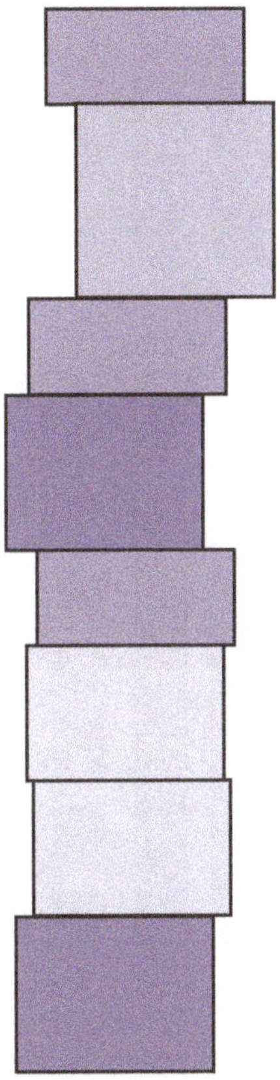

(b)

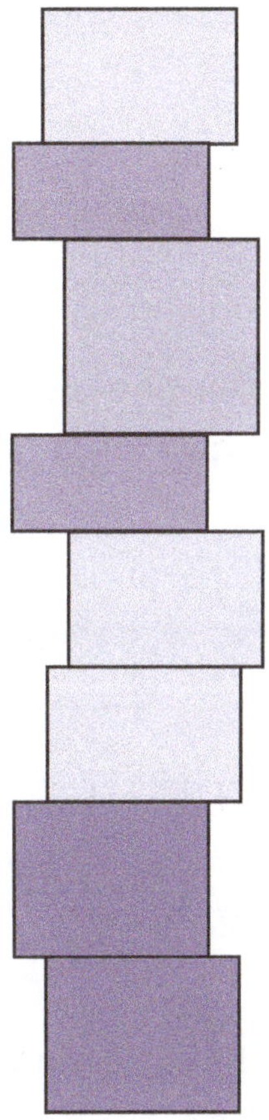

Practice 2: Subtraction of more than 2 numbers

1. Count the number of counting blocks below. If Tya takes 8 blocks and Samir takes 23 blocks, how many are left?

Blocks left = ___ – ___ – ___

= ___ – ___

= ___

So, there are ___ counting blocks left.

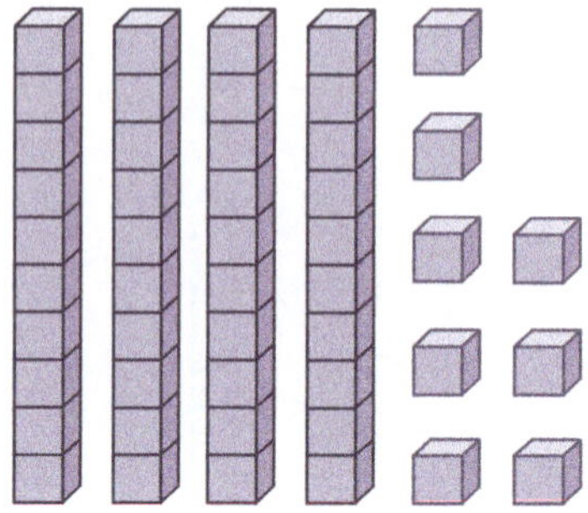

2. There are some counting blocks on a table. Toby takes 17 blocks. Another 15 blocks fall off the table. How many blocks are left?

Blocks left = ___ – ___ – ___

= ___ – ___

= ___

So, there are ___ counting blocks left.

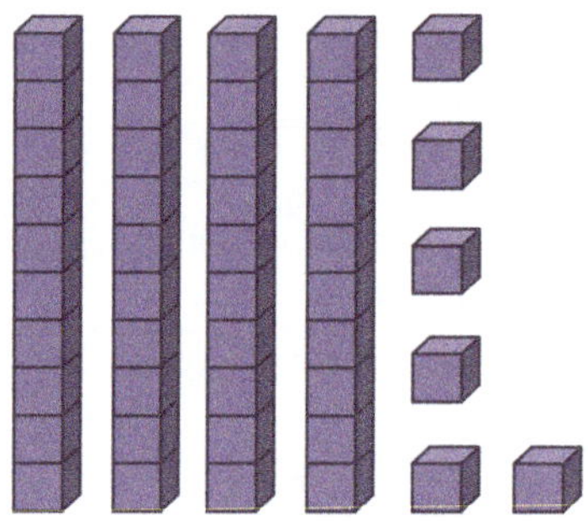

3. Padma and Samir have some counting blocks in a basket. Padma takes out 13 blocks and Samir takes out 24 blocks. How many blocks are left in the basket?

Blocks left = ___ – ___ – ___

= ___ – ___

= ___

So, there are ___ blocks left.

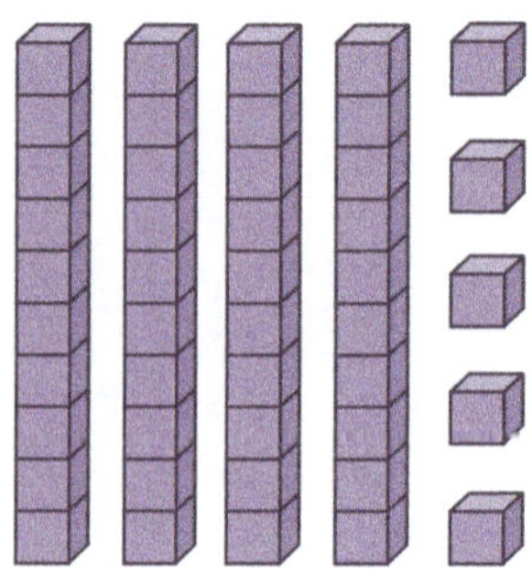

4 A shop in the school canteen makes 36 plates of chicken curry and rice. It sells 13 plates at lunch time and 15 plates after school. How many plates are left?

Plates left = ☐ − ☐ − ☐

= ☐ − ☐

= ☐

So, there are ☐ plates left.

5 A school bus collects 78 learners from school. At the first stop, 26 learners get off. At the second stop, 12 learners get off. How many learners are on the bus now?

Learners left = ☐ − ☐ − ☐

= ☐ − ☐

= ☐

So, there are ☐ learners left on the bus.

6 A bakery has 56 cupcakes ready to sell at the beginning of the week. On Monday it sells 24 and on Tuesday it sells 17. How many cupcakes does the bakery have on sale on Wednesday?

Cupcakes on sale on Wednesday = ☐ − ☐ − ☐

= ☐ − ☐

= ☐

So, there are ☐ cupcakes ready to sell on Wednesday.

7 Complete the following.

(a) $43 - 12 - 9 = 31 - \square$

$= \square$

(b) $38 - 23 - 8 = 15 - \square$

$= \square$

(c) $57 - 21 - 10 = \square - \square$

$= \square - \square$

$= \square$

(d) $45 - 14 - 8 - 6 = \square - \square - \square$

$= \square - \square$

$= \square$

(e) $52 - 25 - 11 - 8 = \square - \square - \square$

$= \square - \square$

$= \square$

(f) $100 - 34 - 23 - 19 = \square - \square - \square$

$= \square - \square$

$= \square$

8 Subtract the following numbers and show your working.

(a) 38 − 10 − 8 = ☐

(b) 45 − 16 − 9 = ☐

(c) 72 − 15 − 41 = ☐

(d) 80 − 51 − 8 = ☐

(e) 55 − 15 − 5 = ☐

(f) 77 − 33 − 11 = ☐

Practice 3: Adding and subtracting near multiples of 10 and 100

1. Draw arrows on the number lines to show the sums.

(a) 35 + 9

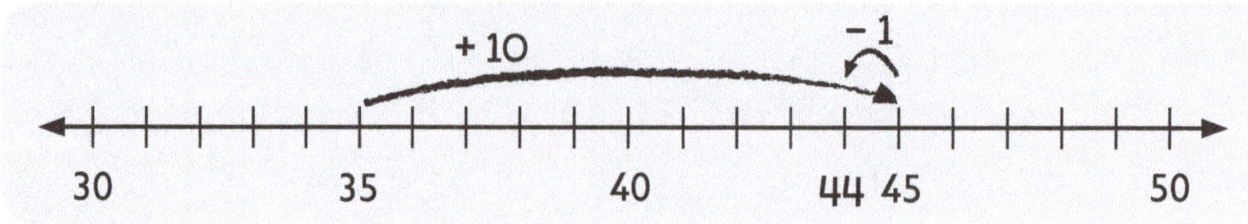

(b) 27 + 19

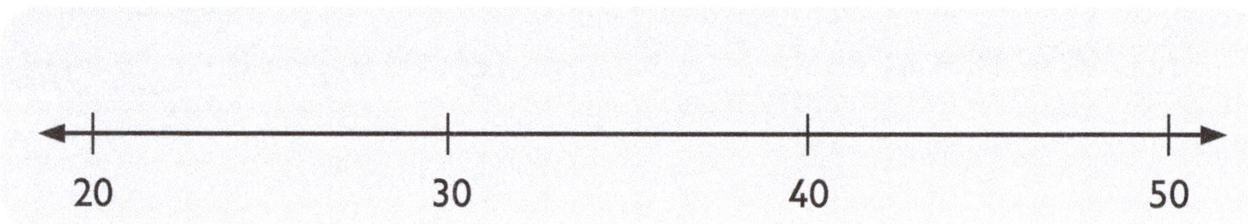

(c) 58 + 17

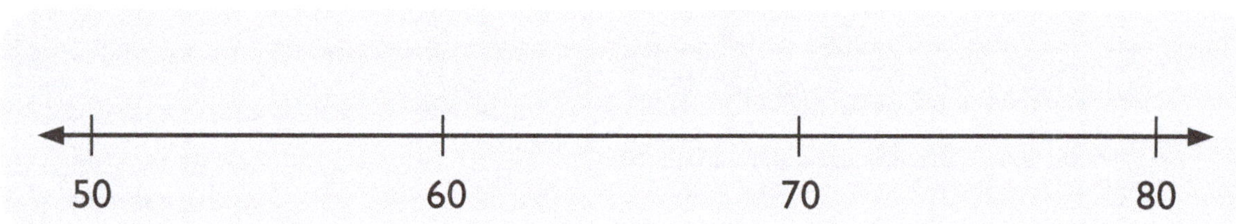

(d) 364 + 99

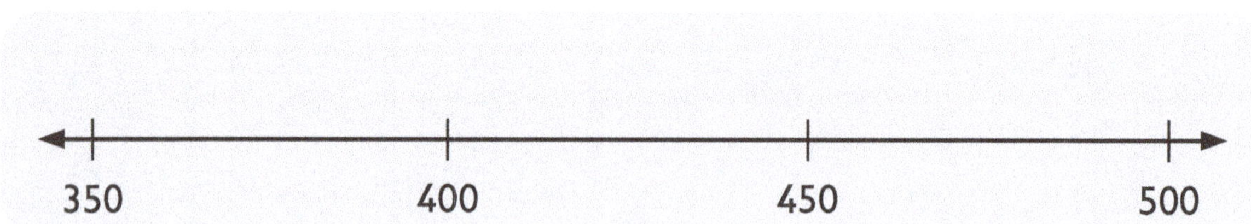

(e) 372 + 98

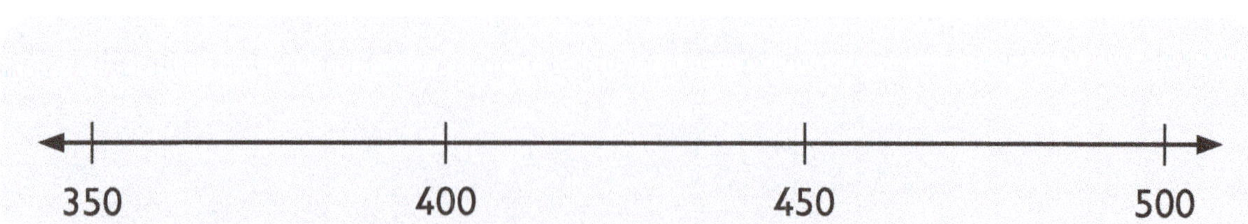

2 Draw arrows on the number lines to show the subtraction equations.

(a) 65 − 19

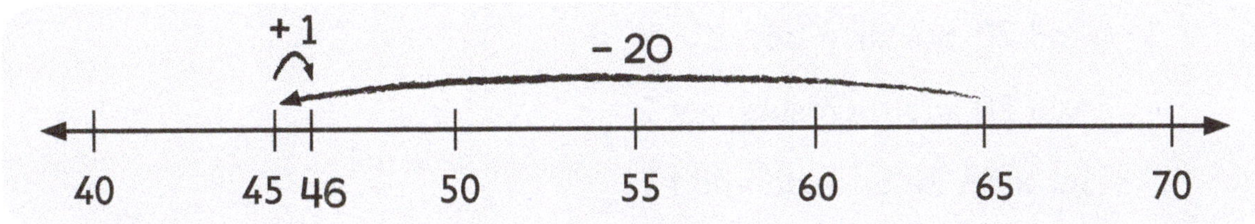

(b) 46 − 9

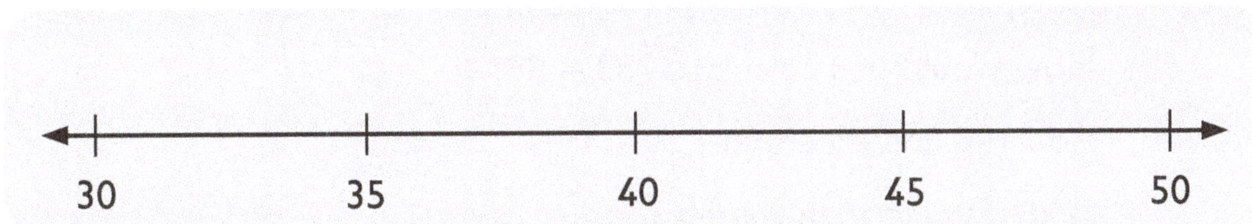

(c) 684 − 99

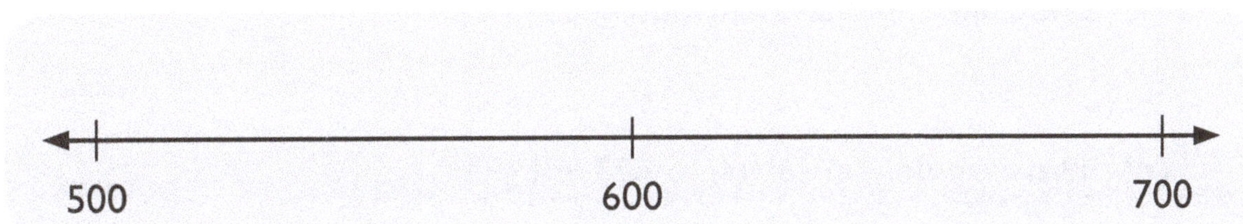

(d) 352 − 97

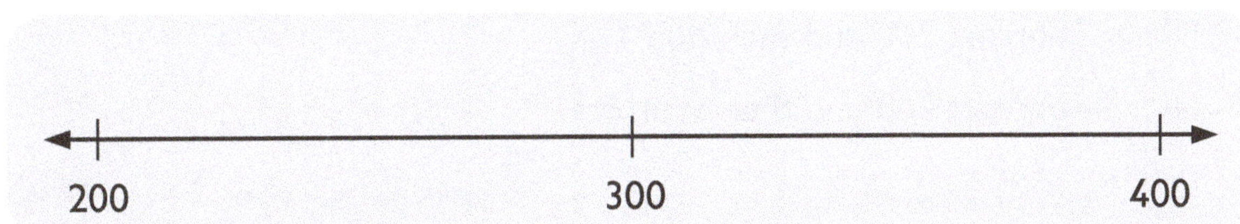

(e) 485 − 49

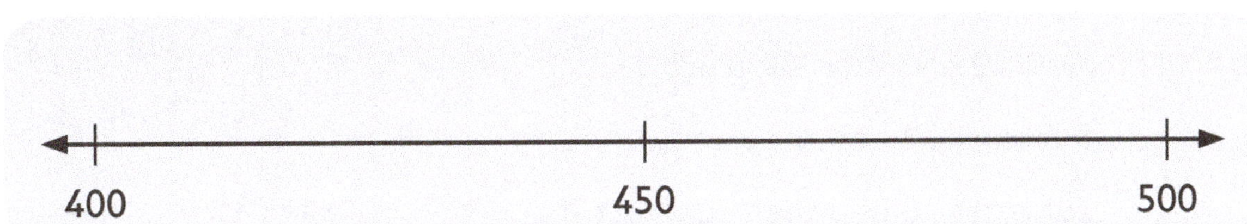

3 Tick the correct statement that explains how to calculate the solution.

(a) How would you calculate 35 + 18?

- Add 20 and then add 2 ☐
- Add 20 and then subtract 2 ☐
- Subtract 20 and then add 2 ☐
- Subtract 20 and then subtract 2 ☐

(b) How would you calculate 783 – 99?

- Add 100 and then add 1 ☐
- Add 100 and then subtract 1 ☐
- Subtract 100 and then add 1 ☐
- Subtract 100 and then subtract 1 ☐

(c) How would you calculate 473 + 199?

- Add 200 and then add 1 ☐
- Add 200 and then subtract 1 ☐
- Subtract 200 and then add 1 ☐
- Subtract 200 and then subtract 1 ☐

(d) How would you calculate 86 – 17?

- Add 20 and then add 3 ☐
- Add 20 and then subtract 3 ☐
- Subtract 20 and then add 3 ☐
- Subtract 20 and then subtract 3 ☐

4. Complete the questions.

(a) 468 + 19 = ☐

(b) 34 − 19 = ☐

(c) 473 − 98 = ☐

(d) 388 + 8 = ☐

(e) 66 − 9 = ☐

(f) 748 + 299 = ☐

(g) 46 + 39 = ☐

(h) 478 − 27 = ☐

(i) 740 + 99 = ☐

(j) 34 + 9 = ☐

(k) 276 − 79 = ☐

(l) 738 − 47 = ☐

5. Find the missing numbers.

(a) 462 − 19 = ☐

(b) 78 + ☐ = 87

(c) 582 + ☐ = 601

(d) ☐ − 18 = 29

(e) 572 − 37 = ☐

(f) ☐ + 99 = 992

(g) 47 + 88 = ☐

(h) 33 + 109 = ☐

(i) 199 + ☐ = 398

(j) ☐ + 299 = 367

(k) 36 − ☐ = 27

(l) 382 − 18 = ☐

Practice 4: Calculating the difference between two near multiples of 1 000

1 Use the number lines to show the difference between these near multiples of 1 000.

(a) What is the difference between 999 and 1 003?

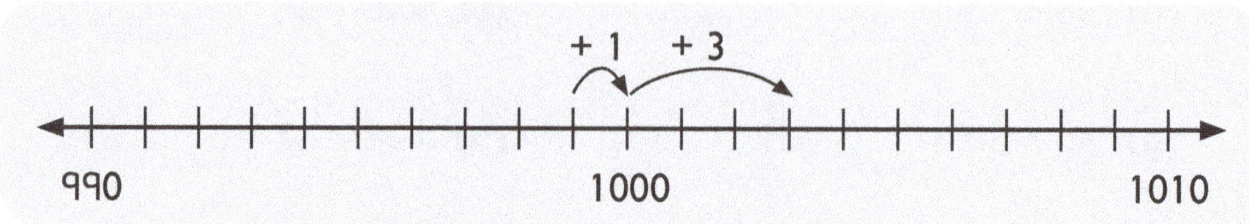

(b) What is the difference between 997 and 1 001?

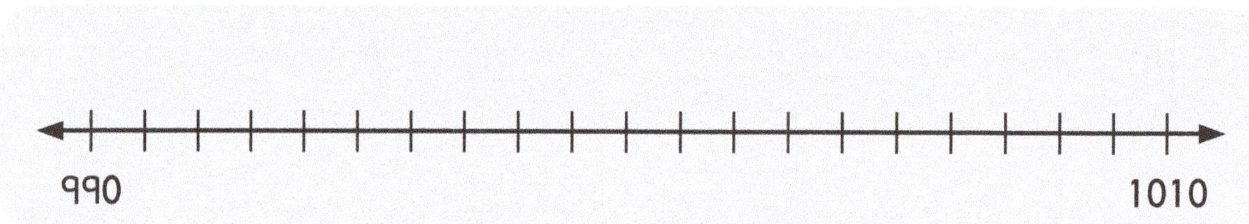

(c) What is the difference between 1 999 and 2 005?

(d) What is the difference between 995 and 1 006?

(e) What is the difference between 3 999 and 4 003?

2 Calculate the difference between these near multiples of 1 000.

(a) What is the difference between 2 998 and 3 001? ☐

(b) What is the difference between 996 and 1 001? ☐

(c) What is the difference between 6 998 and 7 003? ☐

(d) What is the difference between 3 988 and 4 012? ☐

(e) What is the difference between 997 and 1 004? ☐

(f) What is the difference between 7 996 and 8 002? ☐

(g) What is the difference between 2 999 and 3 001? ☐

(h) What is the difference between 3 987 and 4 003? ☐

(i) What is the difference between 1 999 and 2 007? ☐

(j) What is the difference between 3 993 and 4 005? ☐

(k) What is the difference between 999 and 1 005? ☐

(l) What is the difference between 9 999 and 10 003? ☐

Practice 5: Written methods

1. Add these numbers using the column method.

(a)

	6	4	1 .	2	8
+	2	8	9 .	2	7
			.		

(b)

	9	8	8 .	6	5
+	1	2	9 .	4	8
			.		

(c)

	5	1	9	0 .	6
+		7	8	6 .	9
				.	

(d)

	7 .	7	9
+	5 .	5	4
	.		

(e)

				.		
	3	5	4	.	3	7
+	2	1	7	.	4	4
				.		

(f)

				.		
	4	7	8	.	3	9
+	2	1	5	.	3	6
				.		

(g)

					.	
	5	8	3	2	.	7
+	7	3	2	6	.	5
					.	

(h)

			.		
	2	3	.	5	6
+	8	3	.	6	9
			.		

2. Add these numbers together using the column method. Show your working out.

(a) 463.82 + 366.28

(b) 583.09 + 209.22

(c) 168.83 + 345.74

(d) 460.94 + 874.28

3 Answer the questions and show your working.

(a) Samir receives interest of $362.65 every six months from his savings account. How much will he receive in one year?

(b) Jade's brother has already saved $746.58. He saves another $274.47. Has Jade's brother saved enough to buy a $1 000 car yet? Why/why not?

(c) Tya was 157.7 cm tall in January. She grew 8.5 cm in one year. How tall is Tya 12 months later?

(d) At the beginning of spring, Toby's father spreads 6.35 tonnes of gravel on an area in his garden. At the end of summer he spreads another 7.88 tonnes. How much gravel has Toby's father used in his garden?

3 Geometry

Practice 1: Angles review

1 Use the letters to name the angles.

(a)

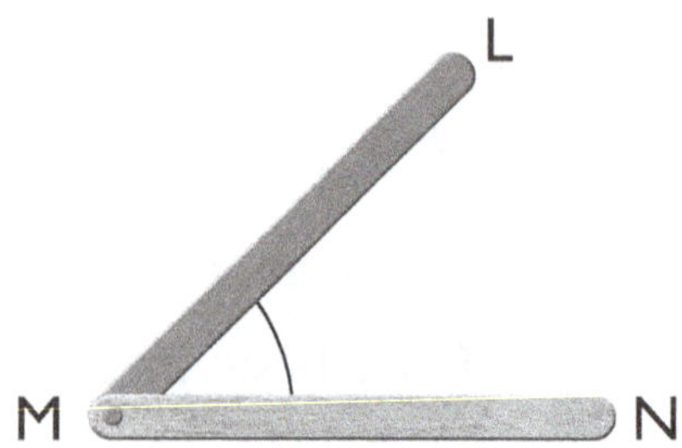

∠ ______

(b)

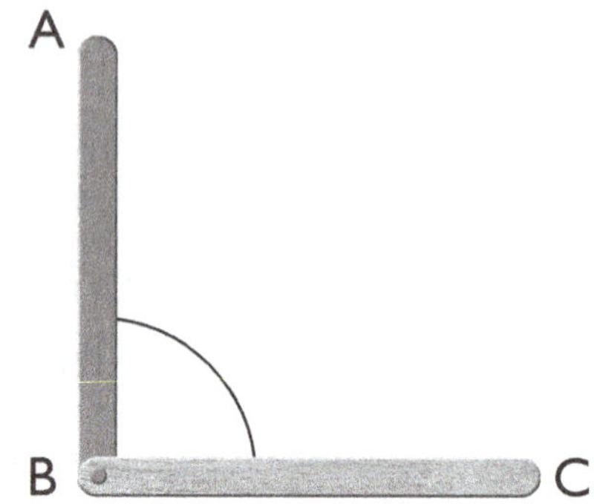

∠ ______

(c)

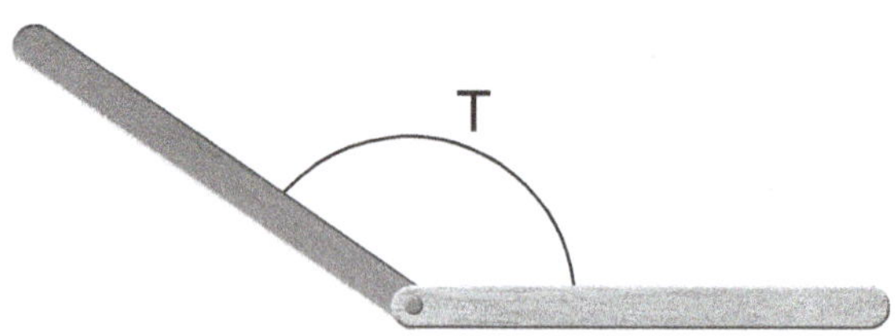

∠ ______

(d)

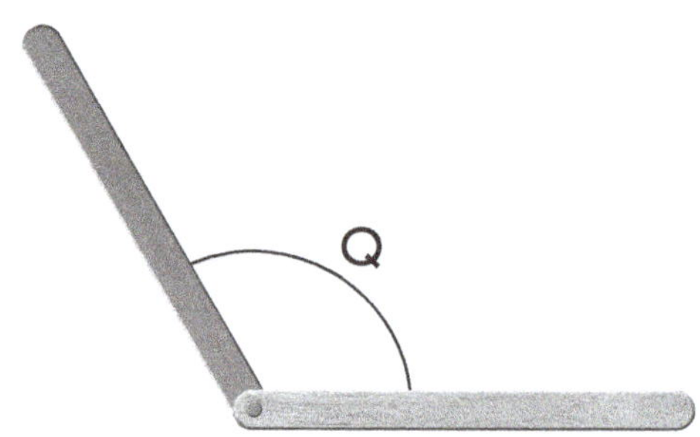

∠ ______

(e)

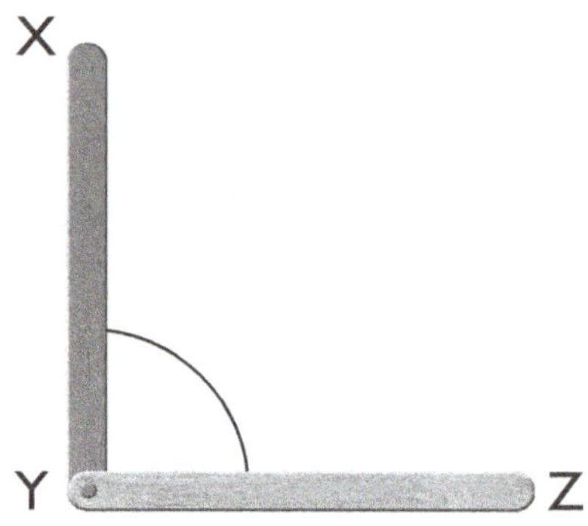

∠ ______

(f)

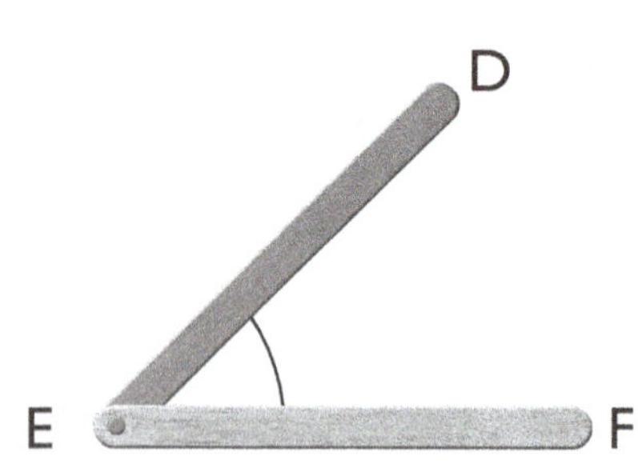

∠ ______

2 Label the angles as acute, obtuse, right or reflex.

(a)

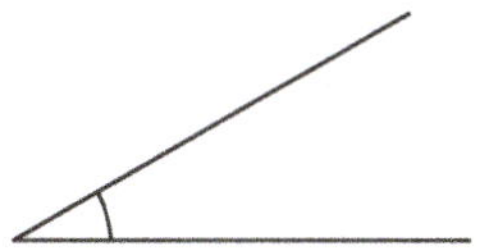

(b)

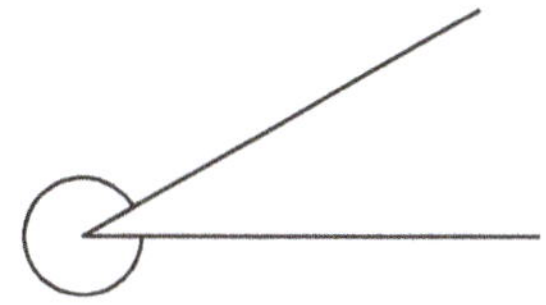

(c)

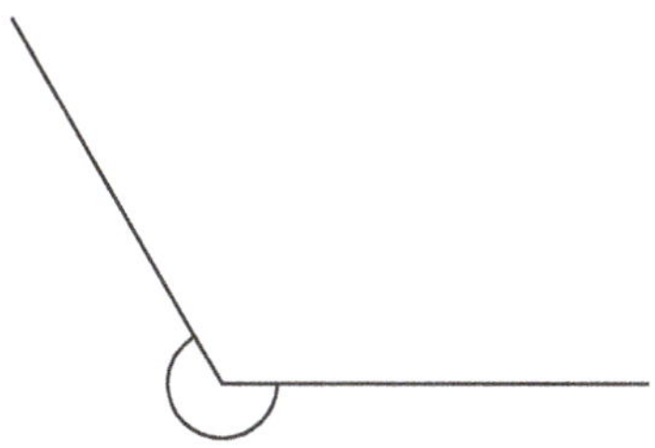

(d)

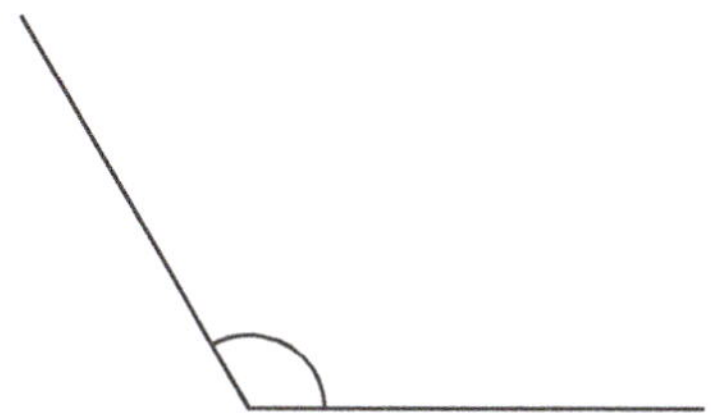

(e)

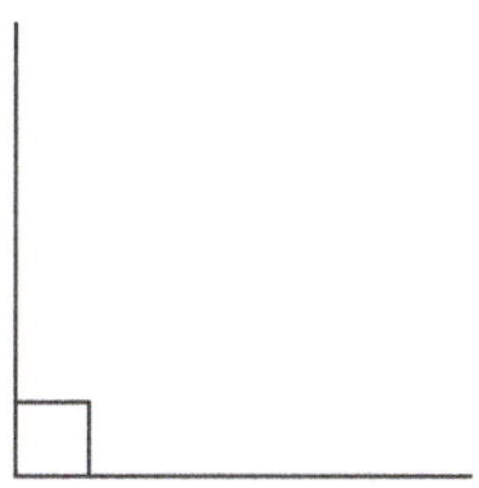

(f)

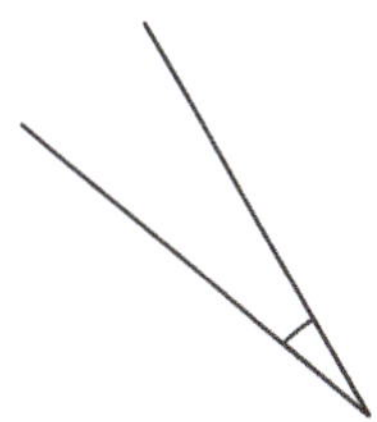

(g)

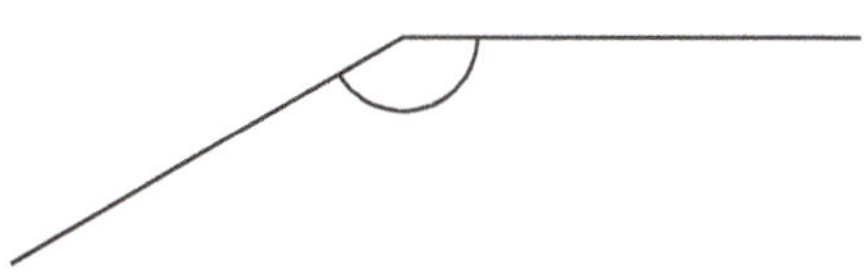

(h)

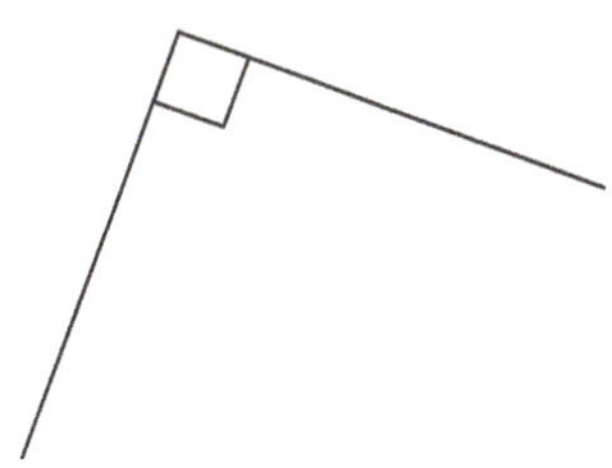

3 Estimate the size of the angles. Then use a protractor to measure them.

(a)

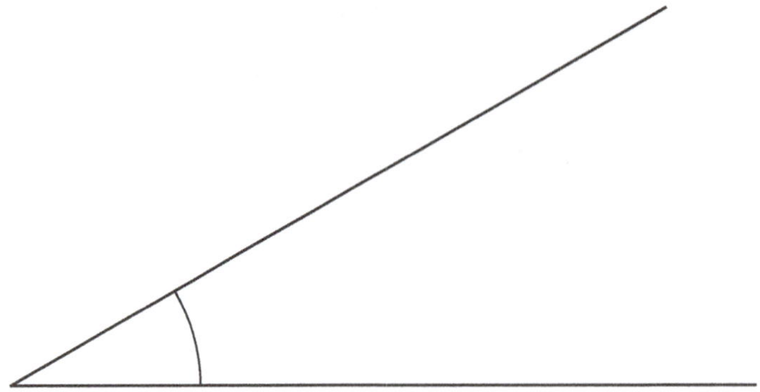

Estimate [ ] Measured [ ]

(b)

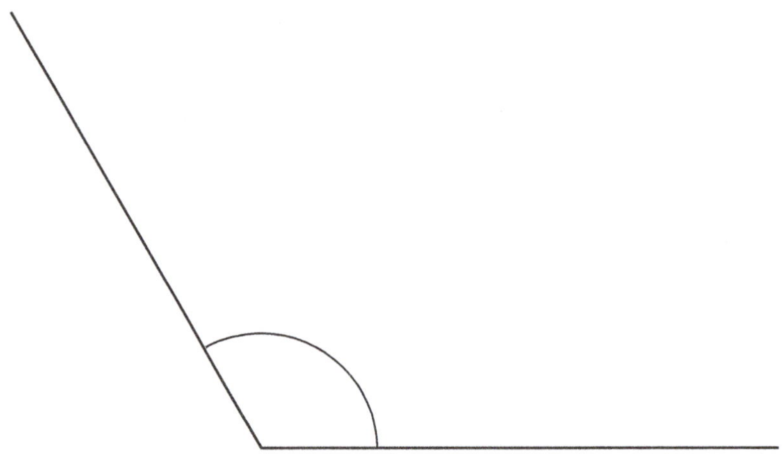

Estimate [ ] Measured [ ]

(c)

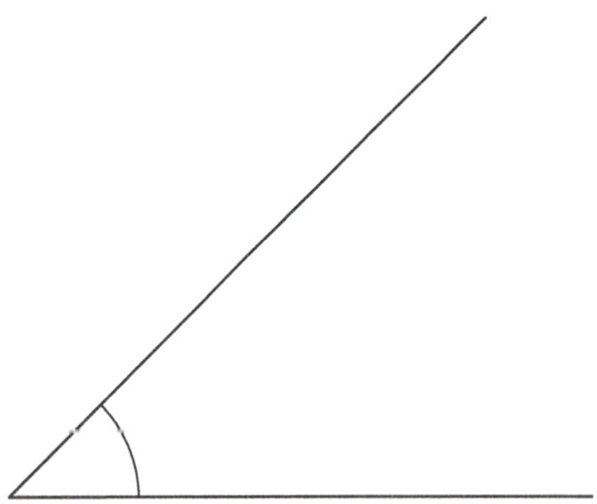

Estimate [ ] Measured [ ]

(d)

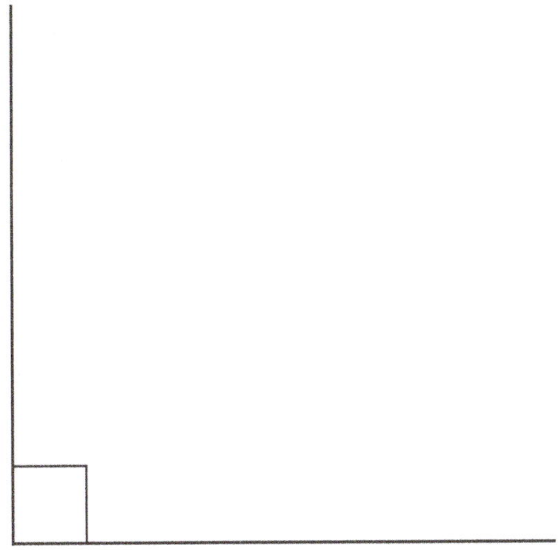

Estimate [ ] Measured [ ]

(e)

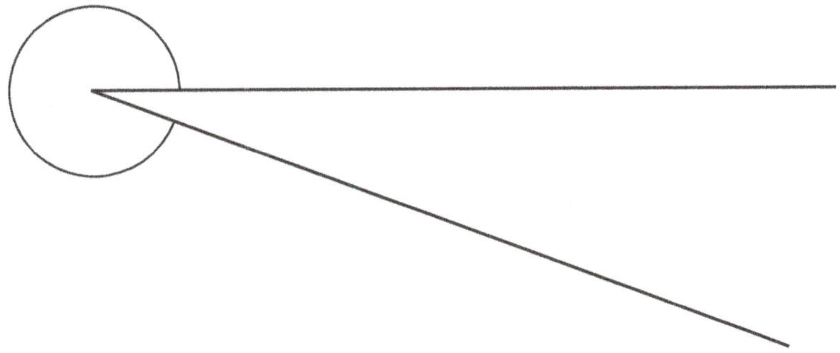

Estimate [ ] Measured [ ]

(f)

Estimate [ ] Measured [ ]

4. Complete the following.

(a) Use a protractor to draw an acute angle of 60°.

(b) Use a protractor to draw an obtuse angle of 130°.

(c) Use a protractor to draw a reflex angle of 220°.

Practice 2: Angles on a straight line

1 Find the missing angle.

(a)

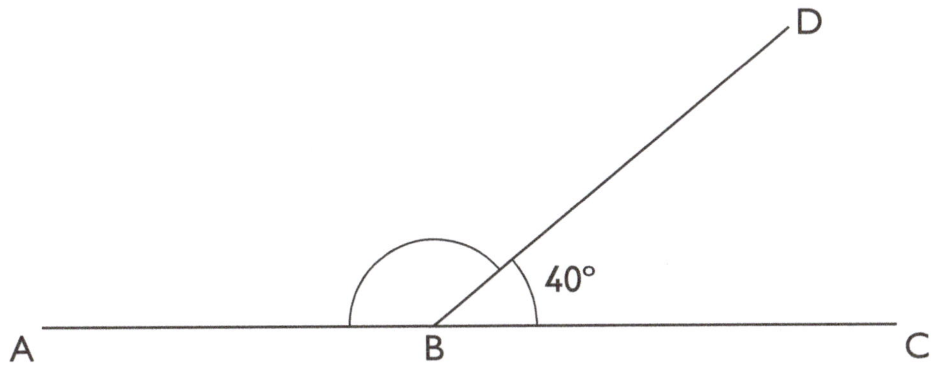

The line ____ is a straight line. The sum of its angles is ____.

∠ABD = ____ – ____

= ____

(b)

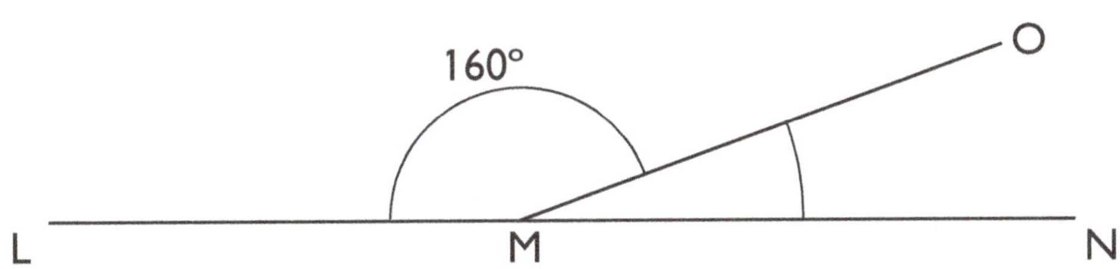

The line ____ is a straight line. The sum of its angles is ____.

∠NMO = ____ – ____

= ____

(c)

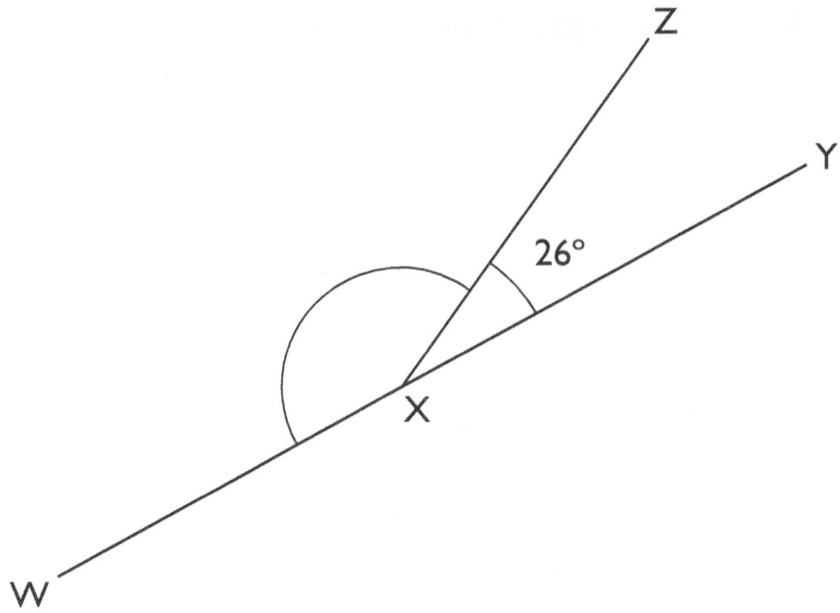

The line ☐ is a straight line. The sum of its angles is ☐.

∠WXZ = ☐ – ☐

= ☐

(d)

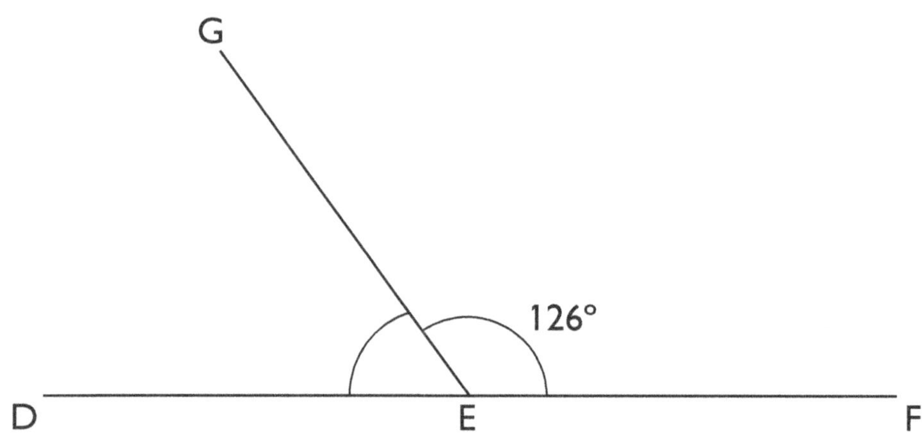

The line ☐ is a straight line. The sum of its angles is ☐.

∠DEG = ☐ – ☐

= ☐

(e) 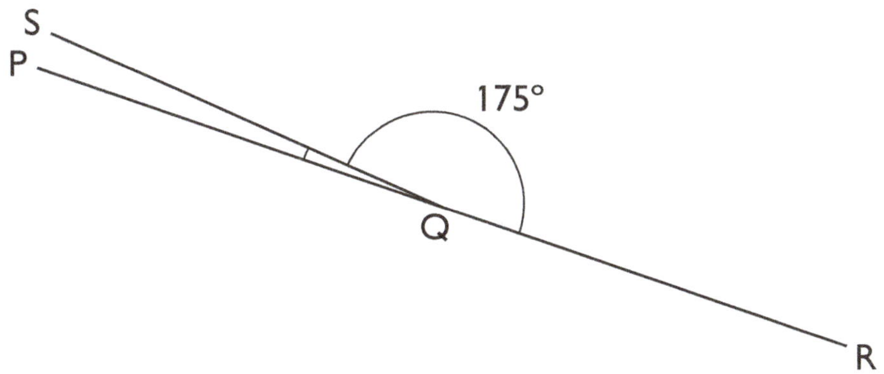

The line ☐ is a straight line. The sum of its angles is ☐.

∠PQS = ☐ – ☐

= ☐

(f) 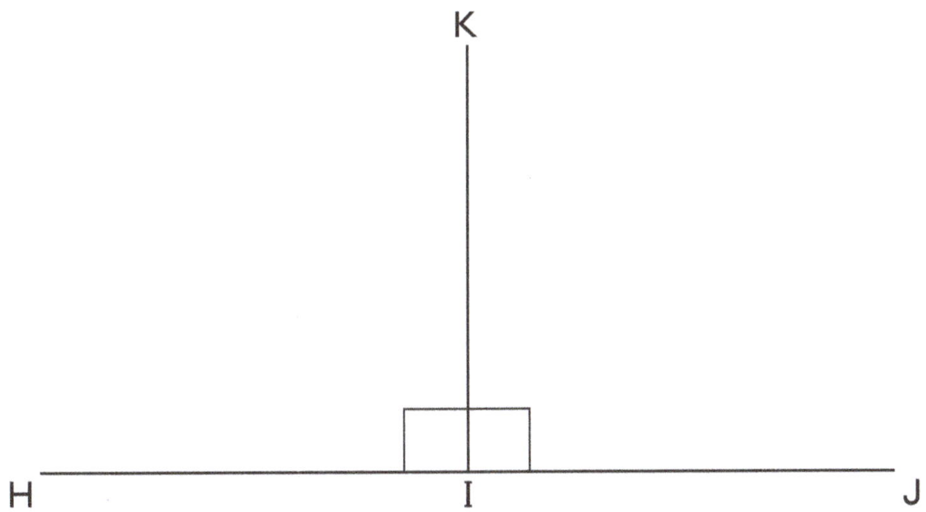

The line ☐ is a straight line. The sum of its angles is ☐.

∠HIK = ∠KIJ = ☐

2 Find the missing angle. Show your working.

(a)

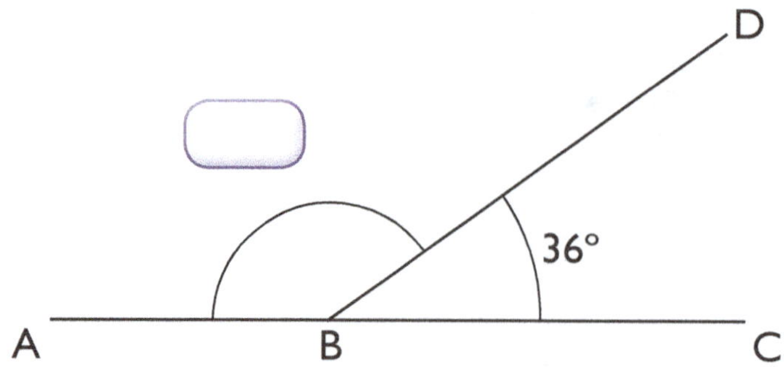

(b)

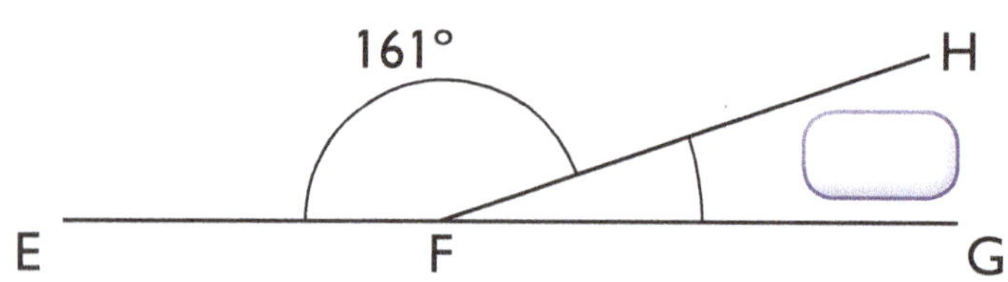

(c)

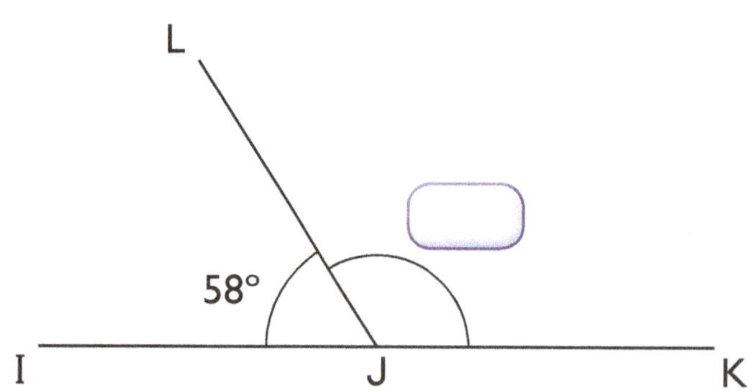

Practice 3: Triangles review

1 Look at each of the triangles and complete the blanks.

(a)

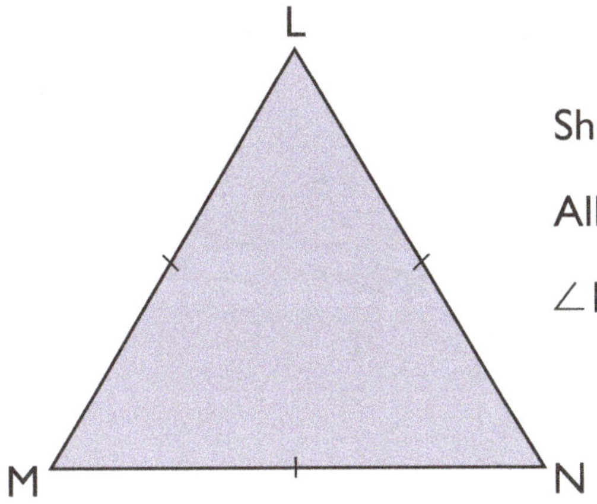

Shape LMN is an ______ triangle.

All of the sides have ______ length.

∠L = ∠M = ∠N = ______°

(b)

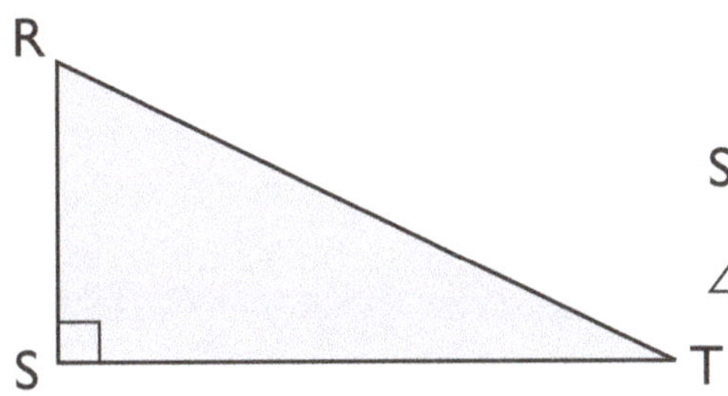

Shape RST is a ______ triangle.

∠S = ______°

(c)

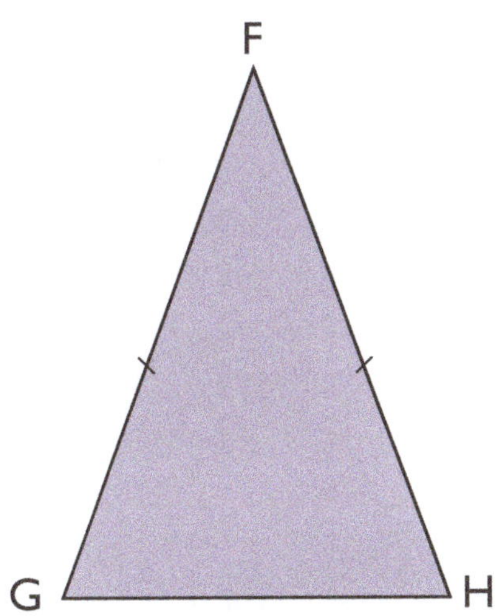

Shape FGH is an ______ triangle.

Side GF has the same length as side ______.

∠G = ∠______

2 Write 'R' next to the right-angled triangles. Write 'I' next to the isosceles triangles. Write 'E' next to the equilateral triangles.

(a)

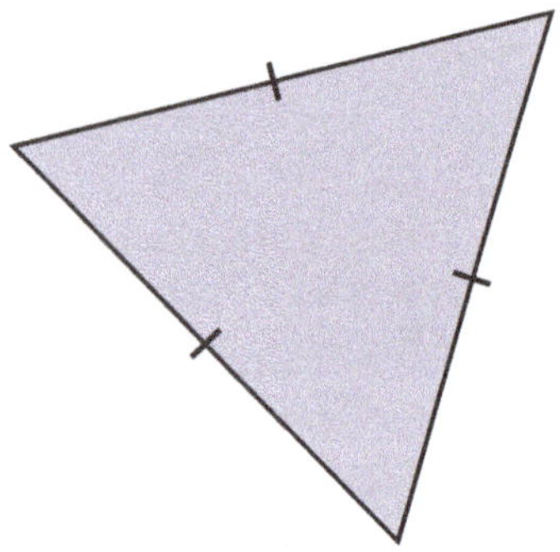

(b)

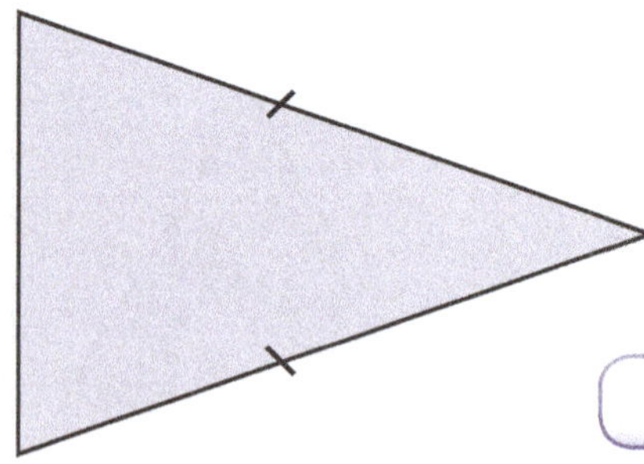

(c)

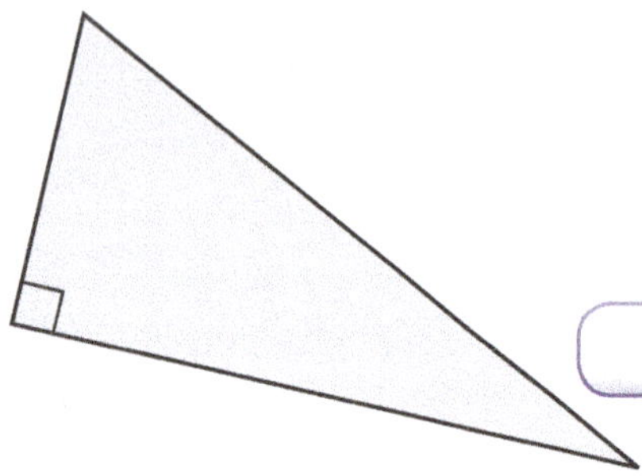

(d)

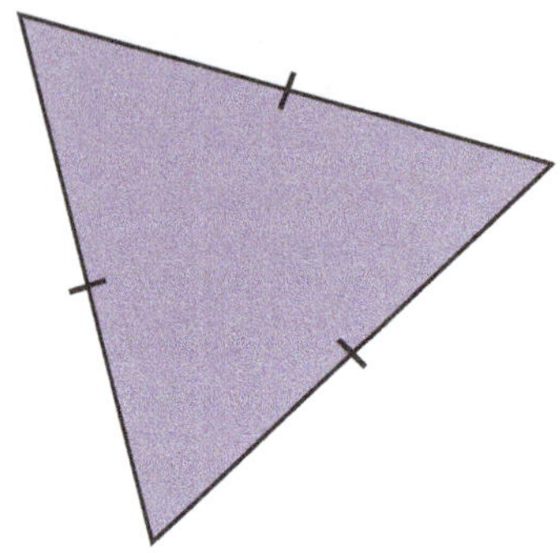

(e)

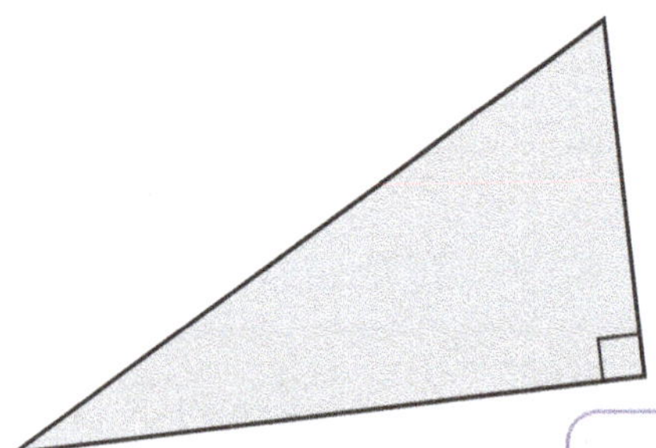

(f)

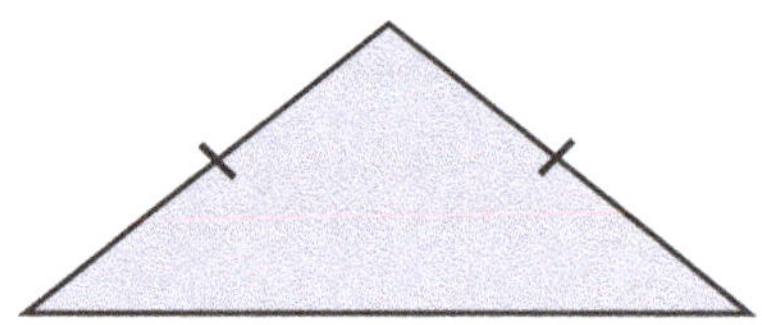

(g)

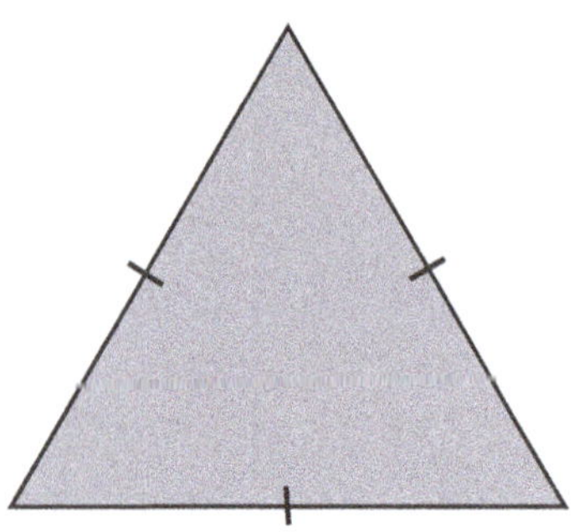

(h)

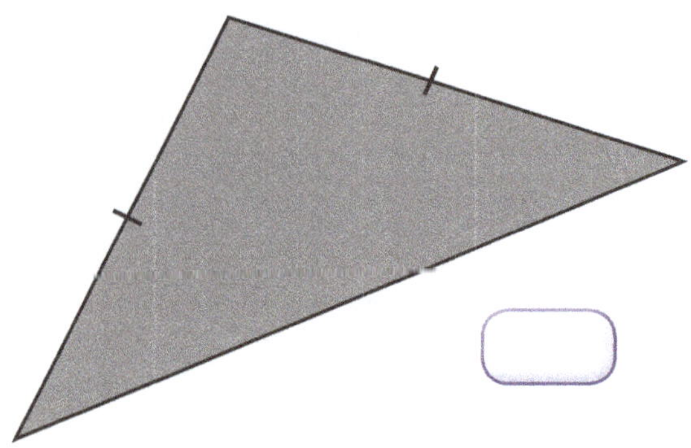

3 Use the grid paper below to draw a right-angled triangle and an isosceles triangle.

4 Use the dotted area below to draw 3 equilateral triangles of different sizes.

Practice 4: Parallel lines

1 Use a set square and ruler to draw the following lines.

(a) Draw and label a line so that AB//CD.

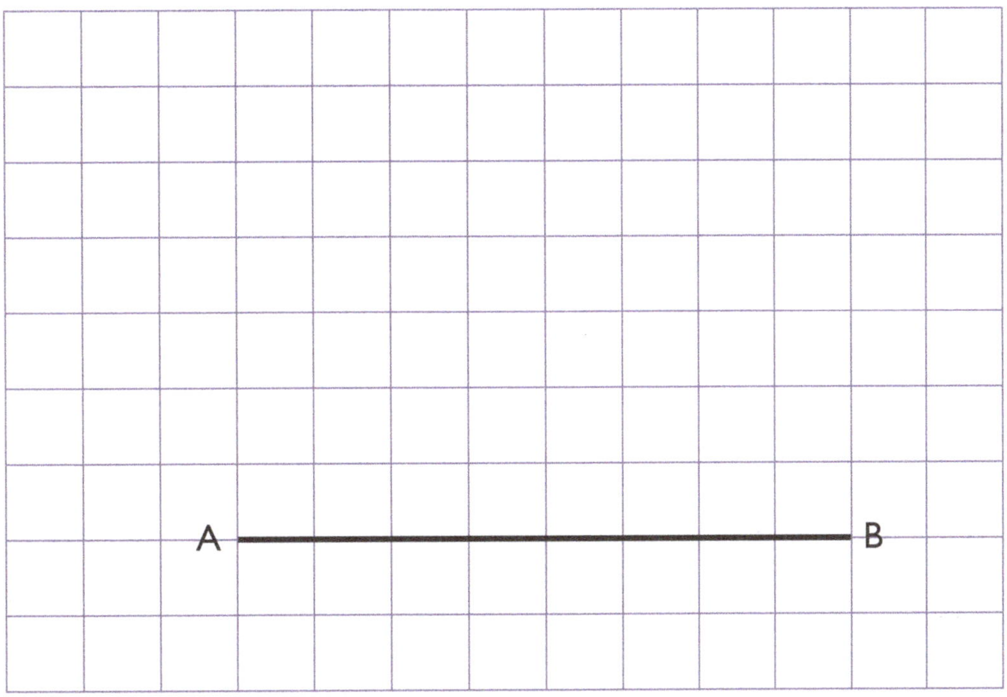

(b) Draw and label 2 lines so that EF//GH//IJ.

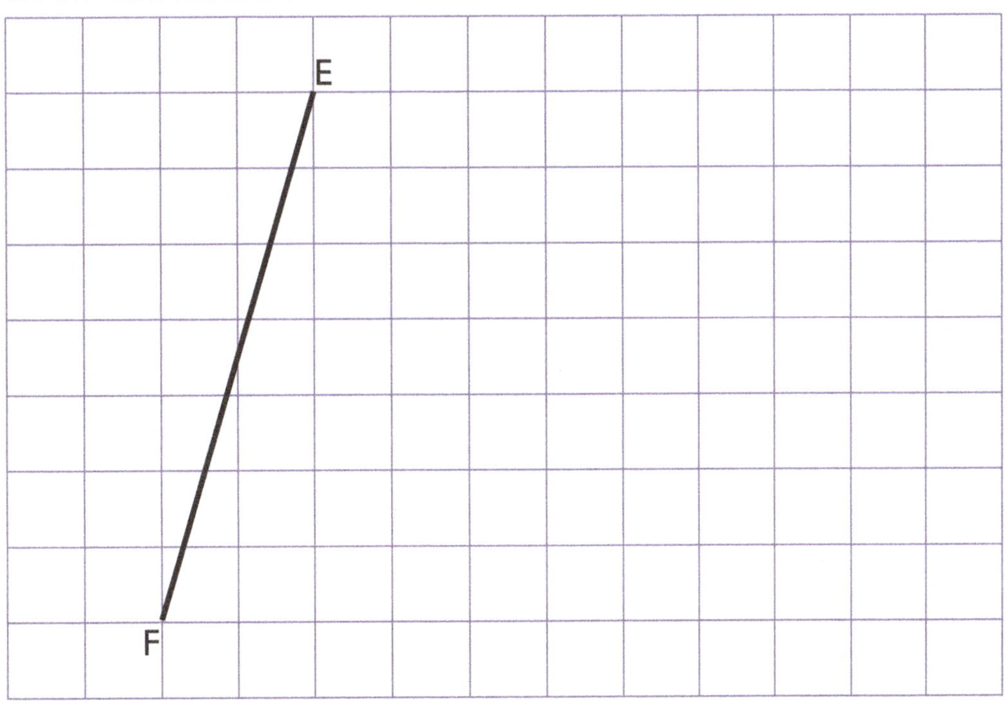

(c) Draw and label 2 lines so that PQ//RS. Draw another line so that MN//PQ.

(d) Draw a 4-sided shape that has 2 pairs of parallel lines.

2 Use a set square and a ruler to check whether the pairs of lines are parallel.

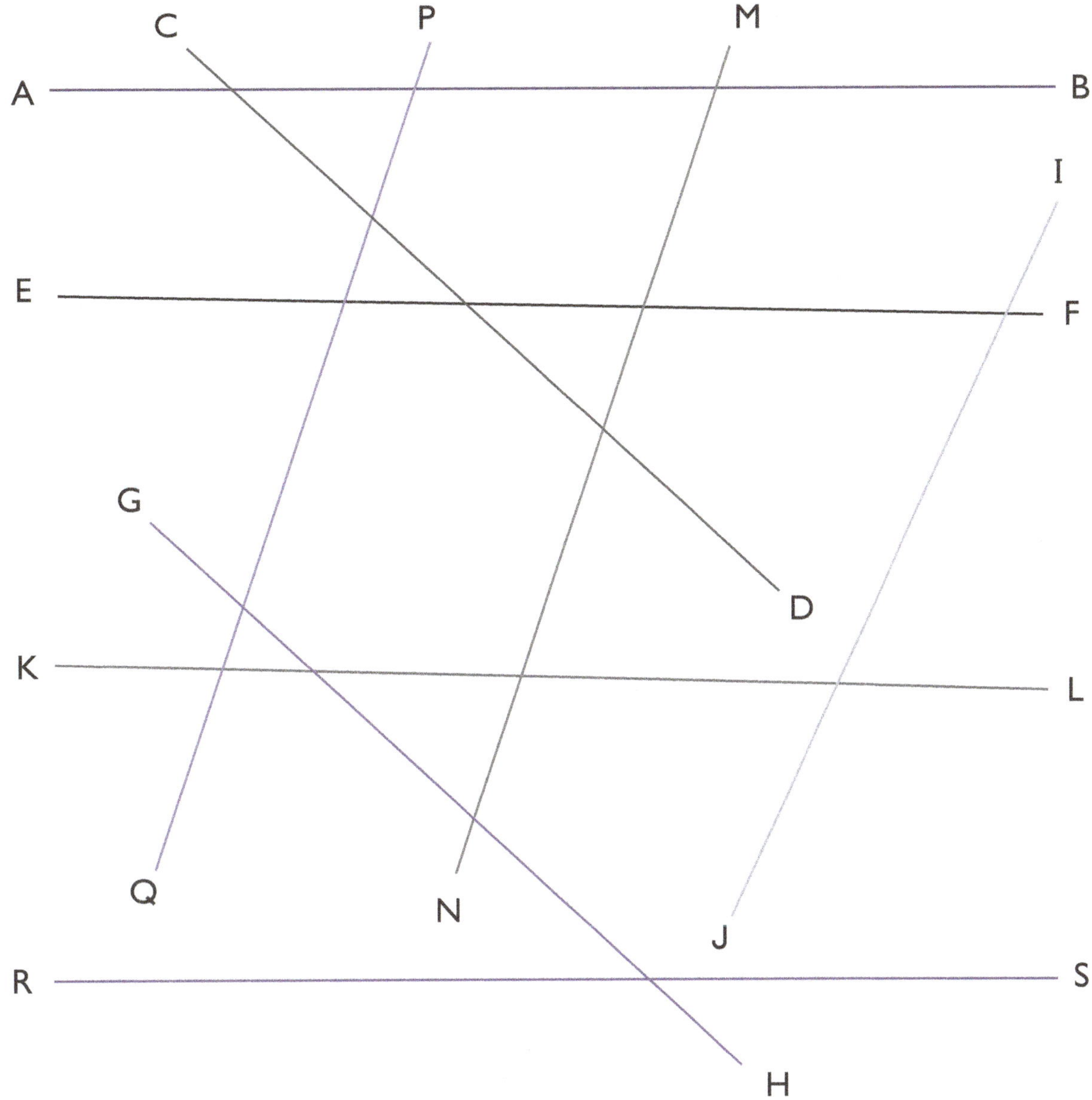

(a) AB // CD ☐ Yes ☐ No

(b) AB // RS ☐ Yes ☐ No

(c) EF // KL ☐ Yes ☐ No

(d) EF // RS ☐ Yes ☐ No

(e) PQ // IJ ☐ Yes ☐ No

(f) MN // PQ ☐ Yes ☐ No

Practice 5: Perpendicular lines

1 Find pairs of lines that are perpendicular.

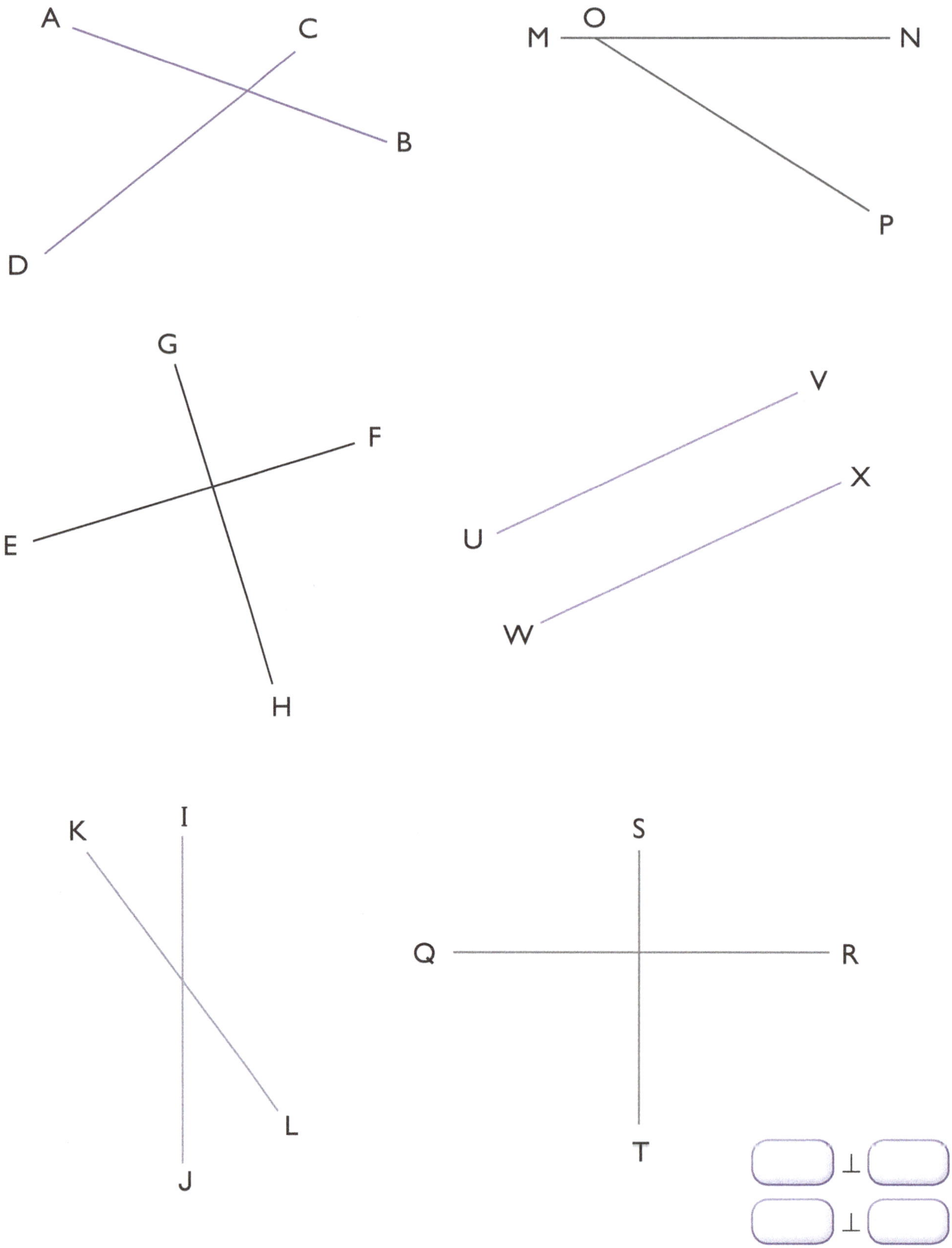

2 Use a set square and ruler to draw the following perpendicular lines.

(a) Draw and label a line so that AB ⊥ CD.

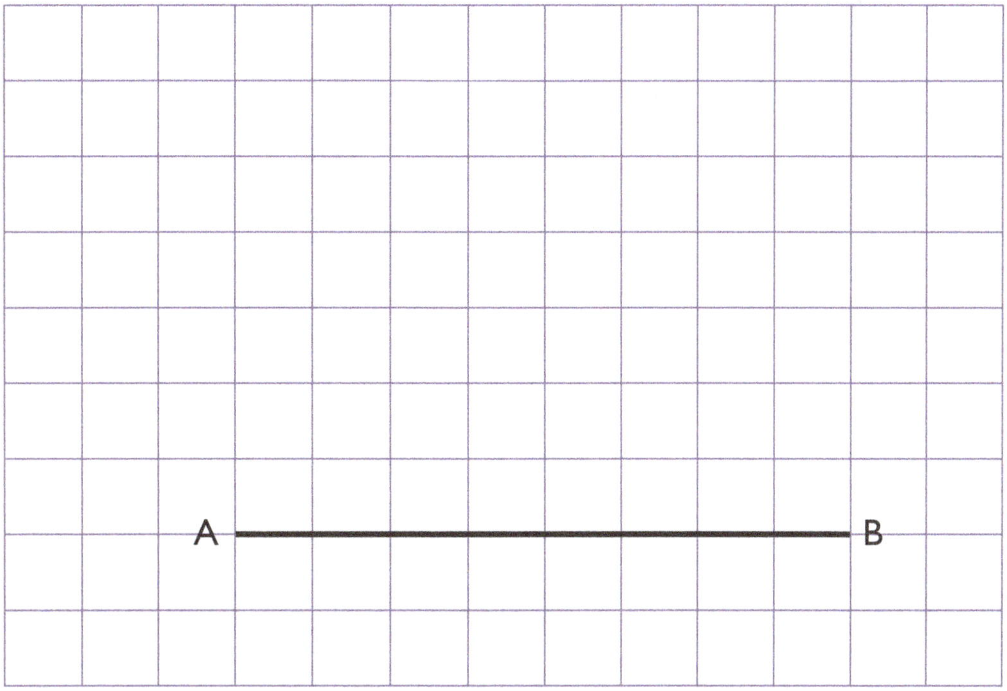

(b) Draw and label 2 lines so that EF ⊥ GH and EF ⊥ JK.

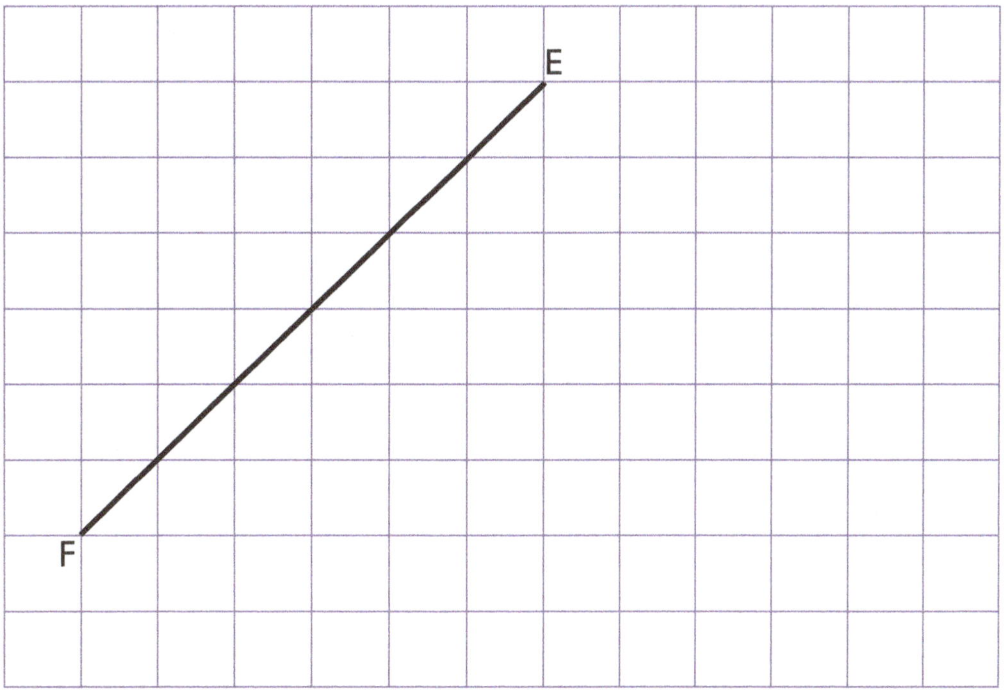

(c) Half a rectangle has been drawn below. Complete the rectangle so that:

- AB ⊥ BD
- AC ⊥ CD
- AB // CD
- AC // BD

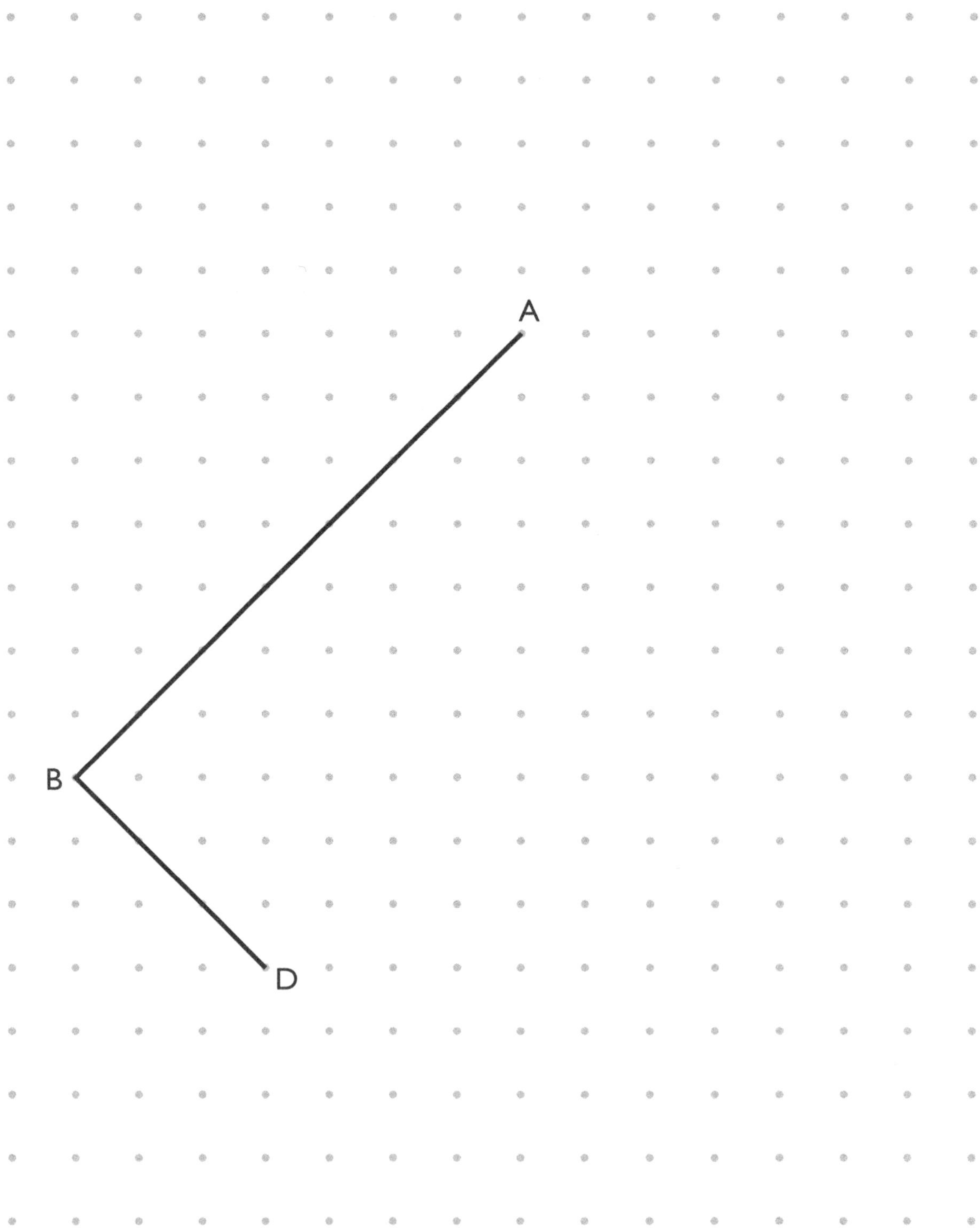

Practice 6: Creating patterns with 2 lines of symmetry

1. Complete the patterns.

(a)

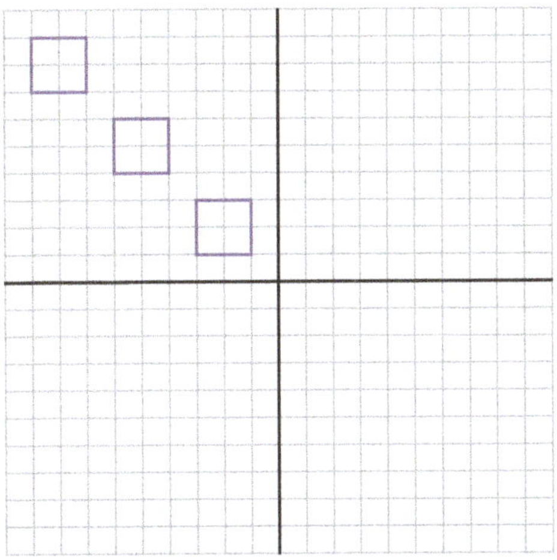

(b)

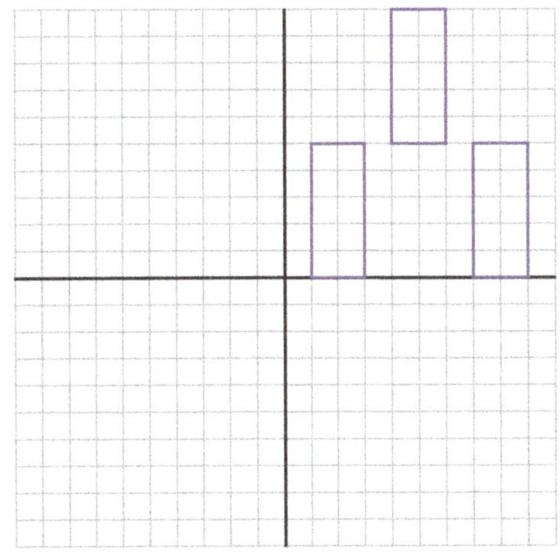

(c)

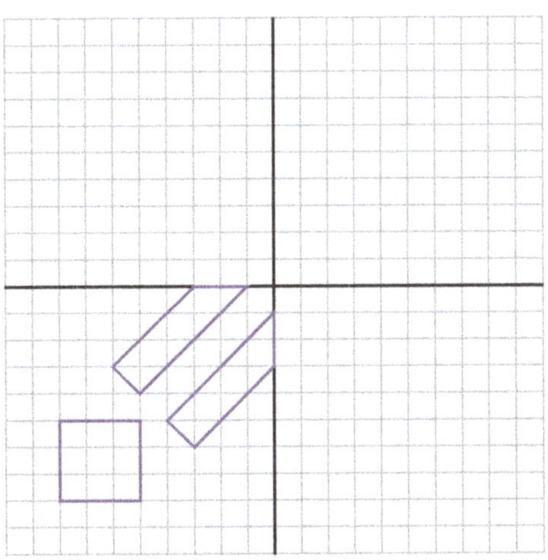

(d)

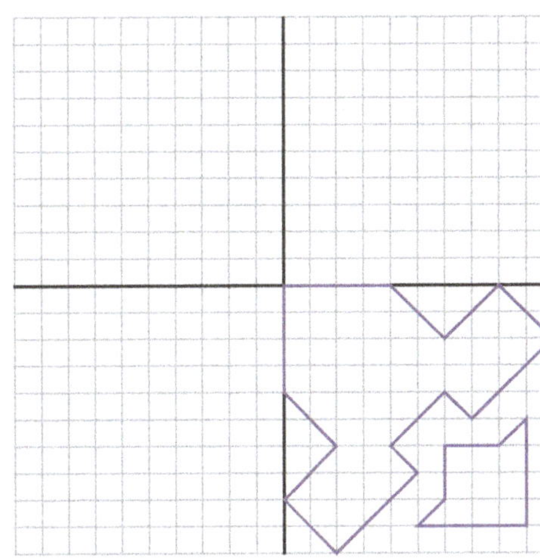

(e)

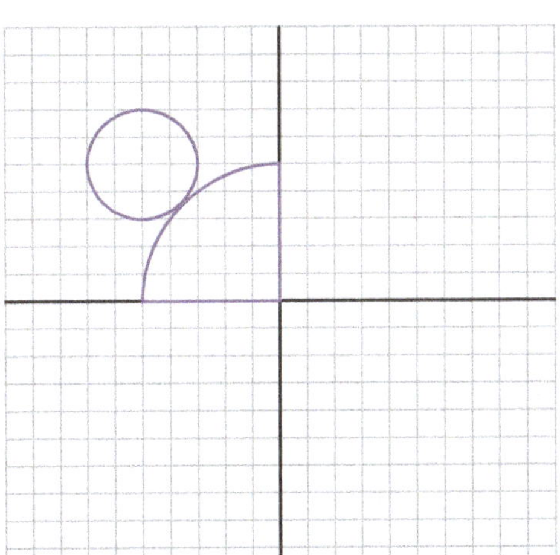

(f)

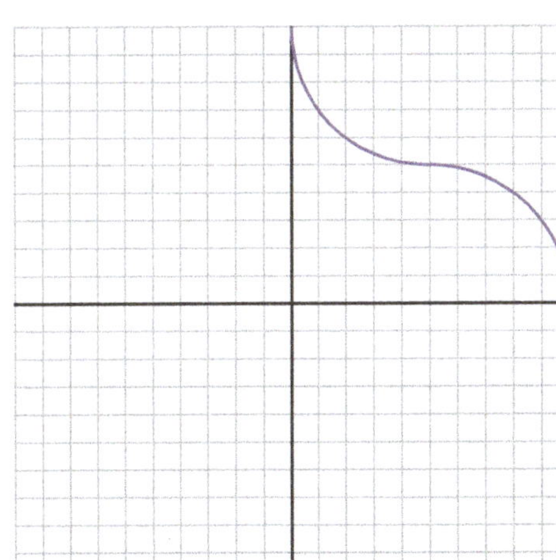

(g)

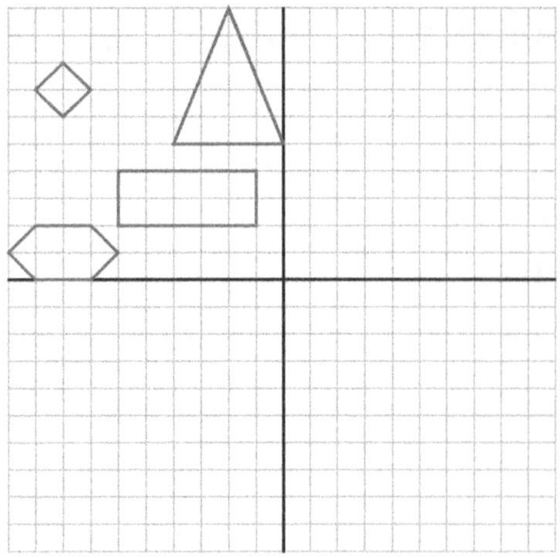

(h)

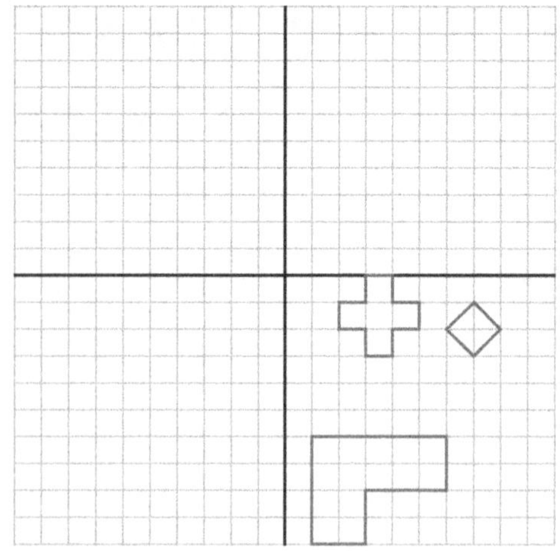

(i)

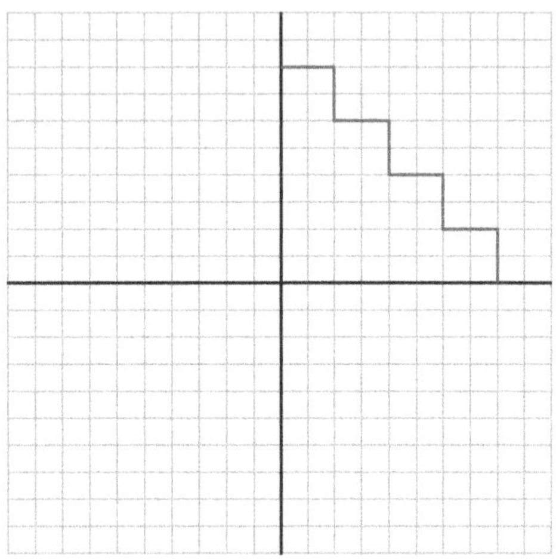

(j)

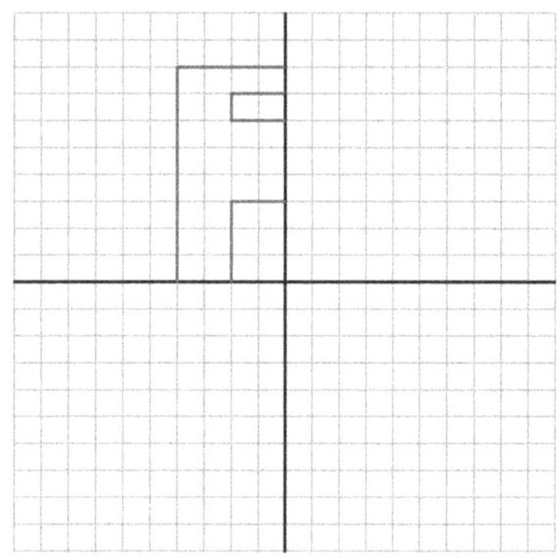

(k)

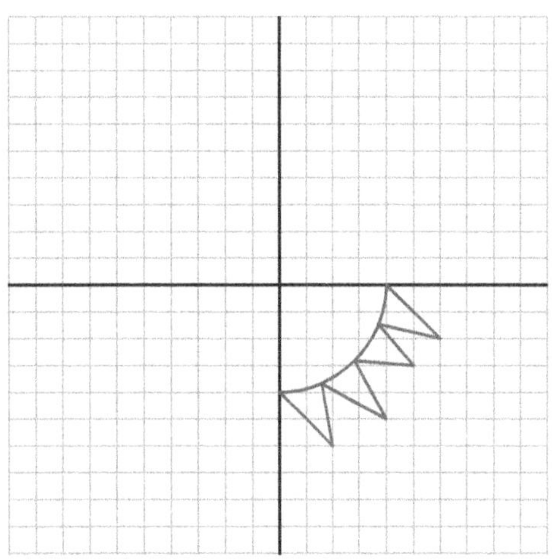

(l)

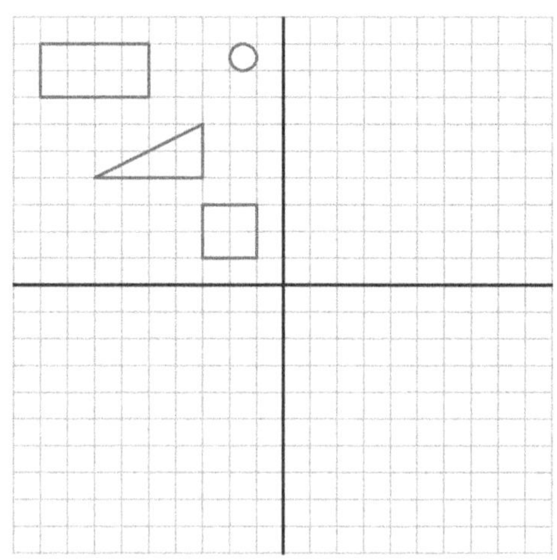

2 Circle the patterns that have two lines of symmetry.

(a)

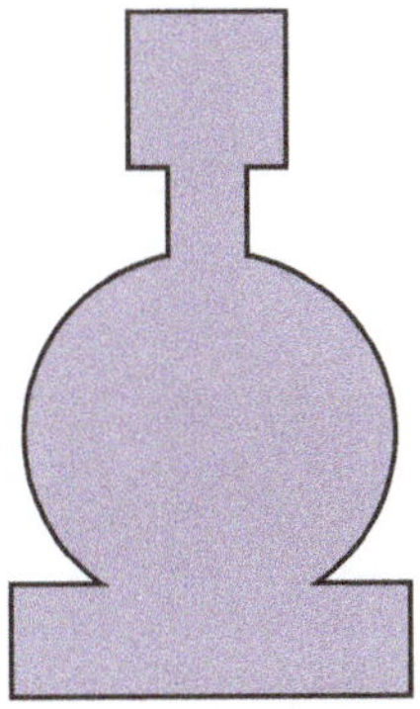

(b)

(c)

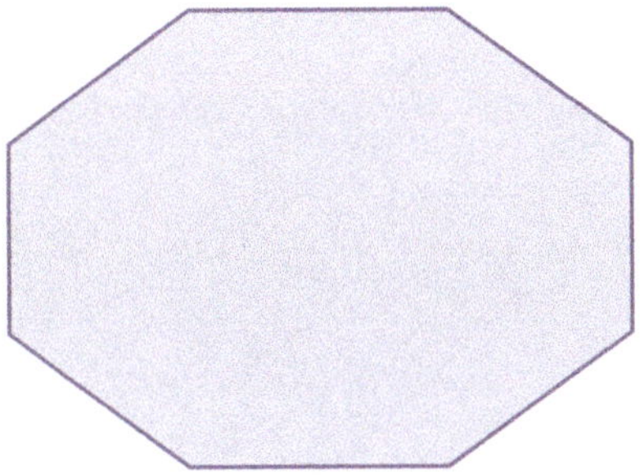

(d)

(e)

(f)

Practice 7: Reflective and rotational symmetry

1 Put a tick next to the shapes with four lines of symmetry and rotational symmetry.

(a)

☐

(b)

☐

(c)

☐

(d)

☐

(e)

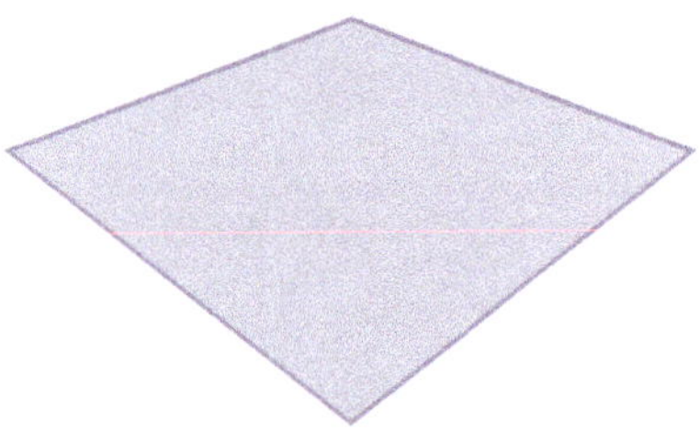

☐

(f)

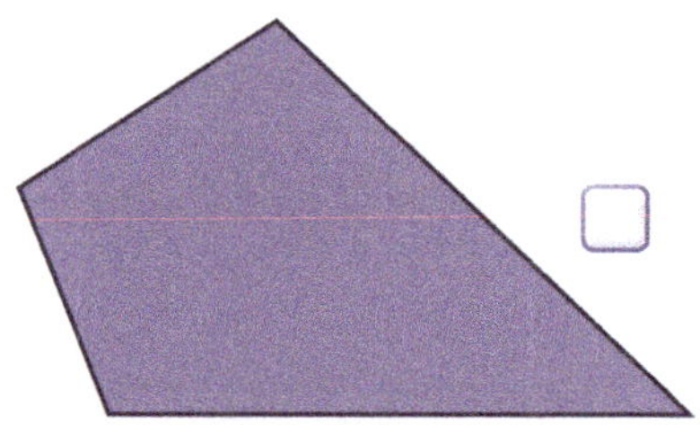

☐

(g)

☐

(h)

☐

2 Draw the lines of symmetry on each of the regular polygons. State the rotational symmetry of each shape.

(a)

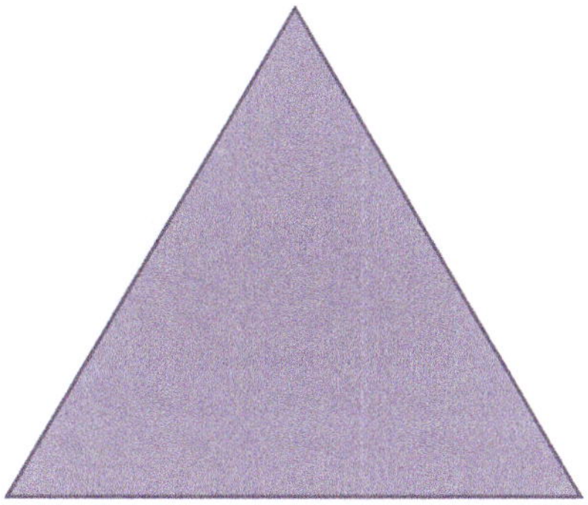

(b)

(c)

(d)

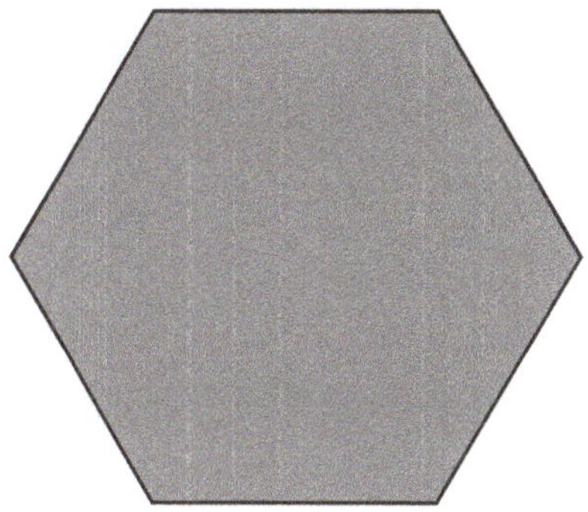

(e)

(f)

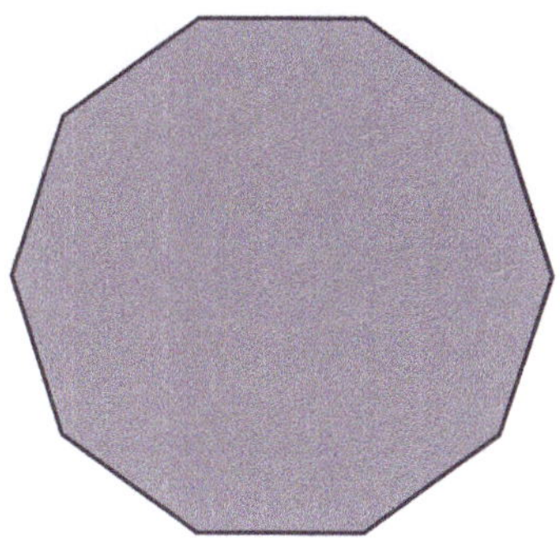

Practice 8: Review of 3D shapes

Name these solids.

(a)

(b)

(c)

(d)

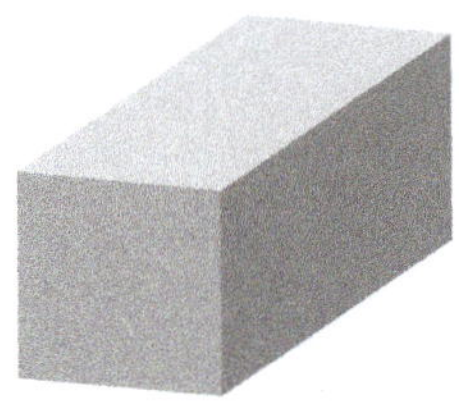

(e)

(f)

(g)

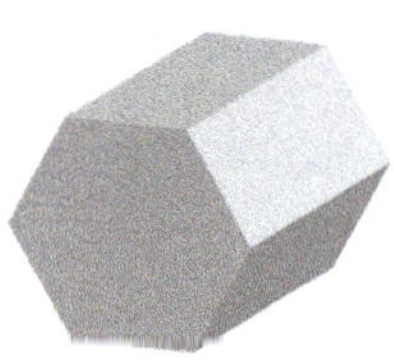

(h)

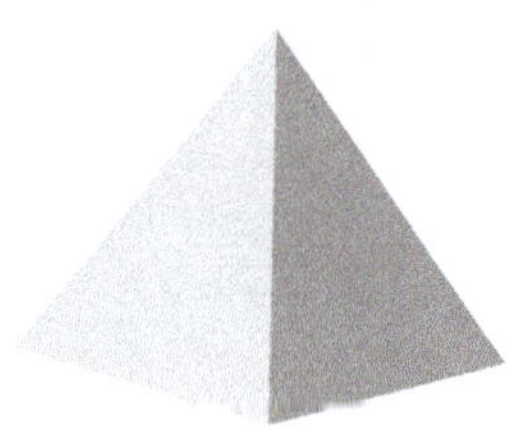

Practice 9: Review of nets of solids

Draw a line from the net to its solid.

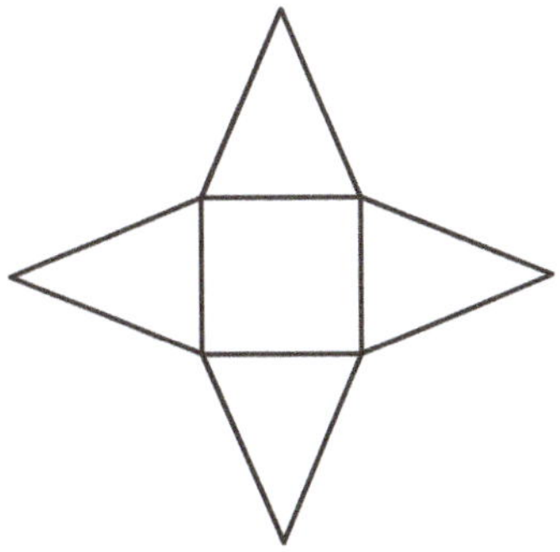

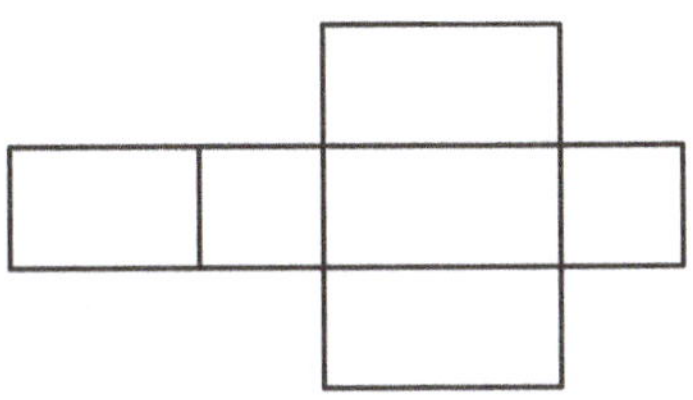

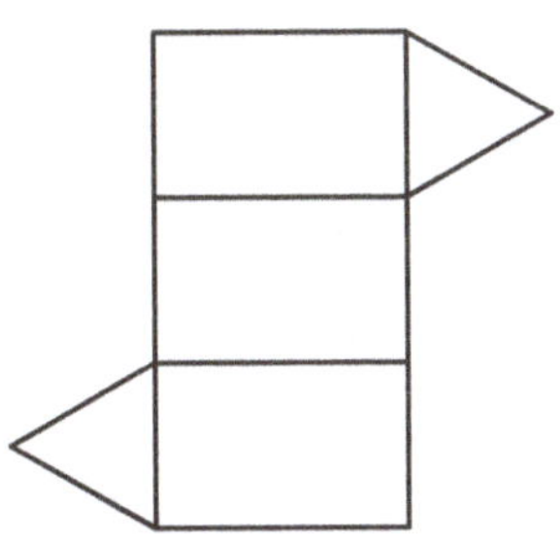

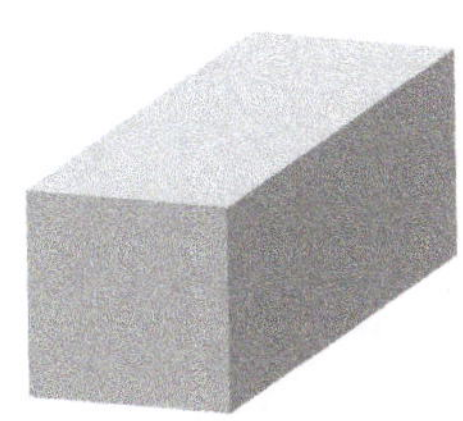

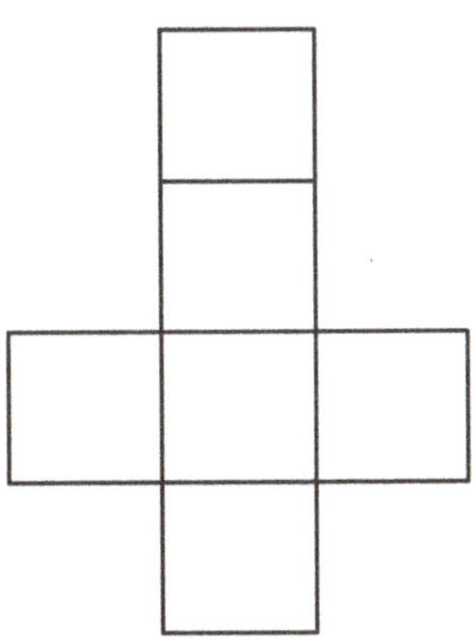

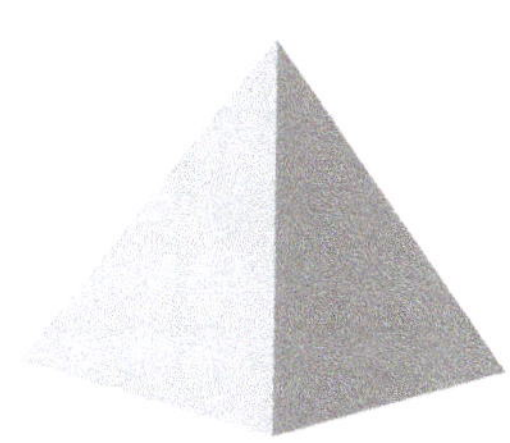

4 Multiplication

Practice 1: Multiplication review

Time yourself to see how quickly you can complete these tables. See if you can improve your time as you move from **(a)** to **(b)** and so on.

(a)

2 × 3 =	4 × 5 =	7 × 4 =	8 × 2 =
10 × 10 =	3 × 7 =	6 × 6 =	2 × 2 =
0 × 4 =	9 × 2 =	3 × 6 =	7 × 1 =
2 × 5 =	4 × 2 =	8 × 3 =	8 × 4 =
8 × 5 =	5 × 6 =	1 × 1 =	3 × 5 =
9 × 8 =	10 × 1 =	10 × 4 =	7 × 6 =
2 × 10 =	5 × 7 =	8 × 2 =	5 × 9 =
9 × 4 =	2 × 5 =	3 × 4 =	4 × 7 =
7 × 9 =	2 × 4 =	1 × 0 =	3 × 4 =
9 × 4 =	6 × 7 =	8 × 3 =	4 × 8 =
10 × 7 =	2 × 6 =	8 × 1 =	2 × 5 =
6 × 7 =	3 × 4 =	9 × 4 =	9 × 9 =

Time

(b)

2 × 4 =	7 × 6 =	10 × 3 =	9 × 4 =
7 × 2 =	5 × 7 =	2 × 1 =	0 × 7 =
4 × 5 =	3 × 7 =	9 × 9 =	7 × 8 =
8 × 8 =	3 × 8 =	9 × 2 =	2 × 6 =
1 × 9 =	3 × 5 =	8 × 3 =	5 × 6 =
2 × 9 =	8 × 4 =	0 × 2 =	5 × 3 =
7 × 4 =	2 × 2 =	7 × 8 =	4 × 6 =
9 × 8 =	10 × 4 =	5 × 10 =	3 × 7 =
2 × 7 =	8 × 3 =	3 × 2 =	9 × 10 =
4 × 4 =	2 × 8 =	4 × 8 =	5 × 4 =
8 × 3 =	8 × 7 =	2 × 5 =	7 × 5 =
9 × 4 =	2 × 9 =	5 × 8 =	9 × 3 =

Time

(c)

0 × 4 =	2 × 5 =	5 × 4 =	8 × 9 =
4 × 5 =	8 × 7 =	9 × 10 =	9 × 3 =
2 × 7 =	5 × 6 =	7 × 9 =	2 × 1 =
4 × 8 =	3 × 7 =	10 × 4 =	7 × 6 =
8 × 3 =	2 × 8 =	3 × 3 =	2 × 7 =
8 × 8 =	9 × 3 =	4 × 7 =	9 × 6 =
1 × 4 =	7 × 8 =	10 × 10 =	4 × 7 =
2 × 4 =	9 × 10 =	7 × 8 =	3 × 8 =
8 × 2 =	7 × 5 =	5 × 5 =	4 × 5 =
10 × 4 =	8 × 2 =	7 × 9 =	6 × 3 =
9 × 5 =	8 × 5 =	1 × 6 =	9 × 2 =
7 × 5 =	4 × 2 =	8 × 5 =	7 × 3 =

Time

2 Answer the following.

(a) Circle the multiples of 4.

8
4 3 6
13
14
16
20
18 19

(b) Circle the multiples of 7.

7 14
8 13
20
28
24 35 32
26 30 37

(c) Circle the multiples of 3.

13
3 4 12
19
8
6 14
18 21
16

(d) Circle the multiples of 9.

16
18
9
6 19
8 36
21
31 45
27

Practice 2: Multiplying multiples of 10 to 90 and multiples of 100 to 900 by a single-digit number

1 Write 4 multiplication facts that you can derive from each of the following.

Example

$3 \times 4 = 12$

$3 \times 40 = 120$ | $40 \times 3 = 120$ | $300 \times 4 = 1200$ | $3 \times 400 = 1200$

(a) $5 \times 6 = 30$

(b) $8 \times 3 = 24$

(c) $9 \times 3 = 27$

(d) $7 \times 6 = 42$

2 Circle the correctly derived multiplication equation.

(a) If $2 \times 8 = 16$, then

$20 \times 8 = 1\,600$

$2 \times 80 = 160$

(b) If $5 \times 6 = 30$, then

$500 \times 6 = 300$

$50 \times 6 = 300$

(c) If $7 \times 3 = 21$, then

$7 \times 300 = 2\,100$

$70 \times 3 = 2\,100$

(d) If $9 \times 4 = 28$, then

$9 \times 40 = 2\,800$

$900 \times 4 = 2\,800$

Practice 3: Multiplying by 19 or 21 mentally

Complete the following multiplication questions. Once you have calculated each answer, write down the steps you took mentally.

(a) $19 \times 6 =$ ☐

(b) $21 \times 4 =$ ☐

(c) $19 \times 12 =$ ☐

(d) 8 × 21 =

(e) 15 × 19 =

(f) 19 × 7 =

Practice 4: Multiplying by 25 mentally

Complete the following multiplication questions. Once you have calculated each answer, write down the steps you took mentally.

(a) $25 \times 6 =$ ☐

(b) $9 \times 25 =$ ☐

(c) $25 \times 18 =$ ☐

(d) 25 × 22 =

(e) 14 × 25 =

(f) 15 × 25 =

Practice 5: Using factors to multiply

Use your knowledge of factors to find the solutions to these questions. Show your working.

(a) $12 \times 16 =$ ______

(b) $18 \times 14 =$ ______

(c) $24 \times 12 =$ ______

(d) $16 \times 8 =$ ______

(e) $22 \times 6 =$ ______

(f) $8 \times 12 =$ ______

Practice 6: Multiplying by a 2-digit number

1 Complete the following.

(a) A banana costs 75 cents at the school canteen. If 37 bananas are sold in 1 day, how much money does the canteen make?

First, let's make an estimate.

☐ ≈ ☐

☐ ≈ ☐

☐ × ☐ = ☐

Let's find the actual product by multiplying rows and columns in a table and adding the results.

×	☐	☐
☐	☐	☐
☐	☐	☐

Now we can add up all of the results.

	☐	☐	☐	☐
		☐	☐	☐
		☐	☐	☐
+			☐	☐
	☐	☐	☐	☐

So, the product of ☐ and ☐ is ☐.

This is close to the estimate of ☐.

So, the canteen makes ☐.

(b) There are 26 tomatoes in a basket. How many tomatoes are there in 115 such baskets?

First, let's make an estimate.

☐ ≈ ☐

☐ ≈ ☐

☐ × ☐ = ☐

Let's find the actual product by multiplying rows and columns in a table and adding the results.

×	☐	☐
☐	☐	☐
☐	☐	☐

Now we can add up all of the results.

+

So, the product of ☐ and ☐ is ☐.

This is close to the estimate of ☐.

So, there are ☐ in ☐ baskets.

(c) A dictionary has 356 pages.
The school library orders 24 dictionaries.
How many pages are there altogether?

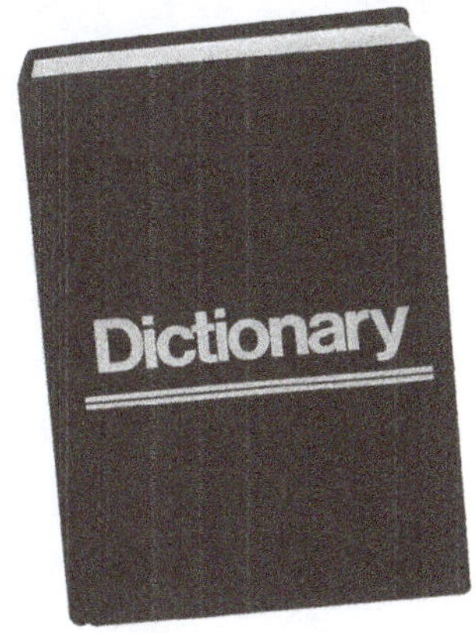

First, let's make an estimate.

☐ ≈ ☐

☐ ≈ ☐

☐ × ☐ = ☐

Let us find the actual product by using the column method.

		☐	☐	☐
×			☐	☐
	☐	☐	☐	☐
+	☐	☐	☐	0
	☐	☐	☐	☐

So, the product of ☐ and ☐ is ☐.

This is close to the estimate of ☐.

So, there are ☐ pages in ☐ dictionaries.

(d) A school is having a party. There will be 147 learners at the party. The school will provide party hats for each learner. If the hats cost 56 cents each, how much money will the school have to spend?

First, let's make an estimate.

[ ] ≈ [ ]

[ ] ≈ [ ]

[ ] × [ ] = [ ]

Let us find the actual product by using the column method.

×

+

So, the product of [ ] and [ ] is [ ].

This is close to the estimate of [ ].

So, the school will have to spend [ ] on the party hats.

2. Complete the following by multiplying rows and columns in a table and adding the results. Show your working.

(a) $49 \times 23 =$ ______

(b) $55 \times 75 =$ ______

(c) $69 \times 33 =$ ______

(d) $179 \times 21 =$ ☐

(e) $262 \times 55 =$ ☐

(f) $36 \times 393 =$ ☐

3. Complete the following using the column method. Show your working.

(a) $19 \times 72 =$ ☐

(b) $24 \times 26 =$ ☐

(c) $35 \times 16 =$ ☐

(d) $47 \times 13 =$ ☐

(e) 61 × 77 =

(f) 132 × 29 =

(g) 258 × 13 =

(h) 93 × 207 =

Problem Solving

In a cooking school there are 2 baking classes. Class A has 34 people. Class B has 43 people. Each person has to bake 28 cookies during the baking class. How many more cookies will Class B bake than Class A?

First, find the number of cookies each class will bake, using the column method.

Class A:

×

+

Class B:

×

+

Then, subtract the number of cookies Class A will bake from the number of cookies Class B will bake.

___ − ___ = ___

Class B will bake ___ more cookies than Class A.

Practice 7: Word problems

1. A company wants to purchase new chairs for its 68 staff. The chairs cost $247 each. How much money does the company need to purchase the chairs?

2. A library wants to buy 139 sets of books. Each set contains 14 books. How many books will the library buy?

3 A new department store is being built. The building will be constructed using large bricks. Each brick has a mass of 9 kg. If a total of 6 586 bricks are used, what will the total mass be? Each brick costs $12. Find the total cost of the bricks.

Break the problem into 2 parts.

Part 1

Part 2

4 A carpenter purchases 67 boxes of nails. Each box contains 258 nails.

(a) How many nails did he purchase altogether?

(b) If 1 box of nails costs 89 cents, how much did he spend altogether?

5. A sandwich costs 95 cents.

(a) How much would it cost to buy sandwiches for 187 students (if each student has one sandwich)?

(b) The teacher gives $200 to pay for the sandwiches. How much change will she receive?

Practice 8: Mixed operations with a pair of brackets

1 Look at the diagrams below. Fill in the blanks to find the total number of items.

(a)

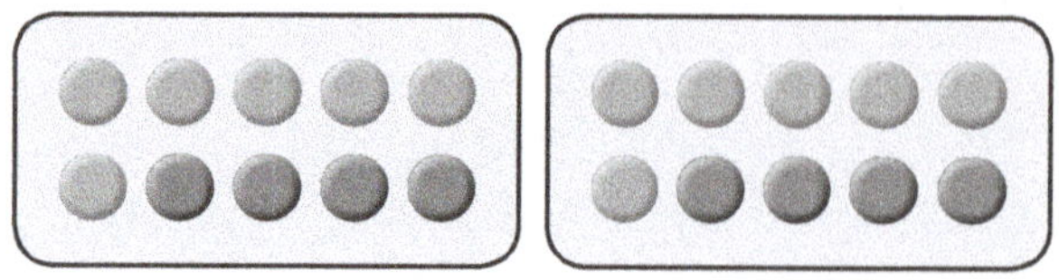

(___ + ___) × ___ = ___

(b)

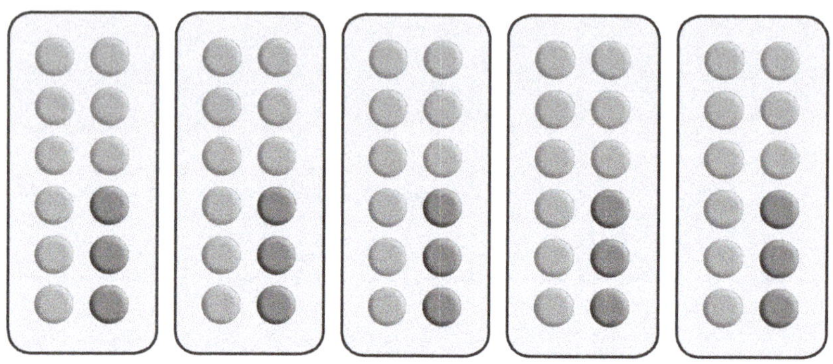

___ × (___ + ___) = ___

(c)

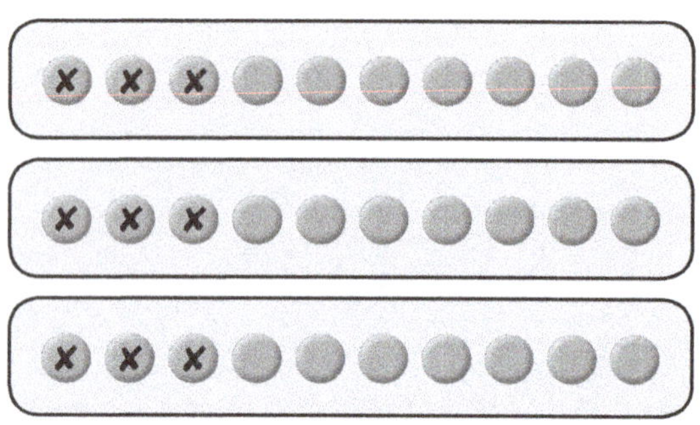

___ × (___ + ___) = ___

(d) 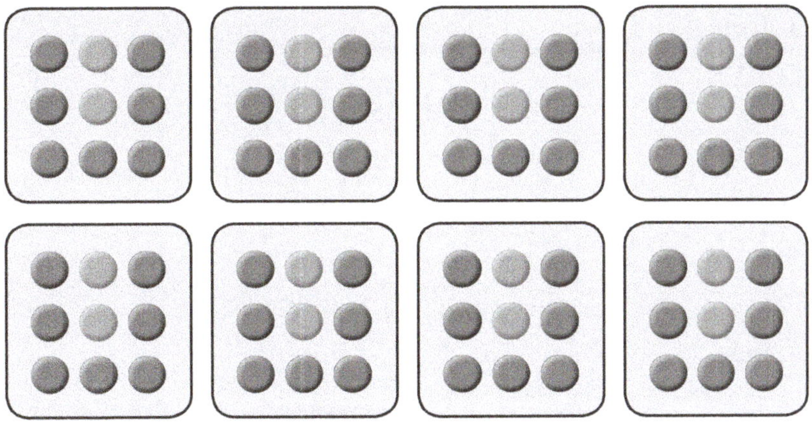

______ __ (______ __ ______) = ______ __ (______)

= ______

(e) 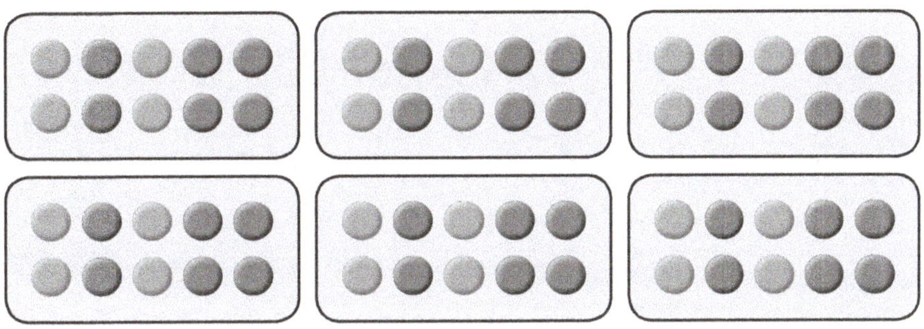

(______ __ ______) __ ______ = (______) __ ______

= ______

(f) 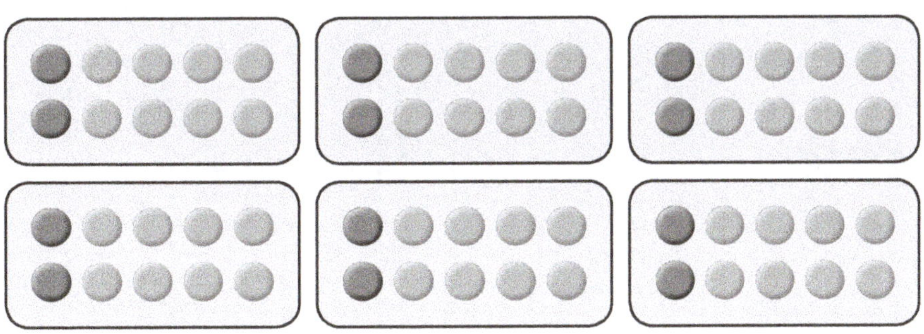

______ __ (______ __ ______) = ______ __ (______)

= ______

2 Complete the following.

(a) $5 \times (8 - 5)$

$= \square \times (\square) = \square$

(b) $(20 - 17) \times 6$

$= (\square) \times \square = \square$

(c) $18 \div (1 + 5)$

$= \square \div (\square) = \square$

(d) $12 + (4 \times 9)$

$= \square + (\square) = \square$

(e) $2 \times (15 + 14)$

$= \square \times (\square) = \square$

(f) $(100 + 50) \times 2$

$= (\square) \times \square = \square$

(g) $56 \div (20 - 13)$

$= \square \div (\square) = \square$

(h) $72 - (19 + 11)$

$= \square - (\square) = \square$

3 Look at the following. Draw the brackets in the correct place.

(a) $5 \times 2 - 2 = 8$

(b) $12 \div 3 + 3 = 2$

(c) $20 - 6 \times 3 = 42$

(d) $30 \div 6 \div 2 = 10$

(e) $13 + 7 - 2 = 18$

(f) $24 \div 6 - 2 = 2$

(g) $75 \times 2 + 15 = 165$

(h) $19 - 2 \times 2 = 34$

4 Look at the diagrams below. Fill in the blanks to find the total number of items.

Example

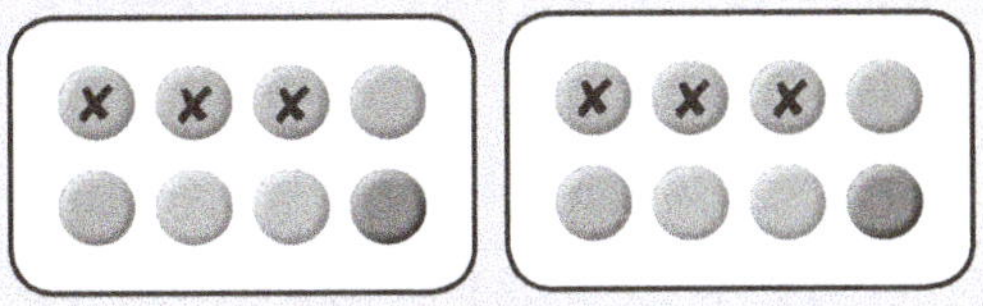

$(8 - 3) \times 2 = (5) \times 2$

$= 10$

(a)

(____ ☐ ____) ☐ ____ = (____) ☐ ____

= ____

(b)

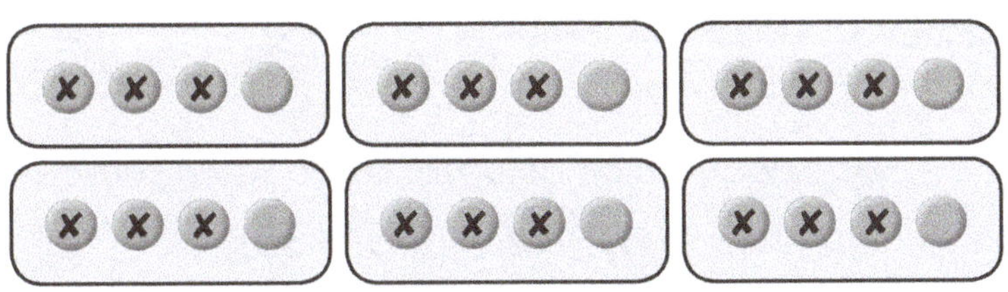

____ ☐ (____ ☐ ____) = ____ ☐ (____)

= ____

(c)

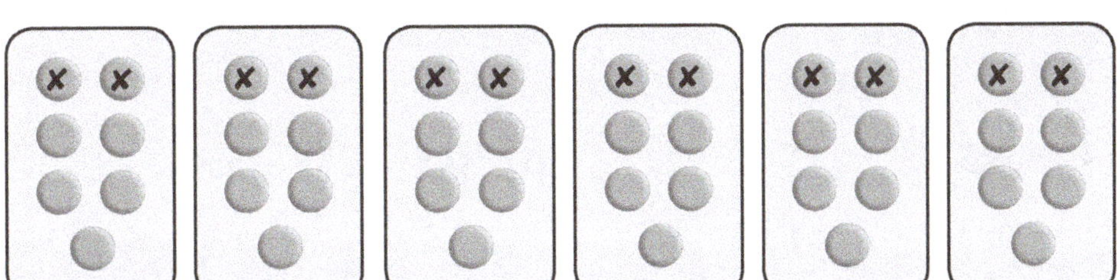

(____ ☐ ____) ☐ ____ = (____) ☐ ____

= ____

5 Complete the following.

(a) $2 \times (3 - 1)$
$= \square \times (\square) = \square$

(b) $(13 - 10) \times 8$
$= (\square) \times \square = \square$

(c) $25 \div (15 - 10)$
$= \square \div (\square) = \square$

(d) $42 \div (1 + 5)$
$= \square \div (\square) = \square$

(e) $60 - (8 \times 4)$
$= \square - (\square) = \square$

(f) $(72 \div 12) + 25$
$= (\square) \times \square = \square$

(g) $100 - (43 + 24)$
$= \square - (\square) = \square$

(h) $64 + (82 - 17)$
$= \square + (\square) = \square$

(i) $4 \times (18 + 12)$
$= \square \times (\square) = \square$

(j) $(100 - 83) \times 2$
$= (\square) \times \square = \square$

(k) $72 \div (20 - 11)$
$= \square \div (\square) = \square$

(l) $64 \div (35 - 33)$
$= \square \div (\square) = \square$

(m) $(11 \times 9) \div 3$
$= (\square) \div \square = \square$

(n) $(48 \div 6) \times 5$
$= (\square) \times \square = \square$

(o) $(16 - 8) + 25$
$= (\square) + \square = \square$

(p) $(45 + 25) - 35$
$= (\square) - \square = \square$

5 Division

Practice 1: Dividing 3-digit numbers by 1-digit numbers

1 Toby received some money from his grandparents. He shared the money equally between himself and his two sisters.

(a) How much money did Toby originally receive? ☐

(b) When Toby shared the money equally, how much did each person receive?

☐

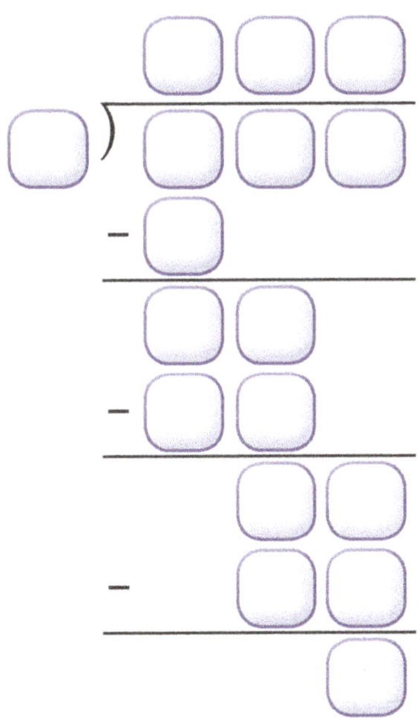

2 Divide the following 3-digit numbers.

(a) 171 ÷ 3 = ☐

(b) 678 ÷ 3 = ☐

(c) 796 ÷ 4 = ☐

(d) 685 ÷ 5 = ☐

3 Complete the following. Show your working.

(a) $748 \div 4 =$ ☐

(b) $340 \div 5 =$ ☐

(c) $522 \div 6 =$ ☐

(d) $259 \div 7 =$ ☐

Practice 2: Division word problems

1. Four legs are needed to make a table. A furniture maker orders 636 such legs. How many tables can be made using these legs?

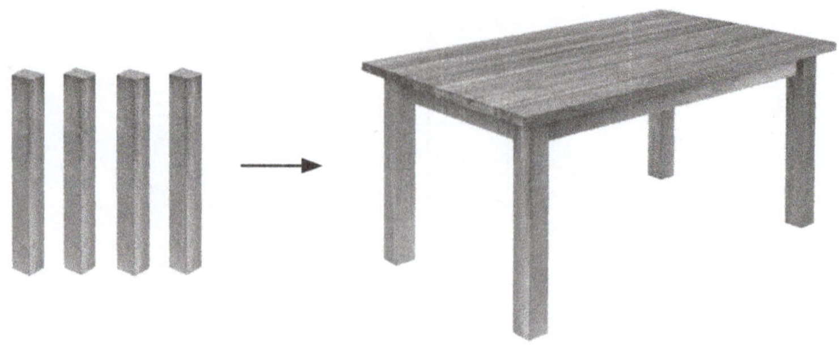

(a) Make a model of the problem.

(b) Solve the problem.

(c) Relate the answer to the problem.

2. A factory produces 792 candles per day. The candles are packed into boxes so that each box contains 9 candles. How many such boxes can be packed with the candles produced in 1 day?

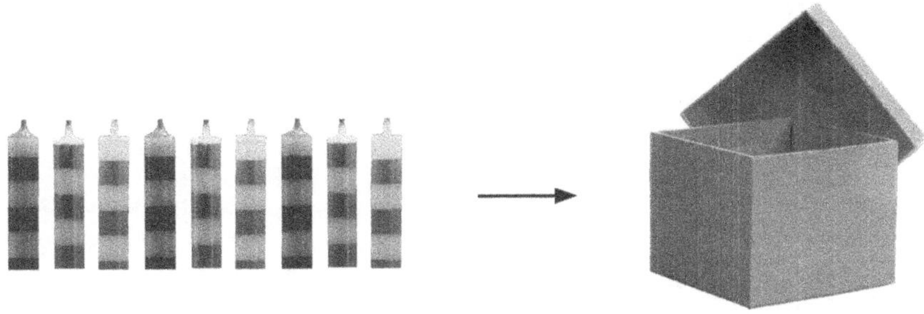

(a) Make a model of the problem.

(b) Solve the problem.

(c) Relate the answer to the problem.

3 Complete these division questions.

(a)

$$\begin{array}{r} \square\square\square \\ 6\overline{)\,8\;\;2\;\;8} \\ -\square \\ \hline \square\square \\ -\square\square \\ \hline \square\square \\ -\;\square\square \\ \hline \square \end{array}$$

(b)

$$\begin{array}{r} \square\square\square \\ 4\overline{)\,6\;\;1\;\;6} \\ -\square \\ \hline \square\square \\ -\square\square \\ \hline \square\square \\ -\;\square\square \\ \hline \square \end{array}$$

(c)

$$\begin{array}{r} \square\square \\ 6\overline{)\,5\;\;2\;\;2} \\ -\square \\ \hline \square\square \\ -\square\square \\ \hline \square\square \\ -\;\square\square \\ \hline \square \end{array}$$

(d)

$$\begin{array}{r} \square\square\square \\ 7\overline{)\,7\;\;5\;\;6} \\ -\square \\ \hline \square\square \\ -\square\square \\ \hline \square\square \\ -\;\square\square \\ \hline \square \end{array}$$

4. Solve these division problems.

(a) $670 \div 5$

(b) $860 \div 4$

(c) $843 \div 3$

(d) $874 \div 2$

Practice 3: Dividing with a remainder

1 Complete these division questions, showing the answer as a remainder.

(a)

4) 6 1 0

(b)

7) 3 6 0

(c)

9) 3 0 0

(d)

8) 8 5 8

2 Complete these division questions. Show your working.

(a) 136 ÷ 3

(b) 450 ÷ 7

(c) 997 ÷ 6

(d) 862 ÷ 9

Practice 4: Expressing a remainder as a fraction

Express the remainders in these division questions as a remainder.

(a) 65 ÷ 3 =

3) 6 5

(b) 88 ÷ 6 =

6) 8 8

(c) 865 ÷ 2 =

2) 8 6 5

(d) 762 ÷ 5 =

5) 7 6 2

Practice 5: Round up or down after division depending on the context

(a) The grassbox on a lawnmower needs to be emptied of grass after cutting 6 lengths of lawn. Assuming the lawnmower is stored empty, how many times are the cuttings removed for a lawn that is 200 lengths in size?

(b) Jade's fitness app beeps every time she has cycled 5 kilometres. Jade cycled 208 kilometres. How many times did her app beep?

(c) Toby's father needs to take his medication every 6 hours. He has taken 7 tablets in the last 50 hours. Has he taken the correct medication? Why/why not?

(d) A factory makes 170 kg of curry each hour. The curry is placed into 3 kg tins to be sold. How many tins are produced per hour?

(e) Han has 100 g of butter. A recipe needs 9 g of butter. How many batches of the recipe can Han make?

6 Area and perimeter

Practice 1: Perimeter of shapes

1 Find the missing length in each shape. Show your working.

(a)

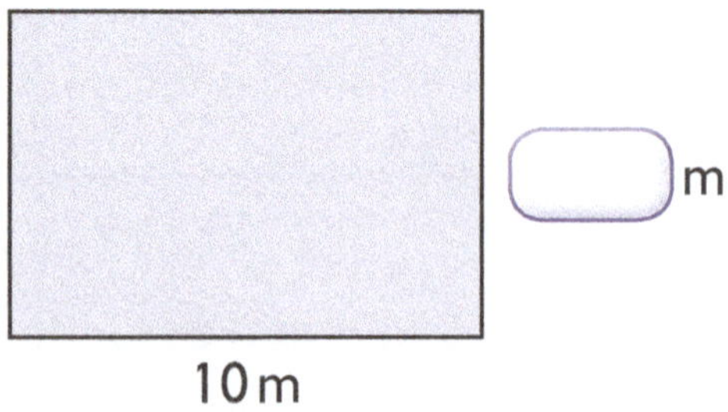

perimeter = 32 m

(b)

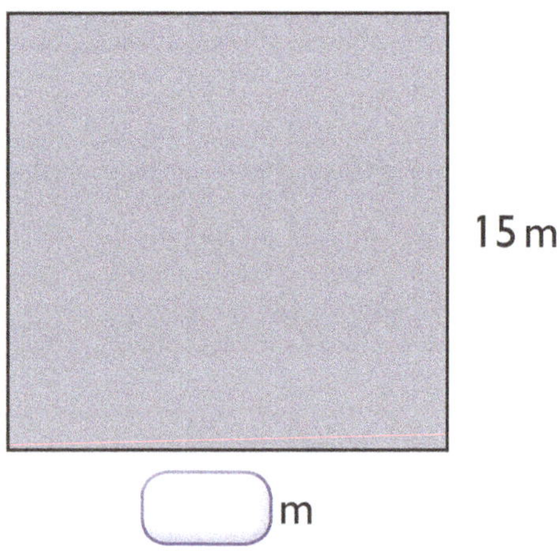

perimeter = 60 m

(c)

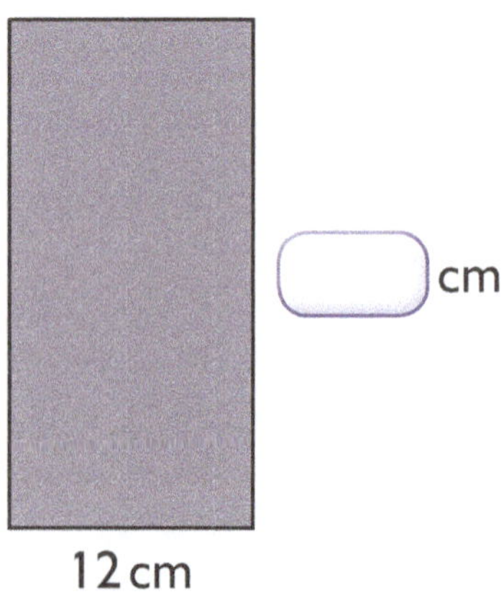

perimeter = 74 cm

(d)

18 cm

cm

perimeter = 136 cm

(e)

m

9 m

perimeter = 40 m

(f)

32 m

m

perimeter = 114 m

2 Find the perimeter of the shapes below. Remember to include the units of length.

(a)

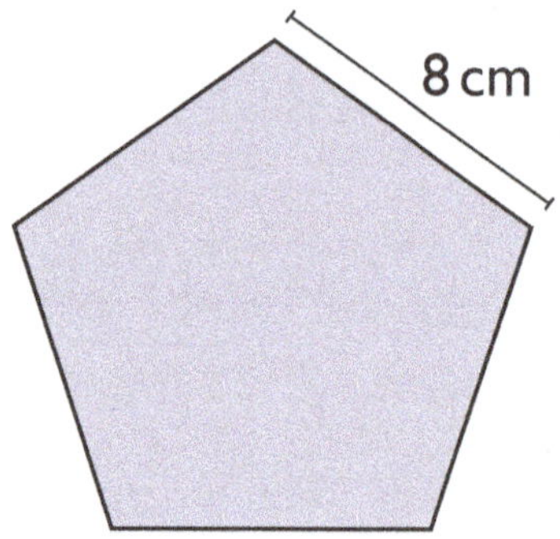

This shape has ☐ sides with equal length.

We can find the perimeter of this shape by:

Perimeter = ☐ × ☐ cm

= ☐ cm

(b)

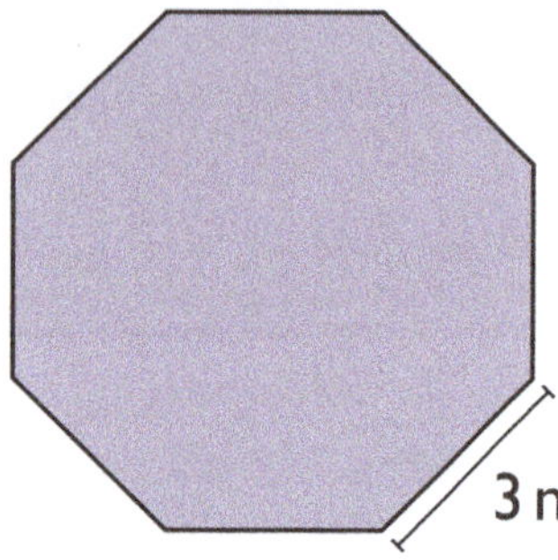

This shape has ☐ sides of equal length.

We can find the perimeter of this shape by:

Perimeter = ☐ × ☐ m

= ☐ m

3 The shape has sides of equal length. Find the missing length of the shape. Show your working.

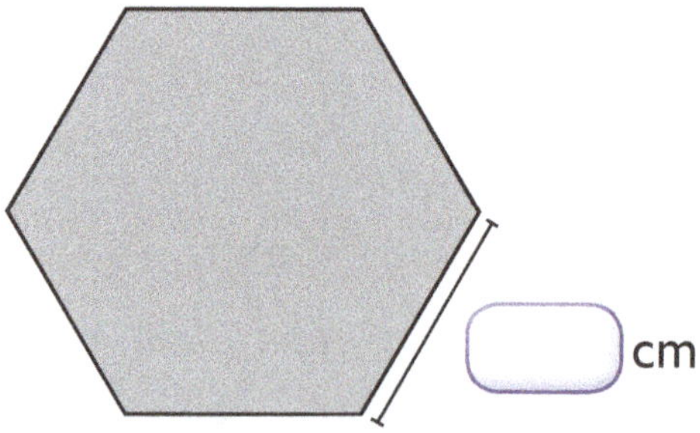

perimeter = 54 cm

Practice 2: Area

1. Find the area of each shape. Each ☐ has an area of 1 cm^2.

(a)

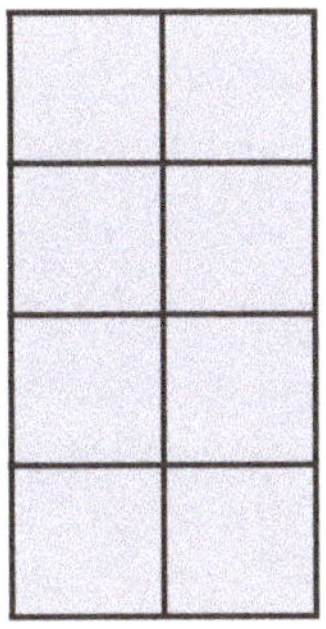

area = ☐ cm^2

(b)

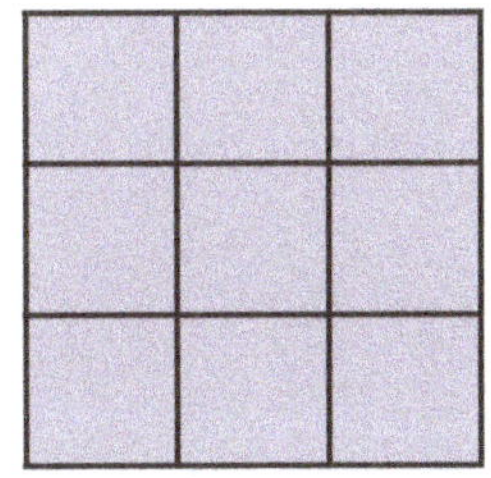

area = ☐ cm^2

(c)

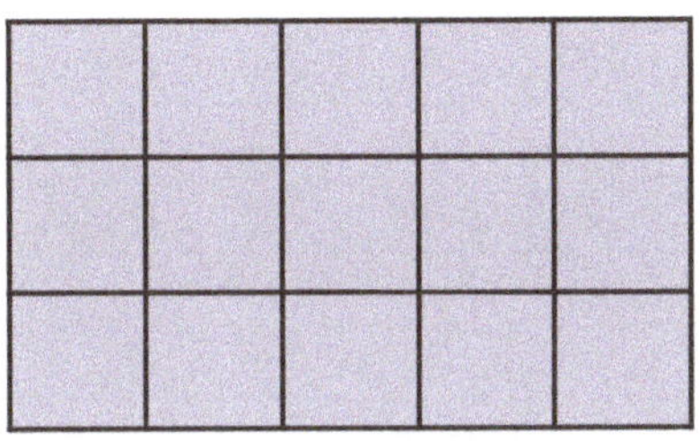

area = ☐ cm^2

(d)

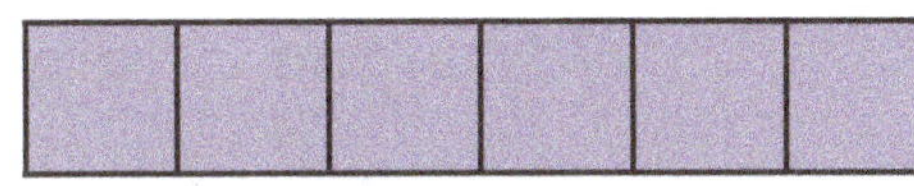

area = ☐ cm^2

(e)

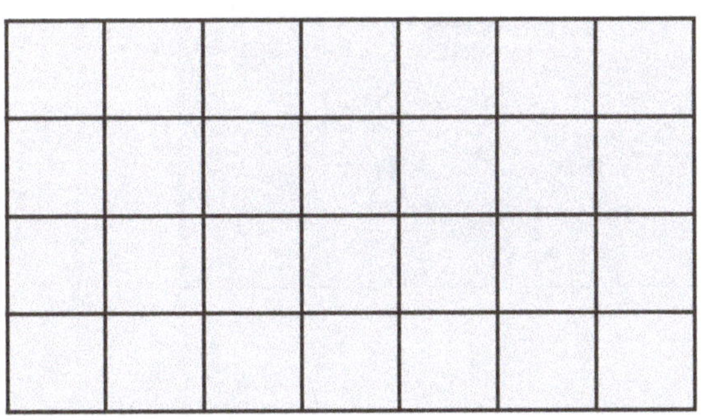

area = ☐ cm^2

(f)

area = ☐ cm^2

2 Complete the following questions.

(a)

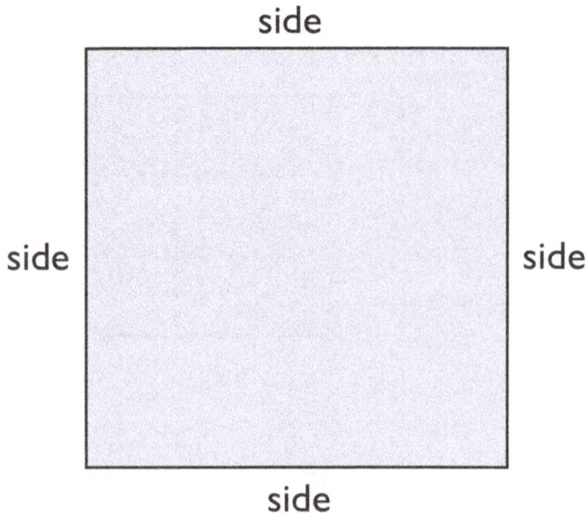

We can find the area of a ________ by:

area = ________ × ________

(b)

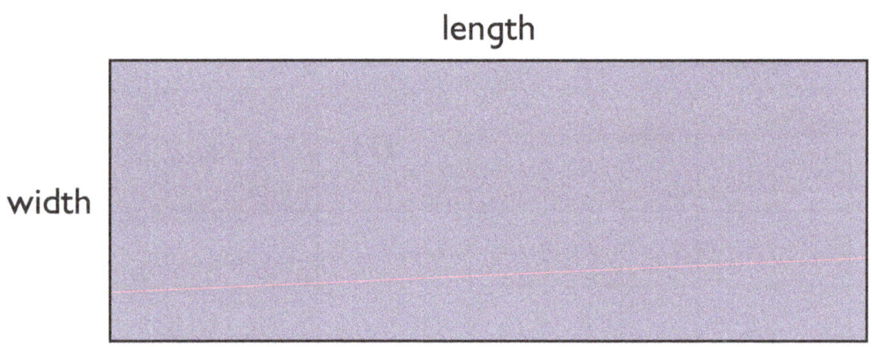

We can find the area of a ________ by:

area = ________ × ________

3. Find the area of these shapes.

(a)

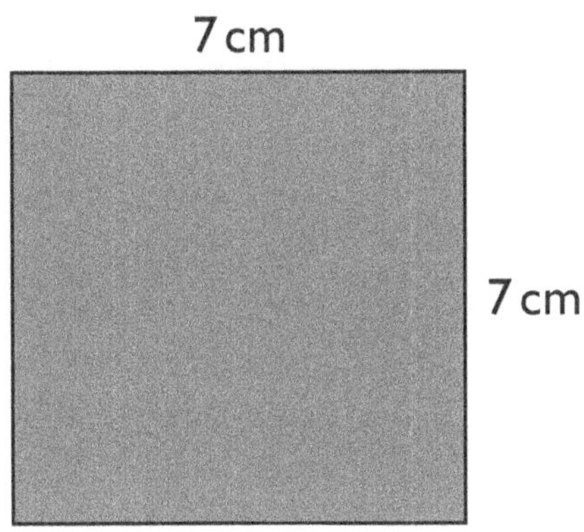

area = ☐ × ☐

= ☐ cm^2

(b)

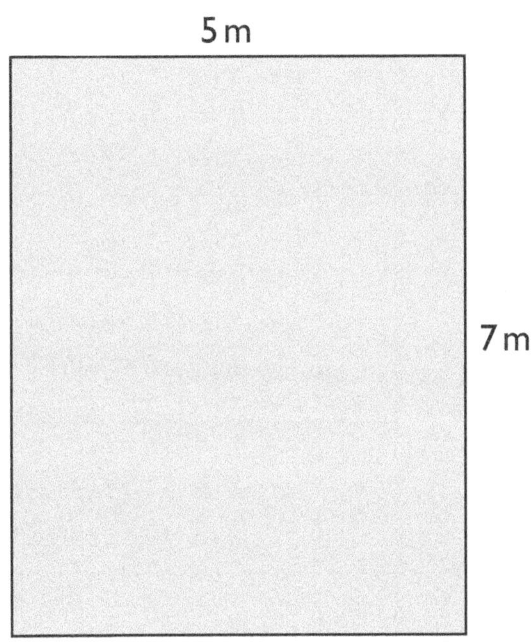

area = ☐ × ☐

= ☐ m^2

(c)

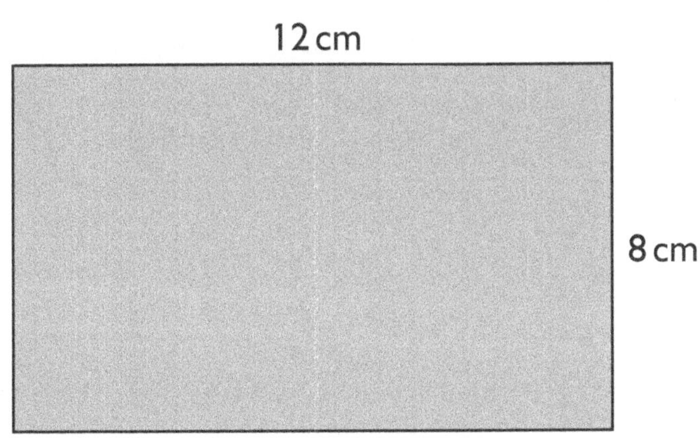

area = ☐ × ☐

= ☐ cm^2

4. Draw the following on the grid paper.

(a) A red rectangle that has an area of $15\,cm^2$.

(b) A blue square that has an area of $25\,cm^2$.

(c) A green rectangle that has an area of $18\,cm^2$.

(d) A yellow square that has an area of $36\,cm^2$.

5 The rectangle shown has an area of 18 cm². Draw 2 other rectangles that have an area of 18 cm² each.

Try to draw some other rectangles that have the same area.

6 Find the missing length of each shape.

(a)

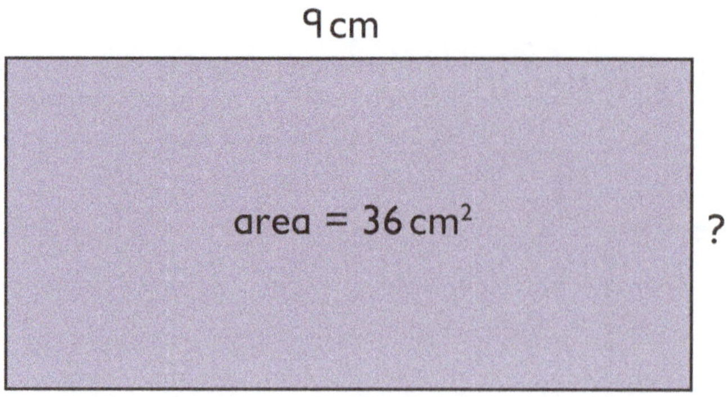

width = ☐ cm

(b)

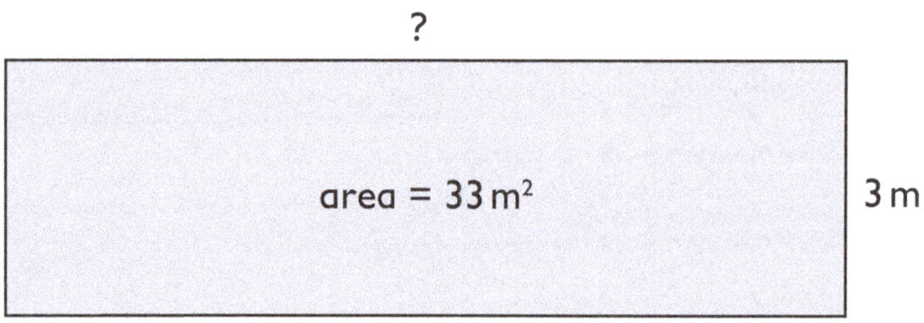

length = ☐ m

(c)

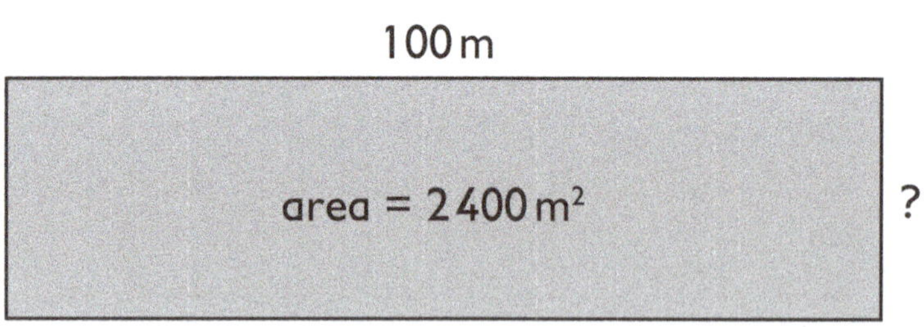

width = ☐ m

Practice 3: Word problems

1 A square coaster has a perimeter of 36 cm.

(a) Find the length of 1 side.

☐ cm

(b) Find the area of the coaster.

☐ cm^2

2 A postage stamp has an area of $6\,cm^2$.

(a) Find 2 possible values for the length and width.
Include units of length.

(i)

length = ☐

width = ☐

(ii)

length = ☐

width = ☐

(b) Which is the common shape of a stamp, shape **(i)** or shape **(ii)**?

3 A kitchen wall is tiled with square tiles.
Each tile has an area of $100\,cm^2$.
Complete the following questions.

(a) Find the length of the side of 1 tile.
Do not forget to include the units of length in your answer.

(b) A total of 250 tiles were used to tile the kitchen wall.
Find the area of the kitchen wall.

cm^2

(c) The kitchen wall is rectangular in shape.
Find 3 possible lengths and widths for the kitchen wall.

Problem Solving

A dairy farmer wants to build a square or rectangular fence for his cows. He bought 120 m of fencing and wants to make an enclosure with the largest possible area. Can you help the farmer to design his fence?

Find the length and width of the fence to create the largest area.

7 Time

Practice 1: Time review

1. Read the times. Then use a ruler to draw the hour and minute hands on the clock face.

(a) Seven o'clock

(b) Quarter past nine

(c) Six twenty-seven

(d) Half past ten

2 Read the time on the clock face. Write the time in numbers and words.

(a)

Numbers:

Words:

(b)

Numbers:

Words:

(c)

Numbers:

Words:

(d)

Numbers:

Words:

3. Complete the chart below.

(a) **1 minute = ☐ seconds**

(b) **1 hour = ☐ minutes**

(c) **1 day = ☐ hours**

(d) **1 week = ☐ days**

(e) **1 year = ☐ days**

4. Convert the following times to seconds.

(a) 1 min 25 s = ☐ s

(b) 2 min 45 s = ☐ s

(c) 3 min 26 s = ☐ s

(d) 3 min 55 s = ☐ s

(e) 9 min = ☐ s

(f) 7 min = ☐ s

(g) 4 min 19 s = ☐ s

(h) 11 min = ☐ s

5. Convert the following times to minutes and seconds.

(a) 121 s = ☐ min ☐ s

(b) 220 s = ☐ min ☐ s

(c) 150 s = ☐ min ☐ s

(d) 318 s = ☐ min ☐ s

(e) 252 s = ☐ min ☐ s

(f) 312 s = ☐ min ☐ s

Practice 2: The 24-hour clock

1 Complete the charts below.

(a) **12-hour clock** **a.m.**

12-hour clock	12.00				4.00				8.00	9.00		11.00
24-hour clock		01:00		03:00		05:00		07:00			10:00	11:00

24-hour clock

(b) **12-hour clock** **p.m.**

12-hour clock	12.00				4.00				8.00	9.00		11.00
24-hour clock		13:00		15:00		17:00		19:00			22:00	23:00

24-hour clock

2 Write the times in words.

(a)

(b)

(c)

(d)

(e)

(f)

3 Look at the times on the clocks. Write 2 possible 24-hour clock times.

(a)

______ or ______

(b)

______ or ______

(c)

______ or ______

(d)

______ or ______

(e)

______ or ______

(f)

______ or ______

4. Draw hands on the 12-hour clock to show the times.

(a) 6 hundred and 15 hours

(b) 13 hundred and 20 hours

(c) 22 hundred hours

(d) 17 hundred and 5 hours

(e) 18 hundred and 45 hours

(f) 15 hundred and 35 hours

5 Match the times to the letters.

What is Tya's favourite time?

					time
16:10	13:45	20:32	19:34	15:14	

Problem Solving

Padma has just finished a meal and wants to know the time.

The digital clock shows this time:

(a) Draw the hands in the clock below to show the time.

(b) Which part of the day is it?

(c) Write this time using a.m. or p.m.

(d) Padma's next meal is in 3 hours. Write the time in digital and analogue time.

Practice 3: Word problems

1. Complete the word problems.

   (a) Jade and Han went on a boat trip. Look at the time they departed and the time they arrived. How long was their trip?

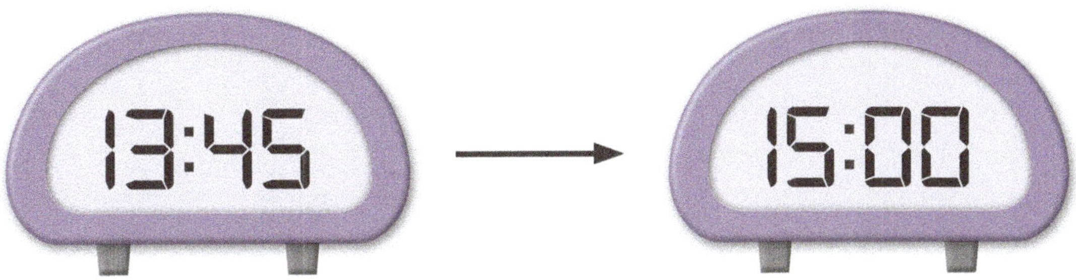

departed arrived

Draw a model to find the answer.

(b) A washing machine is used for 1 h 30 min every day.
How long will it be used for in 1 week?
How long will it be used for in 1 year?

Part 1

Part 2

(c) Padma exercises in the park for 2 h 15 min. It takes her 12 min to get to the park and 12 min to return home. If she leaves home at 11.15 a.m., what time will she return?

8 Fractions

Practice 1: Review of equivalent fractions

1. Put a tick by the pairs of fractions that are equivalent.
   Put a cross by the pairs of fractions that are not equivalent.

(a)
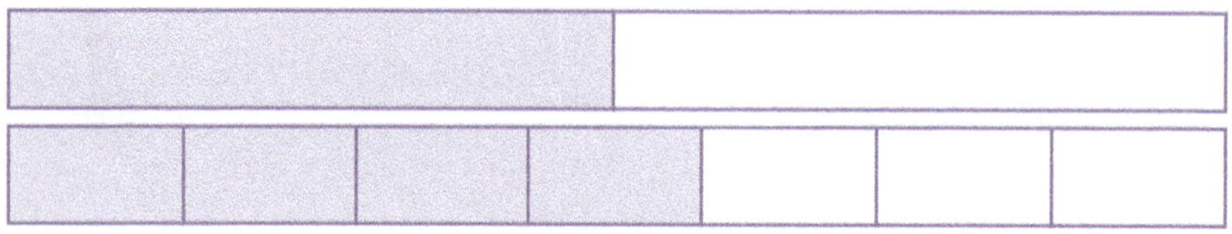
☐

(b)

☐

(c)
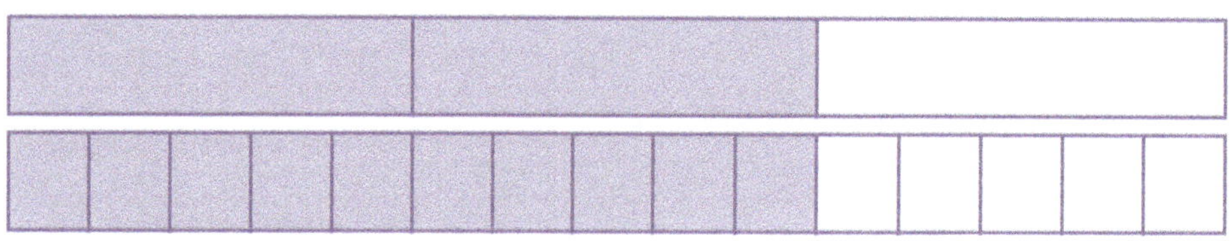
☐

(d)
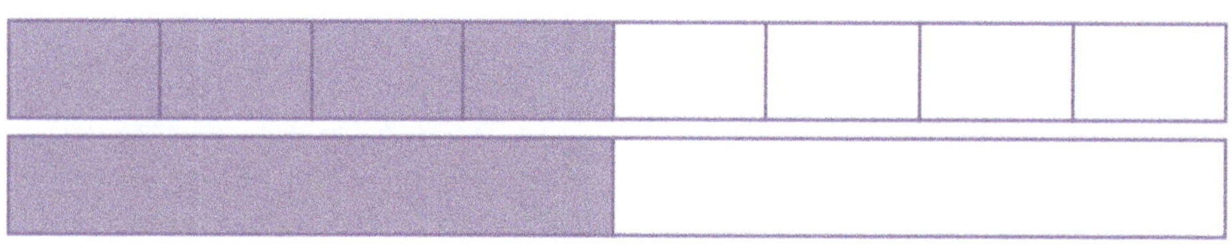
☐

(e)
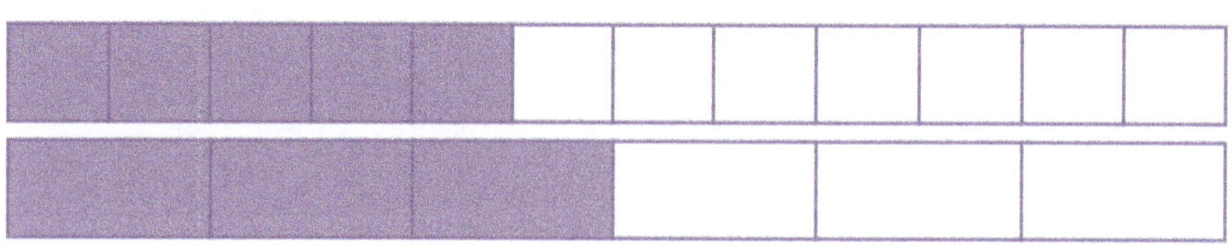
☐

(f)
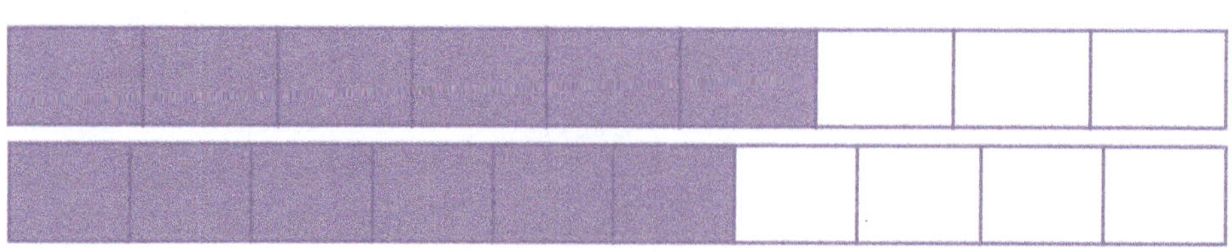
☐

2 Colour the grids below to show the equivalent fractions given.

Example

Divide a bar into 6 parts. Colour 3 parts.

$\frac{3}{6} = \frac{1}{2}$

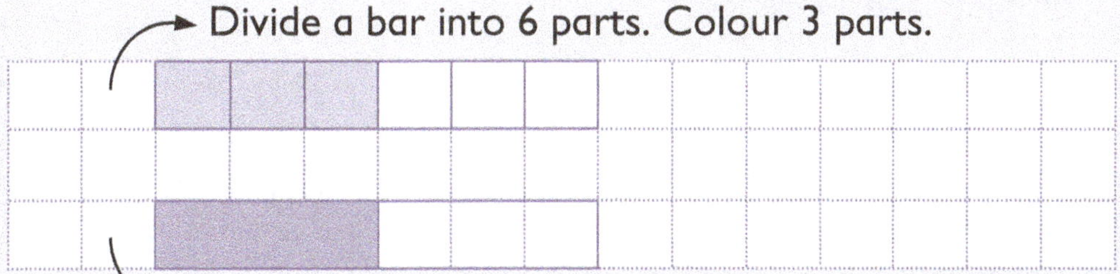

Divide a bar of the same size into 2 parts. Colour 1 part.

(a) $\frac{4}{12} = \frac{1}{3}$

(b) $\frac{1}{4} = \frac{2}{8}$

(c) $\frac{3}{5} = \frac{9}{15}$

Practice 2: Review of decimal and fractional equivalence

1 Complete the sentences.

(a) $\frac{1}{2}$ is equivalent to ☐.

(b) $\frac{\square}{\square}$ is equivalent to 0.1.

(c) $\frac{\square}{\square}$ is equivalent to 0.08.

(d) $\frac{9}{10}$ is equivalent to ☐.

(e) $\frac{1}{100}$ is equivalent to ☐.

(f) $\frac{35}{100}$ is equivalent to ☐.

(g) $\frac{\square}{\square}$ is equivalent to 0.3.

(h) $\frac{\square}{\square}$ is equivalent to 0.78.

2 Match the decimal with the equivalent fraction.

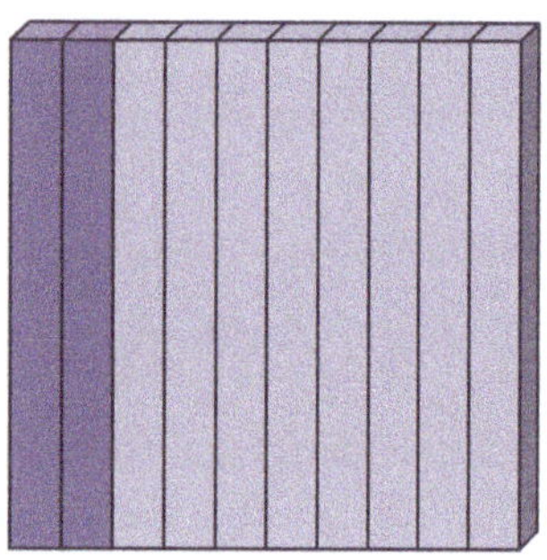

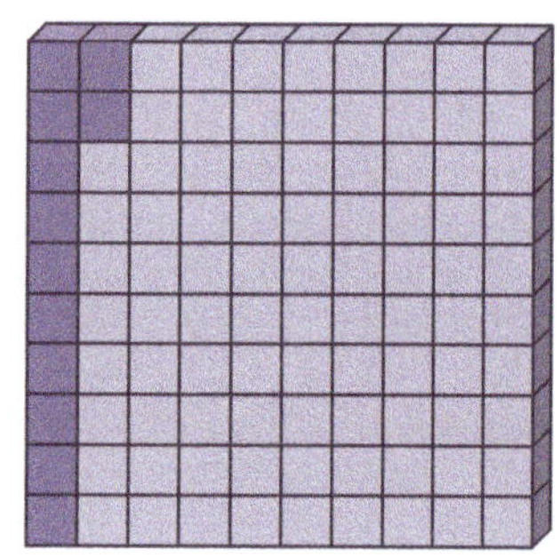

One-tenth

$\frac{1}{2}$

$\frac{12}{100}$

1.2

0.2

one-half

$\frac{1}{10}$

3. Colour in the blocks to show the fraction, then write the decimal equivalent.

(a) $\frac{2}{10}$

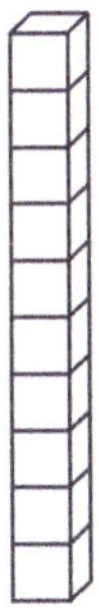

(b) $\frac{65}{100}$

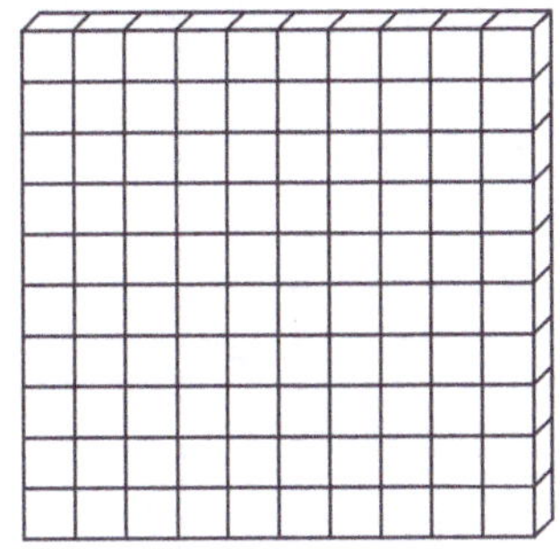

(c) $\frac{8}{10}$

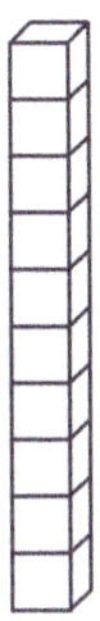

(d) $\frac{3}{10}$

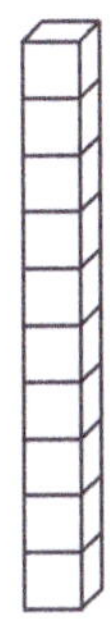

(e) $\frac{90}{100}$

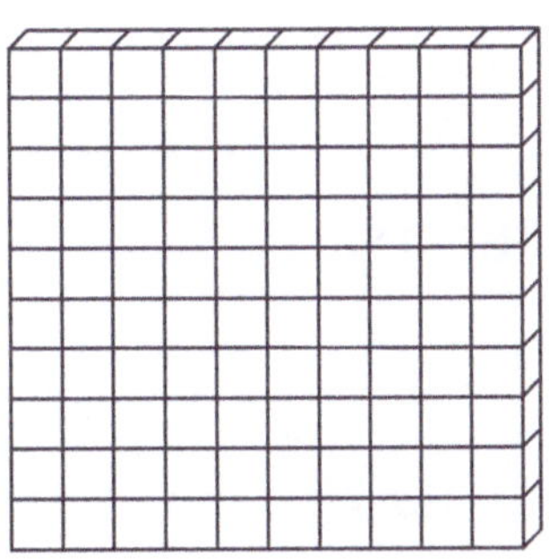

(f) $\frac{42}{100}$

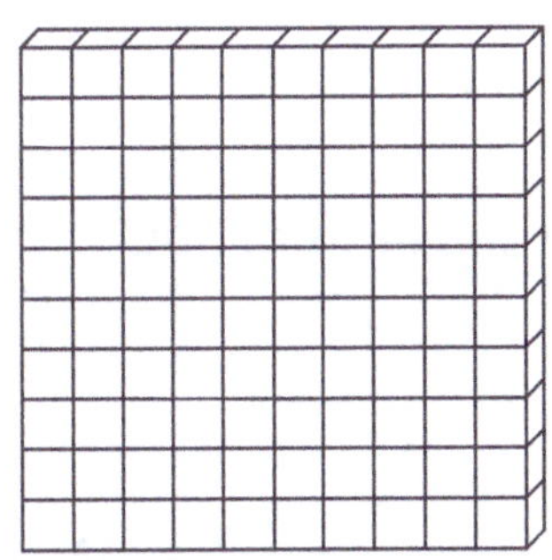

(g) $\frac{1}{10}$

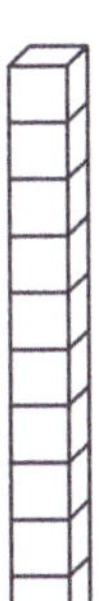

(h) $\frac{1}{100}$

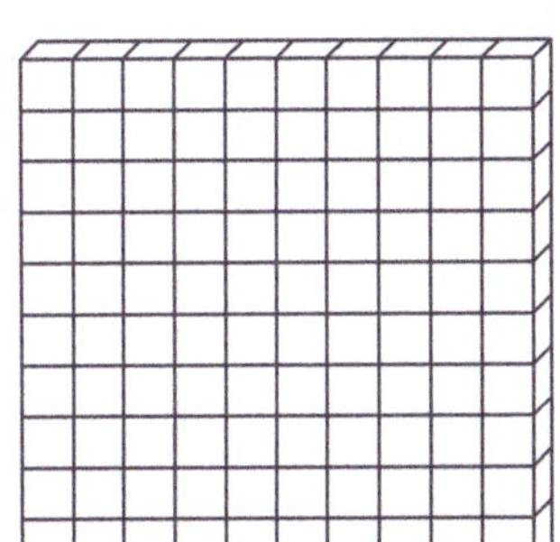

Practice 3: Improper fractions and mixed numbers

1 Write the improper fractions as mixed numbers.

(a) $\frac{3}{2} = \square\frac{\square}{\square}$

(b) $\frac{7}{4} = \square\frac{\square}{\square}$

(c) $\frac{8}{3} = \square\frac{\square}{\square}$

(d) $\frac{7}{5} = \square\frac{\square}{\square}$

(e) $\frac{13}{2} = \square\frac{\square}{\square}$

(f) $\frac{10}{3} = \square\frac{\square}{\square}$

2 Write the mixed numbers as improper fractions.

(a) $1\frac{1}{2} = \frac{\square}{\square}$

(b) $3\frac{2}{3} = \frac{\square}{\square}$

(c) $2\frac{5}{8} = \frac{\square}{\square}$

(d) $4\frac{1}{5} = \frac{\square}{\square}$

(e) $3\frac{4}{7} = \frac{\square}{\square}$

(f) $4\frac{2}{9} = \frac{\square}{\square}$

3 Match these improper fractions and mixed numbers.

$\frac{7}{3}$ $\frac{8}{5}$ $1\frac{3}{5}$ $\frac{9}{4}$ $\frac{11}{4}$

$2\frac{1}{3}$ $2\frac{3}{4}$ $\frac{6}{5}$

$2\frac{1}{4}$ $1\frac{1}{3}$ $\frac{4}{3}$ $1\frac{1}{5}$

4 Change the improper fraction into a mixed number by division with remainder. An example has been done for you.

Example

$\frac{15}{4} \longrightarrow$ 15 ÷ 4 = 3 r 3

The mixed number = $3\frac{3}{4}$

(a) $\frac{9}{2} \longrightarrow$ ☐ ÷ ☐ = ☐ r ☐

The mixed number = ☐ $\frac{☐}{☐}$

(b) $\frac{21}{5} \longrightarrow$ ☐ ÷ ☐ = ☐ r ☐

The mixed number = ☐ $\frac{☐}{☐}$

(c) $\frac{13}{3} \longrightarrow$ ☐ ÷ ☐ = ☐ r ☐

The mixed number = ☐ $\frac{☐}{☐}$

(d) $\frac{25}{4} \longrightarrow$ ☐ ÷ ☐ = ☐ r ☐

The mixed number = ☐ $\frac{☐}{☐}$

(e) $\frac{31}{7} \longrightarrow$ ☐ ÷ ☐ = ☐ r ☐

The mixed number = ☐ $\frac{☐}{☐}$

(f) $\frac{38}{6} \longrightarrow$ ☐ ÷ ☐ = ☐ r ☐

The mixed number = ☐ $\frac{☐}{☐}$

5 Draw on and colour in the grid to make your own mixed numbers.

Write down the fractions as both a mixed number and an improper fraction.

(a)

$\square\frac{\square}{\square} = \frac{\square}{\square}$

(b)

$\square\frac{\square}{\square} = \frac{\square}{\square}$

(c)

$\square\frac{\square}{\square} = \frac{\square}{\square}$

(d)

$\square\frac{\square}{\square} = \frac{\square}{\square}$

Practice 4: Ordering numbers on a number line

Place these numbers on the number line. Convert them all to decimals first to help you.

(a) $\frac{1}{100}$ 0.34 $\frac{25}{100}$ $\frac{5}{100}$ $\frac{4}{10}$

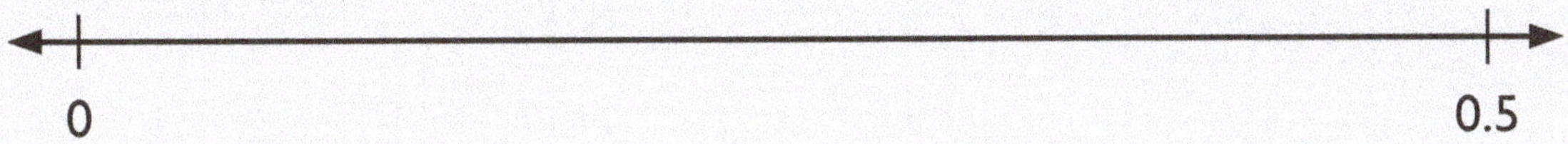

(b) $\frac{5}{2}$ 5.2 $\frac{4}{8}$ $\frac{5}{10}$ 0.75

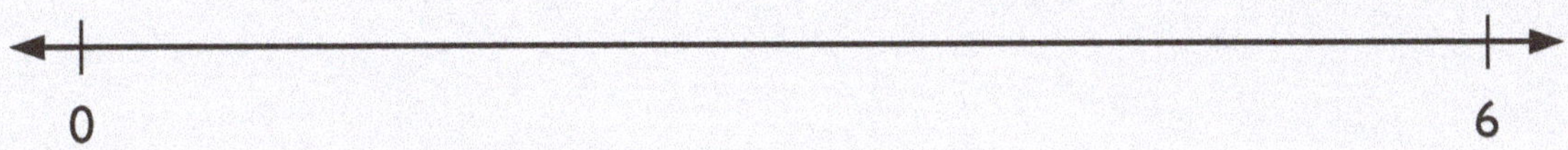

(c) $\frac{6}{10}$ $\frac{1}{4}$ $\frac{82}{100}$ 0.5 $\frac{8}{10}$

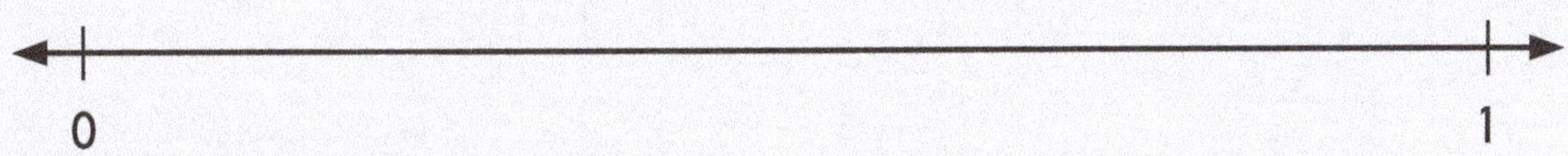

(d) $\frac{6}{1}$ $\frac{13}{2}$ $5\frac{1}{2}$ 6.75   9.1

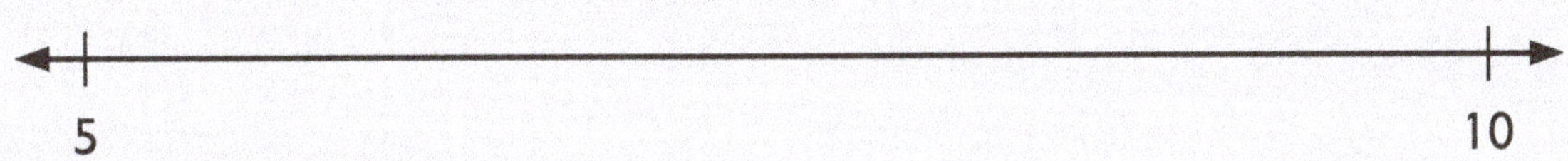

Practice 5: Review of fractions of shapes

1. Shade in $\frac{1}{2}$ of each shape.

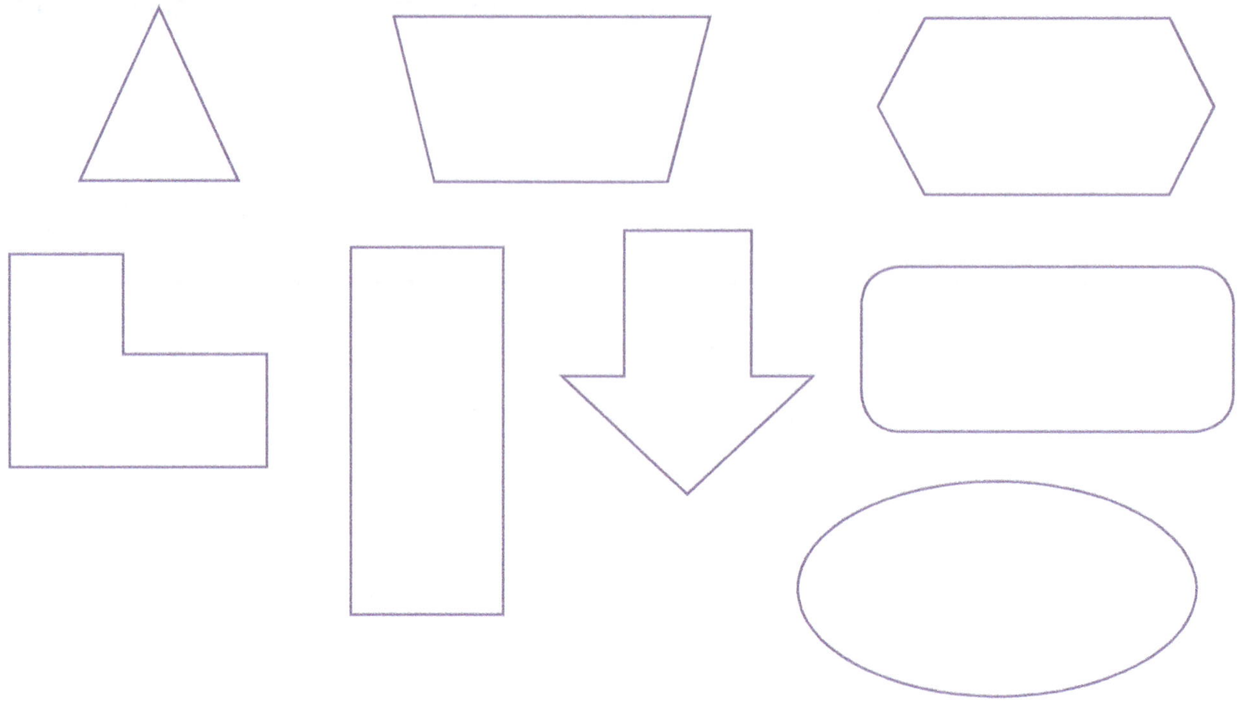

2. Shade in $\frac{1}{4}$ of each shape.

3 Shade $\frac{1}{3}$ of each shape.

4 Shade $\frac{1}{5}$ of each shape.

5 Shade $\frac{1}{8}$ of each shape.

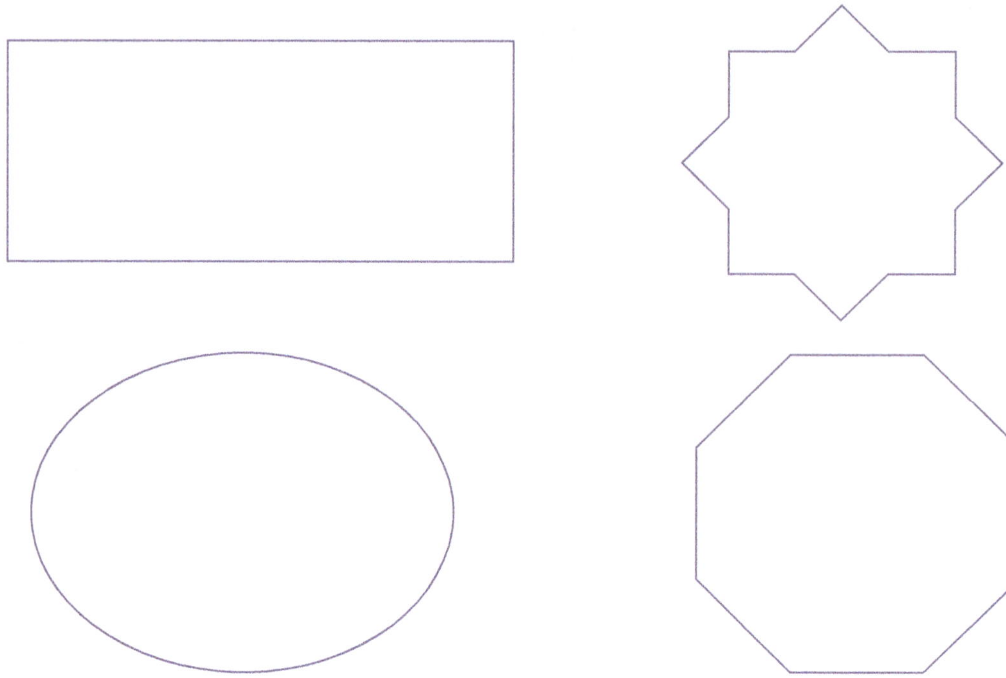

6 Shade $\frac{1}{10}$ of each shape.

7 What fraction of each shape is shaded?

(a)

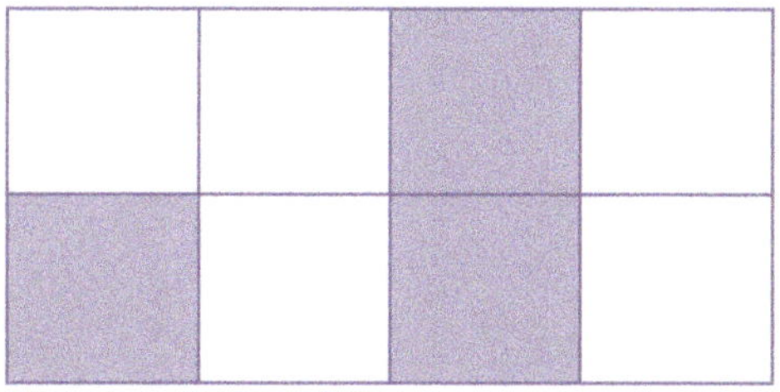

(b)

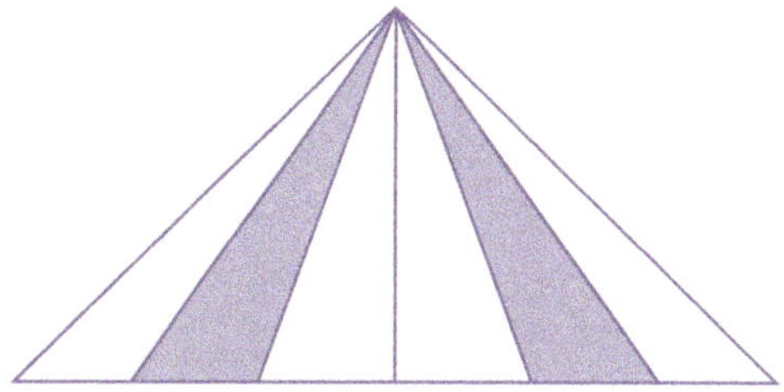

(c)

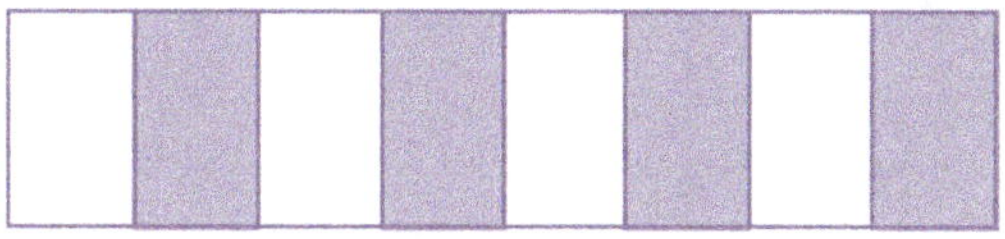

(d)

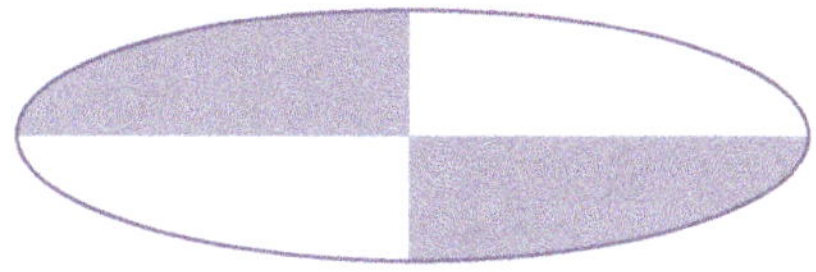

(e)

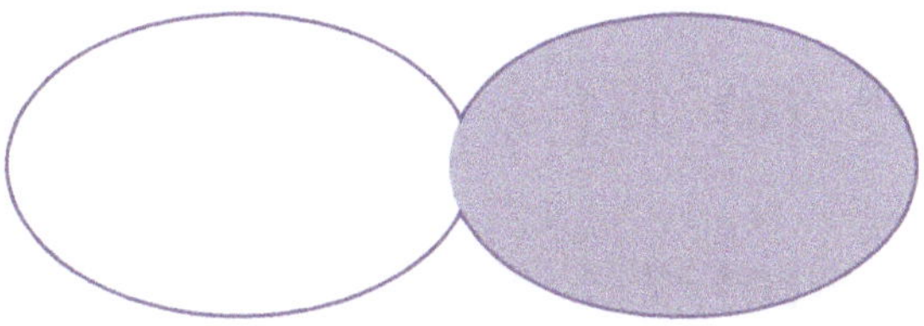

(f)

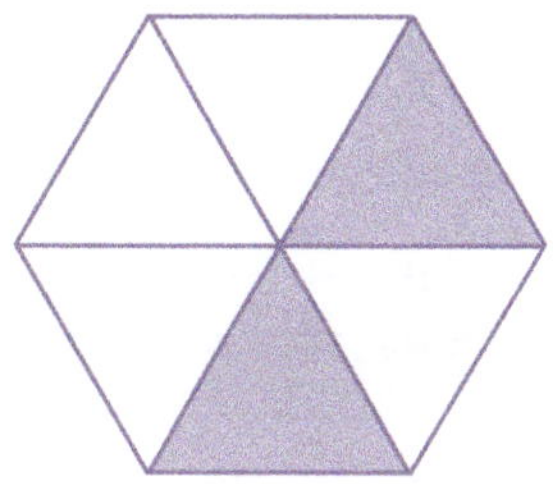

(g)

(h)

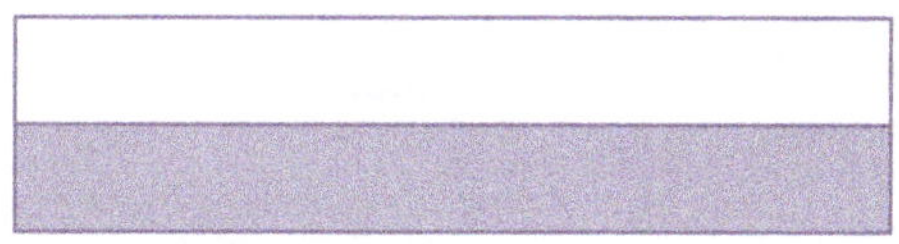

(i)

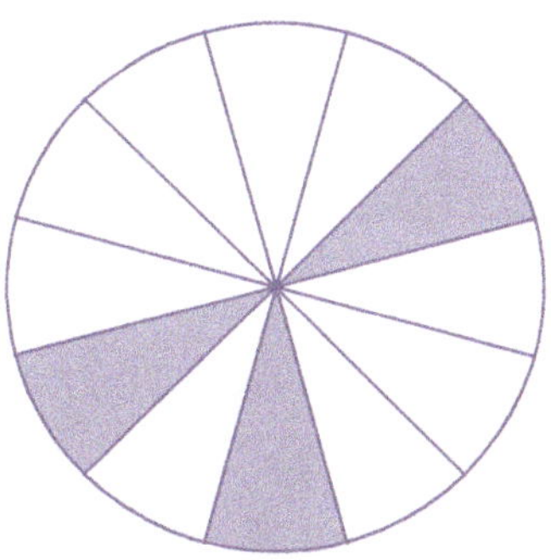

(j)

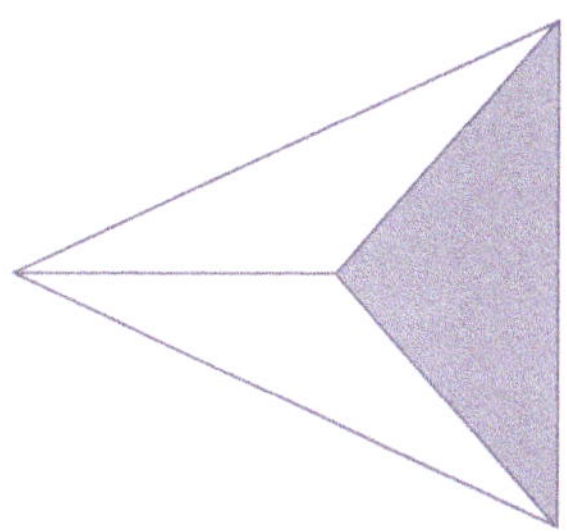

Practice 6: Review of finding fractions of numbers

1. Find $\frac{1}{2}$ of the following numbers.

(a) 20 ☐ (b) 12 ☐

(c) 18 ☐ (d) 24 ☐

(e) 14 ☐ (f) 60 ☐

(g) 30 ☐ (h) 48 ☐

2. Find $\frac{1}{3}$ of the following numbers.

(a) 21 ☐ (b) 12 ☐

(c) 30 ☐ (d) 27 ☐

(e) 15 ☐ (f) 60 ☐

(g) 9 ☐ (h) 18 ☐

3. Find $\frac{1}{4}$ of the following numbers.

(a) 24 ☐ (b) 16 ☐

(c) 20 ☐ (d) 28 ☐

(e) 4 ☐ (f) 12 ☐

(g) 8 ☐ (h) 40 ☐

4 Find $\frac{1}{6}$ of the following numbers.

(a) 30 ☐ (b) 24 ☐

(c) 18 ☐ (d) 42 ☐

(e) 54 ☐ (f) 60 ☐

(g) 12 ☐ (h) 48 ☐

5 Find $\frac{1}{8}$ of the following numbers.

(a) 48 ☐ (b) 64 ☐

(c) 24 ☐ (d) 80 ☐

(e) 72 ☐ (f) 40 ☐

(g) 8 ☐ (h) 16 ☐

6 Find $\frac{1}{10}$ of the following numbers.

(a) 40 ☐ (b) 20 ☐

(c) 90 ☐ (d) 100 ☐

(e) 10 ☐ (f) 60 ☐

(g) 80 ☐ (h) 50 ☐

7 Write the fraction of each number.

(a) 2 is $\frac{\square}{\square}$ of 4.

(b) 4 is $\frac{\square}{\square}$ of 16.

(c) 5 is $\frac{\square}{\square}$ of 15.

(d) 7 is $\frac{\square}{\square}$ of 70.

(e) 12 is $\frac{\square}{\square}$ of 24.

(f) 8 is $\frac{\square}{\square}$ of 56.

(g) 10 is $\frac{\square}{\square}$ of 100.

(h) 17 is $\frac{\square}{\square}$ of 34.

(i) 7 is $\frac{\square}{\square}$ of 42.

(j) 8 is $\frac{\square}{\square}$ of 64.

8 Complete the sentences.

(a) ☐ is $\frac{1}{2}$ of 16.

(b) ☐ is $\frac{1}{10}$ of 30.

(c) ☐ is $\frac{1}{4}$ of 20.

(d) ☐ is $\frac{1}{8}$ of 24.

(e) ☐ is $\frac{1}{3}$ of 27.

(f) ☐ is $\frac{1}{6}$ of 36.

(g) ☐ is $\frac{1}{2}$ of 18.

(h) ☐ is $\frac{1}{4}$ of 16.

(i) ☐ is $\frac{1}{8}$ of 80.

(j) ☐ is $\frac{1}{6}$ of 18.

Practice 7: Fractions as division

1. Show the division of the whole number as a fraction.

   (a) 2 divided by 3

   ☐ becomes the numerator and ☐ becomes the denominator.

   So, ☐ ÷ ☐ = $\frac{☐}{☐}$.

   (b) 7 divided by 11

   ☐ becomes the numerator and ☐ becomes the denominator.

   So, ☐ ÷ ☐ = $\frac{☐}{☐}$.

   (c) 6 divided by 13

   ☐ becomes the numerator and ☐ becomes the denominator.

   So, ☐ ÷ ☐ = $\frac{☐}{☐}$.

   (d) 5 divided by 4

   ☐ becomes the numerator and ☐ becomes the denominator.

   So, ☐ ÷ ☐ = $\frac{☐}{☐}$ = ☐$\frac{☐}{☐}$.

2 Complete the following.

(a) $12 \div 7 = \frac{\square}{\square} = \square\frac{\square}{\square}$

(b) $10 \div 3 = \frac{\square}{\square} = \square\frac{\square}{\square}$

(c) $3 \div 2 = \frac{\square}{\square} = \square\frac{\square}{\square}$

(d) $9 \div 4 = \frac{\square}{\square} = \square\frac{\square}{\square}$

(e) $11 \div 2 = \frac{\square}{\square} = \square\frac{\square}{\square}$

(f) $16 \div 5 = \frac{\square}{\square} = \square\frac{\square}{\square}$

(g) $10 \div 4 = \frac{\square}{\square} = \frac{\square}{\square} = \square\frac{\square}{\square}$

(h) $12 \div 9 = \frac{\square}{\square} = \frac{\square}{\square} = \square\frac{\square}{\square}$

(i) $14 \div 8 = \frac{\square}{\square} = \frac{\square}{\square} = \square\frac{\square}{\square}$

(j) $11 \div 5 = \frac{\square}{\square} = \square\frac{\square}{\square}$

(k) $20 \div 3 = \frac{\square}{\square} = \square\frac{\square}{\square}$

(l) $19 \div 10 = \frac{\square}{\square} = \square\frac{\square}{\square}$

(m) $18 \div 7 = \frac{\square}{\square} = \square\frac{\square}{\square}$

(n) $13 \div 10 = \frac{\square}{\square} = \square\frac{\square}{\square}$

(o) $14 \div 11 = \frac{\square}{\square} = \square\frac{\square}{\square}$

(p) $19 \div 4 = \frac{\square}{\square} = \square\frac{\square}{\square}$

Practice 8: Proportion

1

(a) How many toys are there altogether? ☐

(b) How many cars are there? ☐

(c) What is the proportion of cars in the toy box? $\frac{\square}{\square}$

(d) Which toy shows a proportion of $\frac{3}{8}$ of the toy box? ☐

2

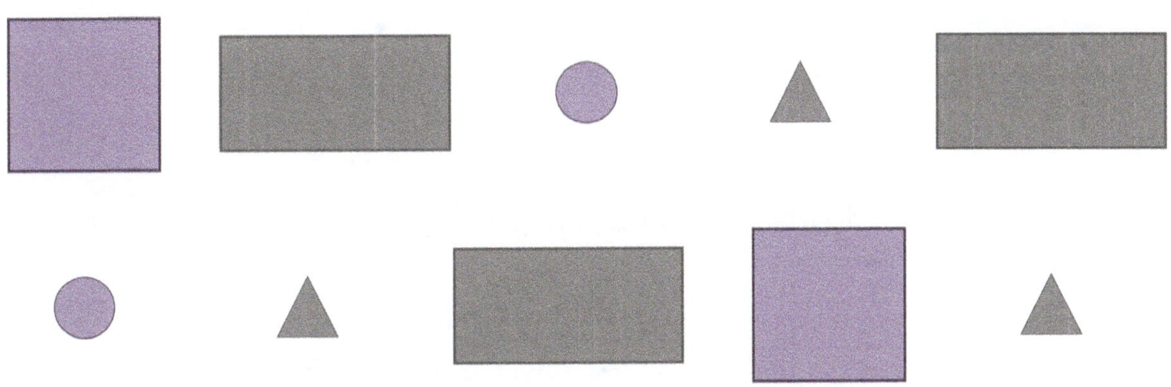

(a) What is the proportion of triangles in the group? $\frac{\square}{\square}$

(b) What is the proportion of purple shapes in the group? $\frac{\square}{\square}$

(c) What is the proportion of big shapes in the group? $\frac{\square}{\square}$

(d) What is the proportion of small shapes in the group? $\frac{\square}{\square}$

3 Look at this set of purple and black sweets. Estimate the proportion of purple sweets.

I estimate the proportion of black sweets to be approximately $\frac{\square}{\square}$.

4 Look at this set of flowers. Estimate the proportion of purple flowers.

I estimate the proportion of purple flowers to be approximately $\frac{\square}{\square}$.

Practice 9: Ratio

1. Complete the following ratio word problems. Show your working out.

   (a) Each sports tracksuit requires 160 m of fabric. How much fabric is required for the school's team of 8?

   (b) Tya's chocolate cake recipe uses 30 g of cocoa. She needs to make 3 cakes and she has 100 g of cocoa left. Will she have enough?

   (c) To make his favourite shade of orange, Samir mixes 5 parts yellow to 2 parts red. He has 6 tins of red paint. How many tins of yellow paint does Samir need if he is to use all of the red paint?

   (d) Padma and Toby run for the same duration every day. Padma always runs 4 km in the time and Toby always runs 3 km. The time they had to run was reduced today, and Padma could only run 2 km. What distance could Toby run in the same time?

(e) The instructions to microwave a dessert say 15 seconds for one portion or 45 seconds for three portions. How long would five portions need to be heated for?

(f) If 6 pens cost 240 cents, how many pens can we buy with 360 cents?

(g) 1 kg of cherries costs $8.00. How much would two-and-a-half kilograms of cherries cost?

(h) If 6 cakes cost $360, how much would 8 cakes cost?

9 Decimals

Practice 1: Review of decimals

1. The big square below is divided into 100 equal parts. Each part is a small square.

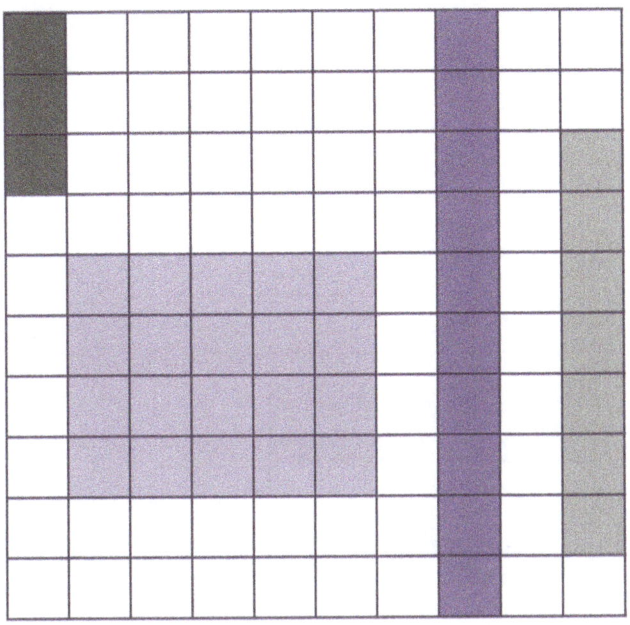

(a) Express the dark grey-coloured squares as a fraction of the whole and as a decimal.

$\frac{\square}{\square} = \square$

(b) Express the light purple-coloured squares as a fraction of the whole and as a decimal.

$\frac{\square}{\square} = \square$

(c) Express the dark purple-coloured squares as a fraction of the whole and as a decimal.

$\frac{\square}{\square} = \square$

(d) Express the light grey-coloured squares as a fraction of the whole and as a decimal.

$\frac{\square}{\square} = \square$

2 Complete the following.

Example

$4\frac{7}{100}$ →

Ones	.	Tenths	Hundredths
4	.	0	7

four point zero seven

(a) $1\frac{4}{10}$ →

Ones	.	Tenths
	.	

(b) $6\frac{23}{100}$ →

Ones	.	Tenths	Hundredths
	.		

(c) $\frac{287}{1\,000}$ →

Ones	.	Tenths	Hundredths	Thousandths
	.			

(d) $89\frac{57}{100}$ →

Tens	Ones	.	Tenths	Hundredths
		.		

(e) $7\frac{558}{1\,000}$ →

Ones	.	Tenths	Hundredths	Thousandths
	.			

Practice 2: Deriving pairs of decimals with a total of 10

1. Add the ones and tenths together to calculate the total of each sum.

(a) 3.4 + 6.6

3 + 3 = ☐

0.4 + 0.6 = ☐

☐ + ☐ = 10

(b) 5.8 + 7.2

5 + 7 = ☐

0.8 + 0.2 = ☐

☐ + ☐ = ☐

(c) 9.1 + 0.9

9 + 0 = ☐

0.1 + 0.9 = ☐

☐ + ☐ = ☐

(d) 2.7 + 7.3

2 + 7 = ☐

0.7 + 0.3 = ☐

☐ + ☐ = ☐

(e) 5.5 + 4.5

5 + 4 = ☐

0.5 + 0.5 = ☐

☐ + ☐ = ☐

(f) 8.8 + 1.2

8 + 1 = ☐

0.8 + 0.2 = ☐

☐ + ☐ = ☐

(g) 2.5 + 7.5

2 + 7 = ☐

0.5 + 0.5 = ☐

☐ + ☐ = ☐

(h) 6.3 + 3.7

6 + 3 = ☐

0.3 + 0.7 = ☐

☐ + ☐ = ☐

2 I have noticed that:

(a) the ones always add up to [ ].

(b) the tenths always add up to [ ].

3 Match pairs of numbers that make a total of 10.

(a) 1.4	•	• 2.5
(b) 5.5	•	• 4.5
(c) 3.7	•	• 8.6
(d) 9.9	•	• 6.3
(e) 7.5	•	• 3.6
(f) 6.4	•	• 0.1

4 Write the other number in the pair that makes a total of 10.

(a) 3.6 [ ] **(b)** 2.7 [ ]

(c) 0.8 [ ] **(d)** 6.5 [ ]

(e) 8.1 [ ] **(f)** 1.4 [ ]

(g) 7.5 [ ] **(h)** 3.9 [ ]

(i) 2.4 [ ] **(j)** 5.5 [ ]

Practice 3: Doubling and halving decimal numbers

1. Complete these sentences.

(a) Double 75 is ☐, so double 7.5 is ☐ and double 0.75 is ☐.

(b) Half of 234 is ☐, so half of 23.4 is ☐ and half of 2.34 is ☐.

(c) Double 86 is ☐, so double 0.86 is ☐ and double 8.6 is ☐.

(d) Half of 152 is ☐, so half of 1.52 is ☐ and half of 15.2 is ☐.

(e) Double 18 is ☐, so double 1.8 is ☐ and double 0.18 is ☐.

(f) Half of 664 is ☐, so half of 66.4 is ☐ and half of 6.64 is ☐.

(g) Double 56 is ☐, so double 5.6 is ☐ and double 0.56 is ☐.

(h) Half of 364 is ☐, so half of 36.4 is ☐ and half of 3.64 is ☐.

2. Halve and double these decimal numbers.

(a) Half of 26.8 is ☐.

(b) Half of 2.70 is ☐.

(c) Double 5.8 is ☐.

(d) Double 0.74 is ☐.

(e) Half of 26.6 is ☐.

(f) Half of 1.78 is ☐.

(g) Double 4.5 is ☐.

(h) Half of 9.9 is ☐.

Practice 4: Ordering decimals

1 Complete the following.

(a) Compare 1.3 and 1.4

☐ is greater than ☐.

☐ is smaller than ☐.

(b) Compare 6.51 and 6.15

☐ is greater than ☐.

☐ is smaller than ☐.

(c) Compare 7.02 and 7.07

☐ is greater than ☐.

☐ is smaller than ☐.

(d) Compare 11.16 and 11.13

☐ is greater than ☐.

☐ is smaller than ☐.

(e) Compare 9.02 and 9.2

☐ is greater than ☐.

☐ is smaller than ☐.

(f) Compare 5.38 and 4.98

☐ is greater than ☐.

☐ is smaller than ☐.

(g) Compare 0.43 and 0.34

☐ is greater than ☐.

☐ is smaller than ☐.

(h) Compare 5.02 and 6.00

☐ is greater than ☐.

☐ is smaller than ☐.

(i) Compare 8 and 7.88

☐ is greater than ☐.

☐ is smaller than ☐.

(j) Compare 10.04 and 10.05

☐ is greater than ☐.

☐ is smaller than ☐.

2 Read the decimal numbers written in words. Tick the smaller decimal number.

(a) ☐ Sixteen point three
☐ Six point nine

(b) ☐ Zero point zero eight
☐ One point six

(c) ☐ Forty-seven point zero two seven
☐ Forty-seven point two seven seven

(d) ☐ One hundred and thirty-three point six five
☐ One hundred and thirty-three point six six

(e) ☐ Eighteen point seven
☐ Eighty point five

(f) ☐ Four point two five eight
☐ Four point eight five two

3 Tick the greater decimal number.

(a) 5.9 ☐ 5.7 ☐

(b) 4.42 ☐ 2.44 ☐

(c) 3.30 ☐ 3.02 ☐

(d) 62.904 ☐ 61.994 ☐

(e) 100.12 ☐ 100.11 ☐

(f) 85.52 ☐ 85.51 ☐

(g) 64.17 ☐ 64.71 ☐

(h) 55.33 ☐ 555.3 ☐

4 Arrange the decimal numbers from the smallest to the greatest.

(a) 4.5 2.1 5.4

smallest → greatest

(b) 0.02 0.25 0.05

smallest → greatest

(c) 3.02 3.01 3.08

smallest → greatest

5 Arrange the decimal numbers from the greatest to the smallest.

(a) 5.99 4.00 4.98

greatest → smallest

(b) 0.01 0.11 0.13

greatest → smallest

(c) 6.20 6.21 6.02

greatest → smallest

Practice 5: Rounding off decimals

Round off each decimal number to the nearest whole number.

Example

2.4

The digit in the [tenths] place is [4].

So, we round [down].

2.4 ≈ [2]

(a) 5.09

The digit in the [ ] place is [ ].

So, we round [ ].

5.09 ≈ [ ]

(b) 37.62

The digit in the [ ] place is [ ].

So, we round [ ].

37.62 ≈ [ ]

(c) 100.52

The digit in the [ ] place is [ ].

So, we round [ ].

100.52 ≈ [ ]

(d) 252.32

The digit in the [ ] place is [ ].

So, we round [ ].

252.32 ≈ [ ]

Practice 6: Written calculations using decimals

1 Use the coloured squares to complete the addition of the decimal numbers.

Example

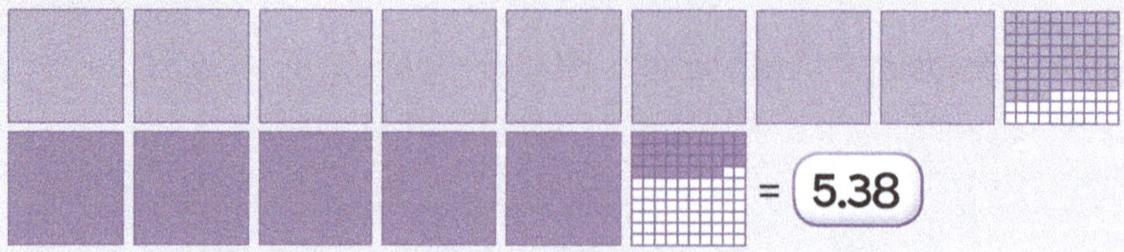

= 8.74

= 5.38

8.74 + 5.38 = 14.12

(a)

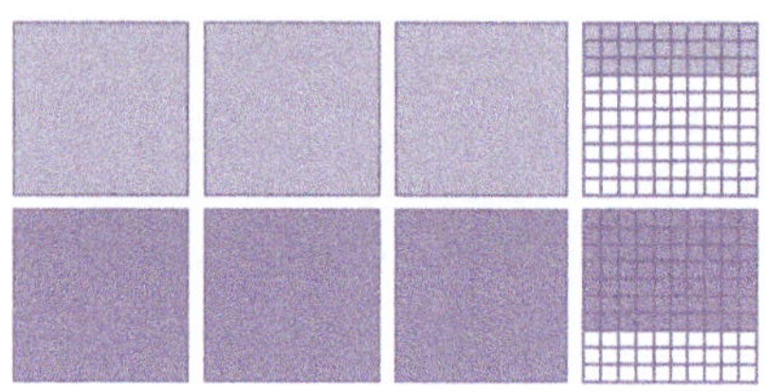

= ____

= ____

____ + ____ = ____

(b)

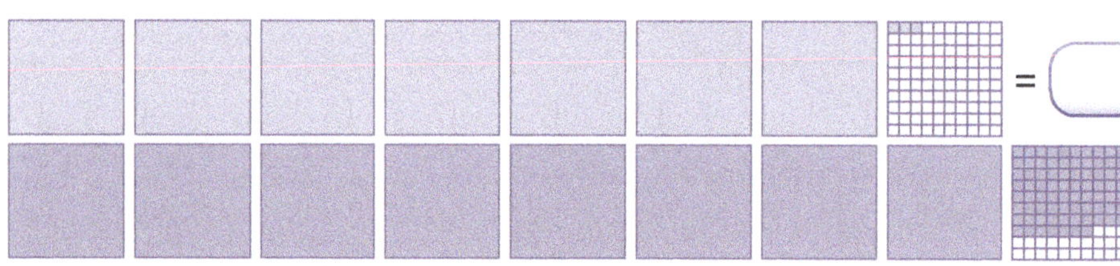

= ____

= ____

____ + ____ = ____

(c)

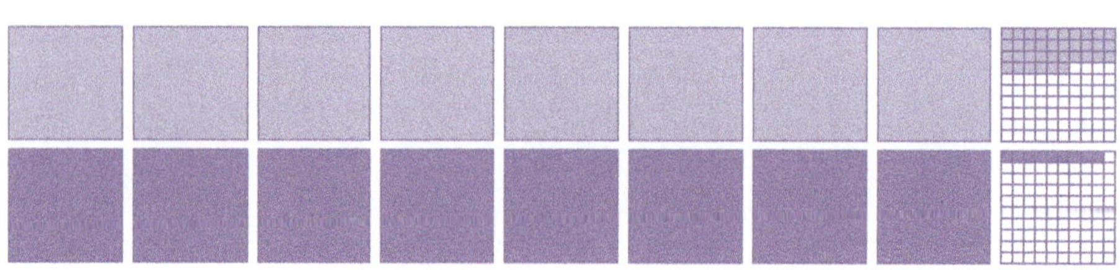

= ____

= ____

____ + ____ = ____

2 Add the decimal numbers.

(a) 1.5 + 1.7 = ☐

(b) 0.4 + 6.6 = ☐

(c) 5.5 + 1.8 = ☐

(d) 18.8 + 19.8 = ☐

(e) 15.2 + 12.9 = ☐

(f) 20.7 + 33.7 = ☐

(g) 65.4 + 22.7 = ☐

(h) 72.8 + 33.6 = ☐

3 Add the decimal numbers.

(a) 0.26 + 1.35 = ☐

☐.☐☐
\+ ☐.☐☐
☐.☐☐

(b) 3.94 + 4.46 = ☐

☐.☐☐
\+ ☐.☐☐
☐.☐☐

(c) 1.56 + 1.99 = ☐

☐.☐☐
\+ ☐.☐☐
☐.☐☐

(d) 2.22 + 4.89 = ☐

☐.☐☐
\+ ☐.☐☐
☐.☐☐

(e) 25.68 + 13.47 = ☐

(f) 46.59 + 27.64 = ☐

4 Use the coloured squares to complete the subtraction of the decimal numbers.

Example

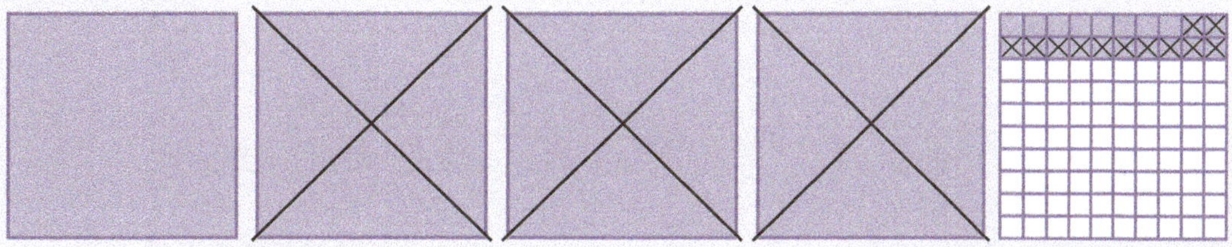

4.20 − 3.12 = 1.08

(a)

☐ − ☐ = ☐

(b)

☐ − ☐ = ☐

(c)

☐ − ☐ = ☐

5 Subtract the decimal numbers.

(a) 7.4 − 1.2 = ☐

☐.☐
− ☐.☐
☐.☐

(b) 6.6 − 5.4 = ☐

☐.☐
− ☐.☐
☐.☐

(c) 9.2 − 1.8 = ☐

☐.☐
− ☐.☐
☐.☐

(d) 30.4 − 12.6 = ☐

☐☐.☐
− ☐☐.☐
☐☐.☐

(e) 20.7 − 13.7 = ☐

☐☐.☐
− ☐☐.☐
☐☐.☐

(f) 15.5 − 4.7 = ☐

☐☐.☐
− ☐☐.☐
☐☐.☐

(g) 45.7 − 7.7 = ☐

☐☐.☐
− ☐☐.☐
☐☐.☐

(h) 73.2 − 62.8 = ☐

☐☐.☐
− ☐☐.☐
☐☐.☐

6 Subtract the decimal numbers.

(a) 0.89 − 0.56 = ☐

$$\begin{array}{r} \square.\square\square \\ -\ \square.\square\square \\ \hline \square.\square\square \end{array}$$

(b) 5.74 − 4.12 = ☐

$$\begin{array}{r} \square.\square\square \\ -\ \square.\square\square \\ \hline \square.\square\square \end{array}$$

(c) 7.22 − 4.36 = ☐

$$\begin{array}{r} \square.\square\square \\ -\ \square.\square\square \\ \hline \square.\square\square \end{array}$$

(d) 6.85 − 3.39 = ☐

$$\begin{array}{r} \square.\square\square \\ -\ \square.\square\square \\ \hline \square.\square\square \end{array}$$

(e) 24.02 − 13.15 = ☐

(f) 51.72 − 27.84 = ☐

Practice 7: Word problems

1 Jade weighs 23.45 kg. Her father weighs 68.79 kg.

(a) How much heavier is Jade's father than Jade?

Jade's father is ☐ kg heavier than Jade.

(b) What is the total mass of Jade and her father?

The total mass of Jade and her father is ☐ kg.

(c) Jade's father lost 4.25 kg. What is his new weight?

Jade's father's mass is now ☐ kg.

2 A garden is split into 2 sections. One section is 6.32 m long and the other is 34.64 m long. How long is the garden in total?

The garden is ☐ m long in total.

3 Jade is playing with her toy truck and toy train. The truck measures 17.3 cm long and 2.5 cm high. The train measures 35.45 cm long and 14.8 cm high.

(a) Jade lines her toy truck and toy train up. What is the length of the two toys together?

The total length of the 2 toys is ☐ cm.

(b) Then Jade places her toy truck on top of the train. What is the height of the two toys together?

The total height of the 2 toys is ☐ cm.

4 Padma must carry 3 boxes, each weighing 7.3 kg. What is the total weight Padma will carry?

5 Samir's foot length is 9.8 cm long. If he put his two feet one in front of the other, what would the total length be?

The total length would be [ ] cm.

6 The width of a plant is 7.5 cm. What distance would be covered by 8 plants planted next to each other?

The distance covered by 8 plants would be [ ] cm.

7 A brick is 6.8 cm high. 8 bricks are stacked on top of each other. How high is the pile of bricks?

The pile of bricks is [ ] cm.

10 Percentages

Practice 1: Percentages

1. There are 100 ice creams in 4 different flavours – vanilla, strawberry, lemon and chocolate. Count the number of ice creams for each flavour. Then answer the questions that follow.

(a) How many of the ice creams are lemon flavoured? ☐

(b) What fraction of the ice creams are lemon flavoured? $\frac{\square}{\square}$

(c) Write the number of lemon-flavoured ice creams as a percentage of the total number of ice creams. ☐

(d) How many of the ice creams are chocolate flavoured? ☐

(e) What fraction of the ice creams are chocolate flavoured? $\frac{\square}{\square}$

(f) Write the number of chocolate-flavoured ice creams as a percentage of the total number of ice creams. ☐

(g) How many of the ice creams are strawberry flavoured? ☐

(h) What fraction of the ice creams are strawberry flavoured? $\frac{\square}{\square}$

(i) Write the number of strawberry-flavoured ice creams as a percentage of the total number of ice creams. ☐

(j) Write the number of vanilla-flavoured ice creams as a percentage of the total number of ice creams. ☐

2 The big square below is divided into 100 small squares of equal size. Some of the small squares are coloured.

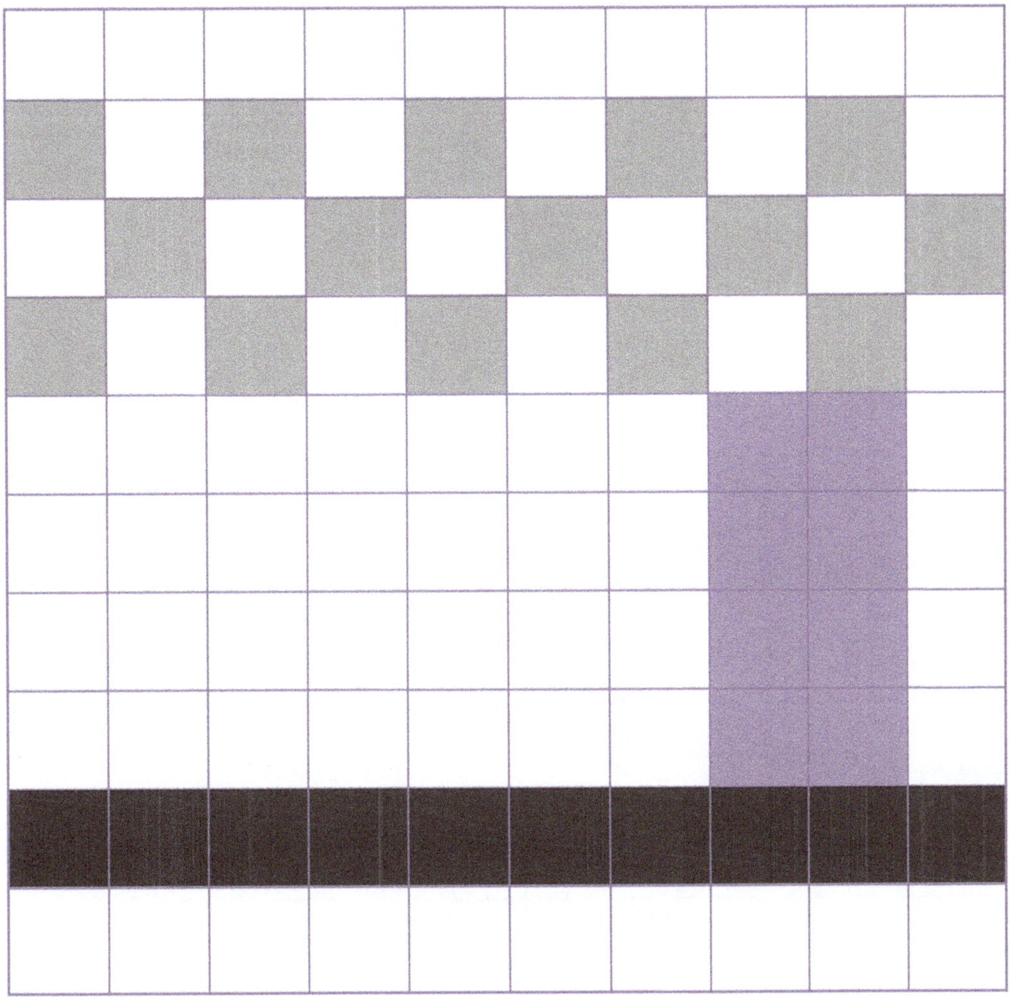

(a) What percentage of the big square is coloured grey? ☐

(b) What percentage of the big square is coloured purple? ☐

(c) What percentage of the big square is coloured black? ☐

(d) What percentage of the big square is coloured black or purple? ☐

(e) What percentage of the big square is coloured grey or black? ☐

(f) What percentage of the big square is not coloured? ☐

3 The big square below is divided into 100 small squares of equal size. Answer the questions that follow.

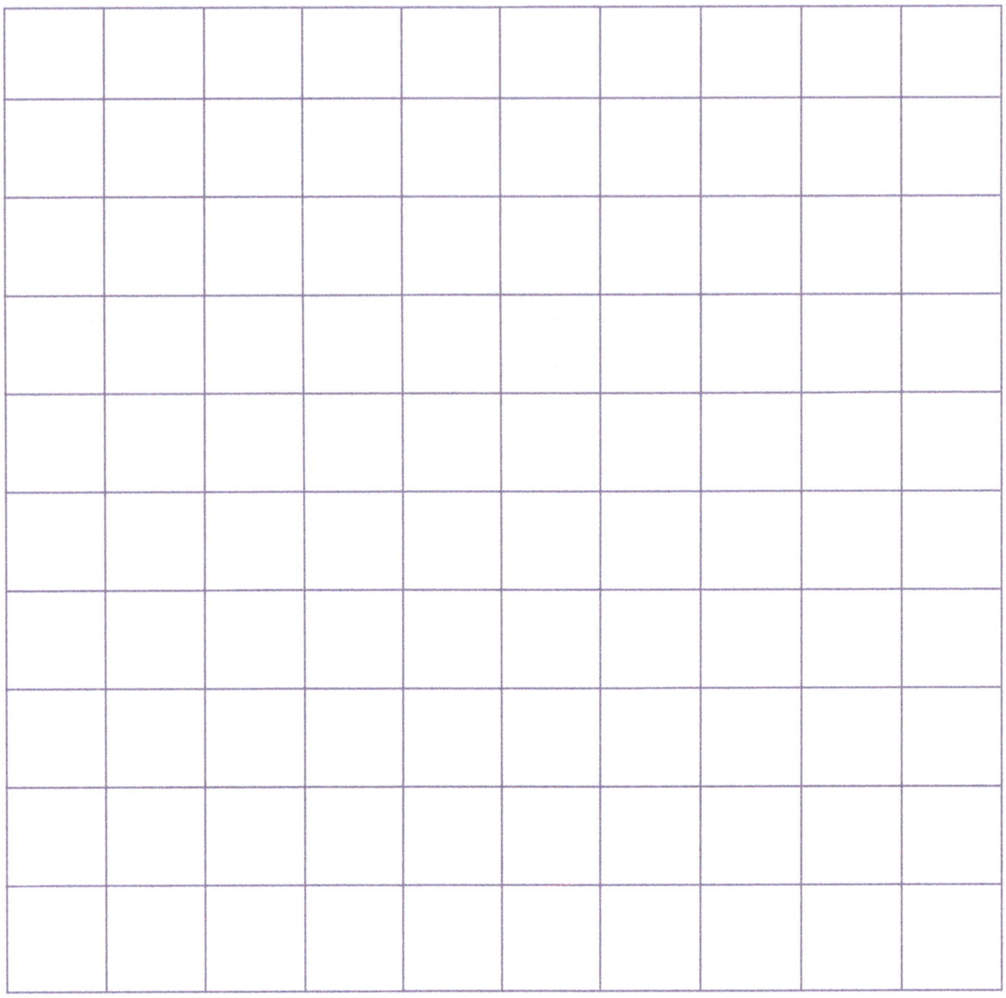

(a) Colour 23% of the big square green.

(b) Colour 5% of the big square blue.

(c) Colour eighteen per cent of the big square yellow.

(d) Colour twenty-eight per cent of the big square red.

(e) What percentage of the big square is not coloured? ☐

(f) What percentage of the big square is not coloured blue? ☐

4. Write each percentage in words.

(a) 7% [ ]

(b) 11% [ ]

(c) 36% [ ]

(d) 50% [ ]

(e) 44% [ ]

(f) 92% [ ]

(g) 100% [ ]

(h) 0% [ ]

5. Read and write each percentage.

(a) Thirteen out of one hundred [ ]

(b) Fifty-nine out of one hundred [ ]

(c) Forty-six out of one hundred [ ]

(d) Seventy-seven out of one hundred [ ]

(e) Thirteen out of one hundred [ ]

(f) Eighty-one out of one hundred [ ]

(g) Ninety-nine out of one hundred [ ]

(h) Sixty-three out of one hundred [ ]

6 Find these percentages of 240.

(a) 10% ☐ (b) 20% ☐

(c) 50% ☐ (d) 60% ☐

(e) 5% ☐ (f) 75% ☐

7 Find these percentages of 300.

(a) 1% ☐ (b) 10% ☐

(c) 100% ☐ (d) 5% ☐

(e) 50% ☐ (f) 25% ☐

8 Find these percentages of 500.

(a) 10% ☐ (b) 5% ☐

(c) 20% ☐ (d) 25% ☐

(e) 50% ☐ (f) 75% ☐

9 Find these percentages of 420.

(a) 10% ☐ (b) 50% ☐

(c) 30% ☐ (d) 25% ☐

(e) 80% ☐ (f) 1% ☐

11 Length, mass and volume

Practice 1: Review of units of length, mass and volume

1 Fill in the blanks.

Example

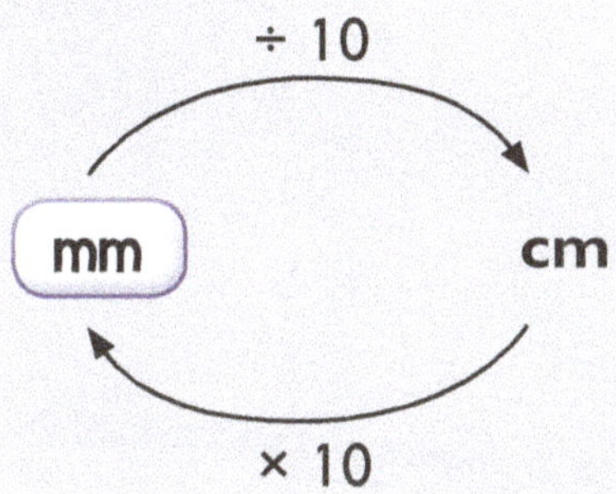

To convert [mm] to cm, we [divide] by 10.

(a)

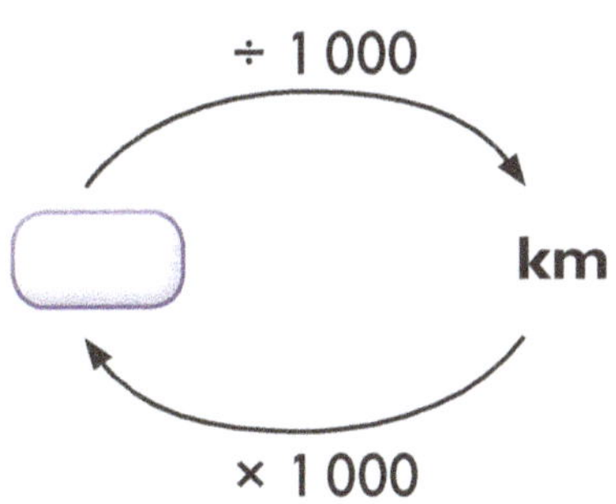

To convert [ ] to km, we [ ] by 1 000.

(b)

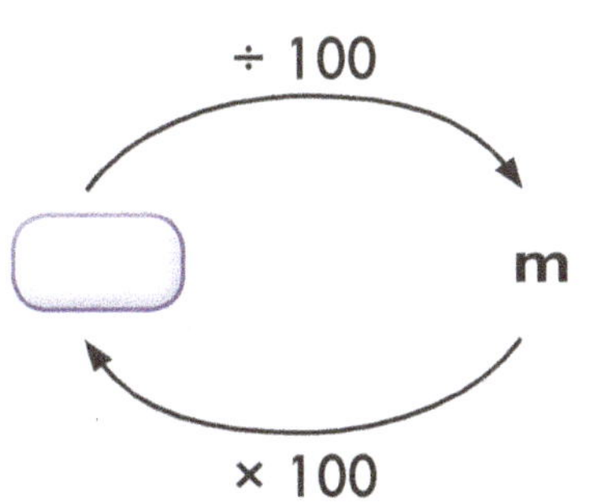

To convert [ ] to m, we [ ] by 100.

(c)

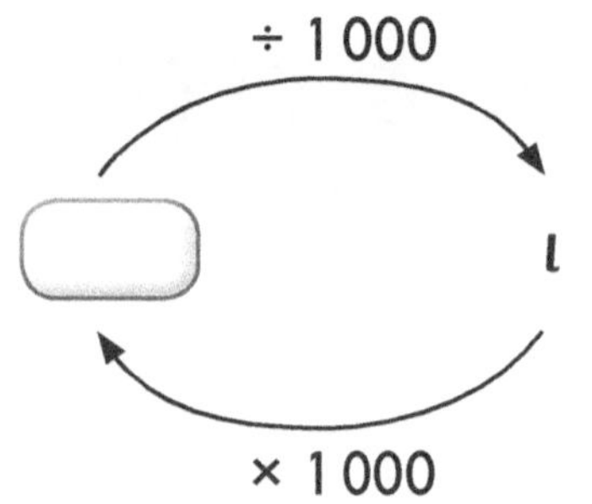

To convert ☐ to l, we ☐ by 1 000.

(d)

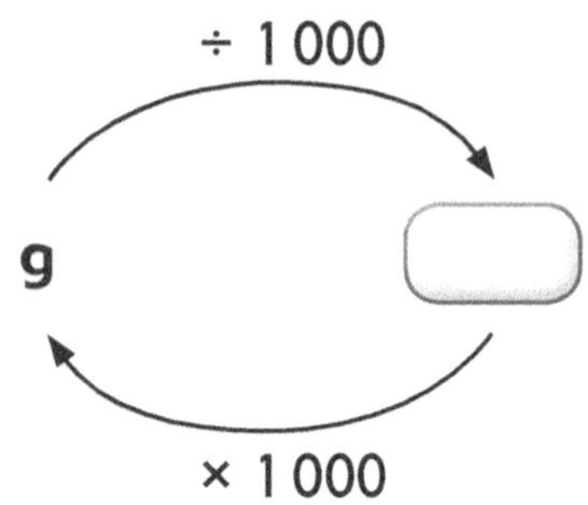

To convert ☐ to g, we ☐ by 1 000.

(e)

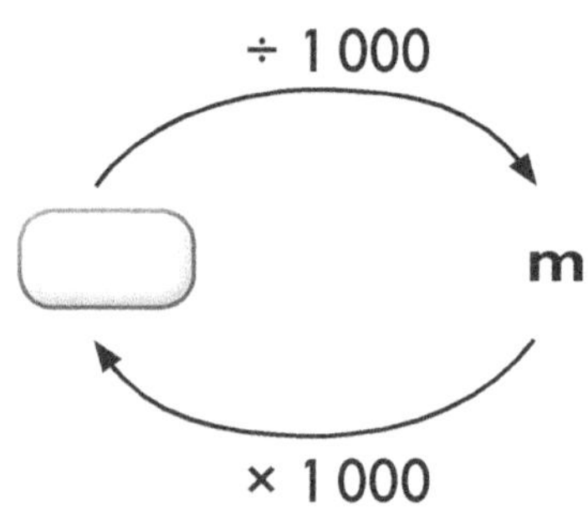

To convert ☐ to m, we ☐ by 1 000.

(f)

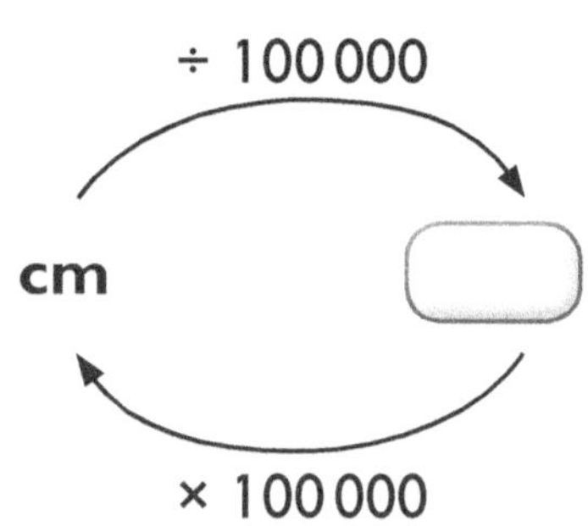

To convert ☐ to cm, we ☐ by 100 000.

2 Convert the following.

(a) Convert 17 kg to grams.

To convert kilograms to grams, we [ ] by [ ].

[ ] ☐ [ ] = [ ]

So, 17 kg = [ ] g.

(b) Convert 128 cm to millimetres.

To convert centimetres to millimetres, we [ ] by [ ].

[ ] ☐ [ ] = [ ]

So, 128 cm = [ ] mm.

(c) Convert 2 km to metres.

To convert kilometres to metres, we [ ] by [ ].

[ ] ☐ [ ] = [ ]

So, 2 km = [ ] m.

(d) Convert 3 000 g to kilograms.

To convert grams to kilograms, we [ ] by [ ].

[ ] ☐ [ ] = [ ]

So, 3 000 g = [ ] kg.

(e) Convert 5 l to millilitres.

To convert litres to millilitres, we [ ] by [ ].

[ ] □ [ ] = [ ]

So, 5 l = [ ] ml.

(f) Convert 700 mm to centimetres.

To convert millimetres to centimetres, we [ ] by [ ].

[ ] □ [ ] = [ ]

So, 700 mm = [ ] cm.

(g) Convert 9000 ml to litres.

To convert millilitres to litres, we [ ] by [ ].

[ ] □ [ ] = [ ]

So, 9000 ml = [ ] ml.

(h) Convert 30 000 m to kilometres.

To convert metres to kilometres, we [ ] by [ ].

[ ] □ [ ] = [ ]

So, 30 000 m = [ ] km.

Practice 2: Length, mass and volume in decimal form

1. Convert the following lengths to metres. Write the correct unit of measurement.

   (a) 42 cm ÷ 100 = ☐

   (b) 438 cm ÷ 100 = ☐

   (c) 552 cm ÷ 100 = ☐

   (d) 1 065 cm ÷ 100 = ☐

2. Convert the following lengths to kilometres. Write the correct unit of measurement.

   (a) 76 m ÷ 1 000 = ☐

   (b) 3 m ÷ 1 000 = ☐

   (c) 116 m ÷ 1 000 = ☐

   (d) 2 375 m ÷ 1 000 = ☐

3. Convert the following masses to kilograms. Write the correct unit of measurement.

   (a) 99 g ÷ 1 000 = ☐

   (b) 102 g ÷ 1 000 = ☐

   (c) 472 g ÷ 1 000 = ☐

   (d) 6 110 g ÷ 1 000 = ☐

4. Convert the following volumes to litres. Write the correct unit of measurement.

   (a) 65 ml ÷ 1 000 = ☐

   (b) 236 ml ÷ 1 000 = ☐

   (c) 809 ml ÷ 1 000 = ☐

   (d) 8 342 ml ÷ 1 000 = ☐

5. Convert the following lengths to millimetres. Write the correct unit of measurement.

(a) 58 cm × 10 = ☐ **(b)** 154 cm × 10 = ☐

(c) 6 m × 1 000 × 10 = ☐ **(d)** 10.2 m × 100 × 10 = ☐

6. Convert the following lengths to metres and centimetres. Write the correct units of measurement.

(a) 0.2 m × 100 = ☐

(b) 0.04 m × 100 = ☐

(c) 0.376 m × 100 = ☐

(d) 1.7 m × 100 = ☐

(e) 34.01 m × 100 = ☐

(f) 100.3 m × 100 = ☐

7. Complete the following.

(a) 1.4 km × 1 000 = ☐ km ☐ m

(b) 18.01 km × 1 000 = ☐ km ☐ m

(c) 6.3 kg × 1 000 = ☐ kg ☐ g

(d) 16.004 kg × 1 000 = ☐ kg ☐ g

(e) 7.093 ml × 1 000 = ☐ l ☐ ml

(f) 89.103 ml × 1 000 = ☐ l ☐ ml

8. Complete the following conversions.

(a) A glass contains 235 ml of milk. How many litres is that?

To convert millilitres to litres, we ☐ by ☐.

☐ ☐ ☐ = ☐

So, 235 ml = ☐ l.

(b) A book is 20.5 cm long. How many metres is that?

To convert centimetres to metres, we ☐ by ☐.

☐ ☐ ☐ = ☐

So, 20.5 cm = ☐ m.

(c) A child weighs 19.7 kg. How many grams is that?

To convert kilograms to grams, we ☐ by ☐.

☐ ☐ ☐ = ☐

So, 19.7 kg = ☐ g.

(d) An apple weighs 45.2 g. How many kilograms is that?

To convert grams to kilograms, we ☐ by ☐.

☐ ☐ ☐ = ☐

So, 45.2 g = ☐ kg.

(e) A road is 2.07 km long. How many metres is that?

To convert kilometres to metres, we ☐ by ☐.

☐ ☐ ☐ = ☐

So, 2.07 km = ☐ m.

(f) A car's petrol tank contains 80.71 l of petrol. How many millilitres is that?

To convert litres to millilitres, we ☐ by ☐.

☐ ☐ ☐ = ☐

So, 80.71 l = ☐ ml.

(g) A paper clip is 3.61 cm long. How many millimetres is that?

To convert centimetres to millimetres, we ☐ by ☐.

☐ ☐ ☐ = ☐

So, 3.61 cm = ☐ mm.

(h) A path is 507 m long. How many kilometres is that?

To convert metres to kilometres, we ☐ by ☐.

☐ ☐ ☐ = ☐

So, 507 m = ☐ km.

Practice 3: Ordering measurements in mixed units

1 Order these units of length from shortest to longest. Convert them all to the same unit of measurement first.

(a) 34 mm 3.7 cm 2 cm 8 mm 32 mm 3.6 cm

shortest → longest

(b) 89 cm 1.2 m 1 m 88 cm 136 cm 2.02 m

shortest → longest

(c) 98.4 km 8 934 cm 100.1 km 78 km 98 m 8 893 m

shortest → longest

2 Order these units of mass from heaviest to lightest. Convert them all to the same unit of measurement first.

(a) 50.2 kg 4 500 g 4 kg 480 g 5 389 g 49.33 kg

heaviest → lightest

(b) 2 307 g | 24.32 kg | 22 kg 180 g | 2 319 g | 25.01 kg

heaviest → lightest

(c) 18.84 kg | 846 g | 30.467 kg | 15 kg 73 g | 2 280 g

heaviest → lightest

3 Order these units of capacity from largest to smallest. Convert them all to the same unit of measurement first.

(a) 2 305 ml | 25.4 l | 22 l 85 ml | 2 320 ml | 24.65 l

largest → smallest

(b) 1.3 l | 1 103 ml | 1.25 l | 1 l 880 ml | 1.45 l

largest → smallest

(c) 15.38 l | 1 845 ml | 22 l 20 ml | 54.15 l | 2 461 ml

largest → smallest

Practice 4: Review of measuring length, mass and volume

Place the most appropriate unit of measurement next to each object.
Choose from millimetres (mm), centimetres (cm), metres (m), grams (g), kilograms (kg), millilitres (ml), litres (l).

(a)

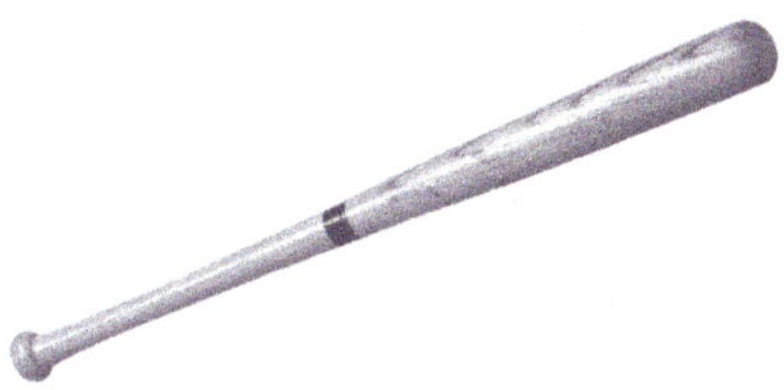

The length should be measured in ☐.

(b)

The capacity should be measured in ☐.

(c)

The capacity should be measured in ☐.

(d)

The distance should be measured in ☐.

(e)

The mass should be measured in ☐.

(f)

The mass should be measured in ☐.

Practice 5: Interpreting a reading that lies between two divisions on a scale

1 What is the mass shown on these scales?

(a)

(b)

(c)

(d)

2 What is the volume in these measuring jugs and cylinders?

(a)

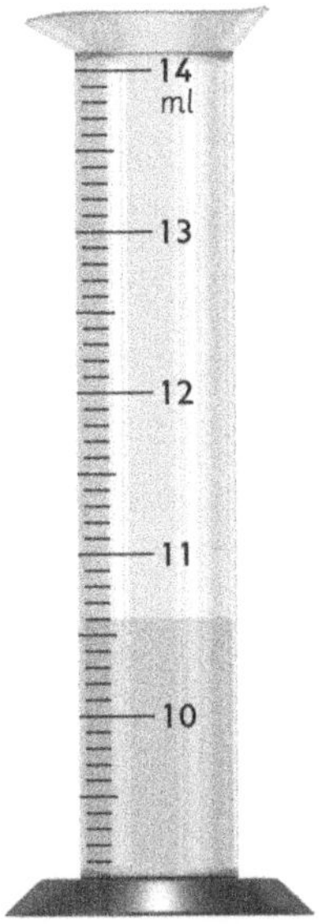

(b)

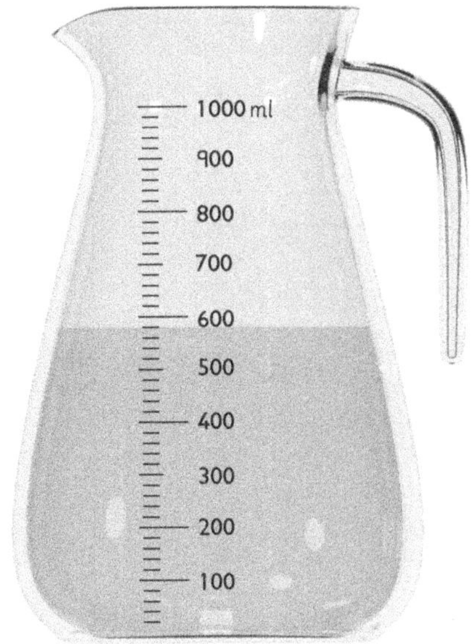

(c)

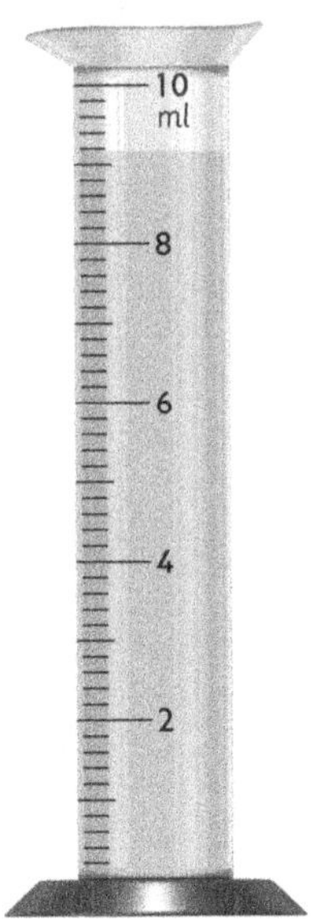

(d)

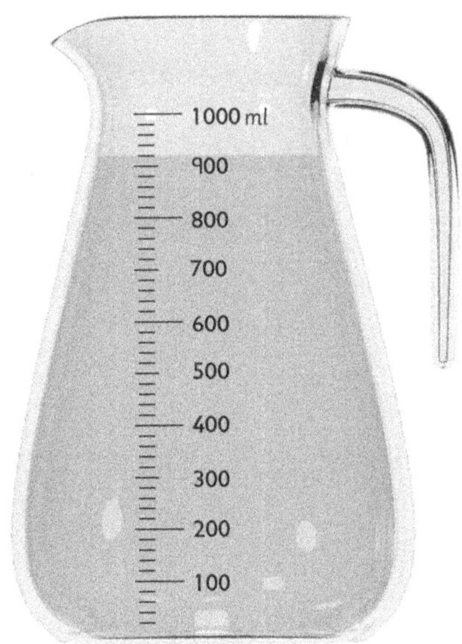

3 What is the length on these rulers?

(a)

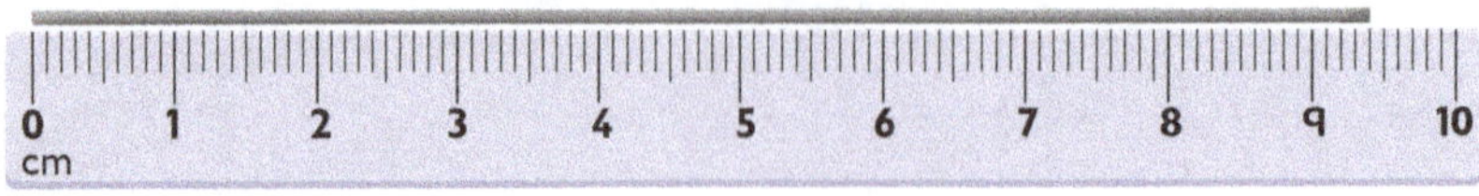

(b)

(c)

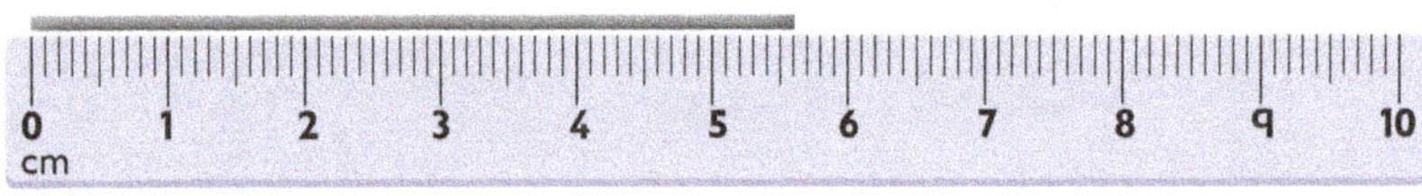

(d)

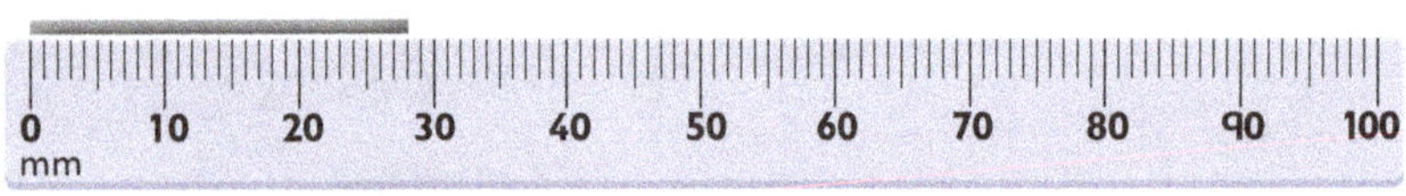

(e)

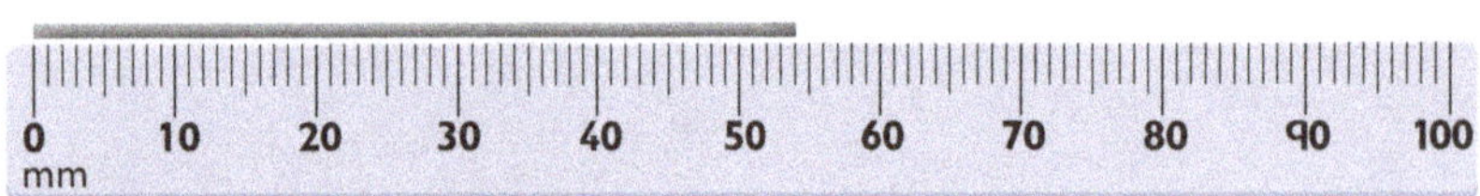

(f)

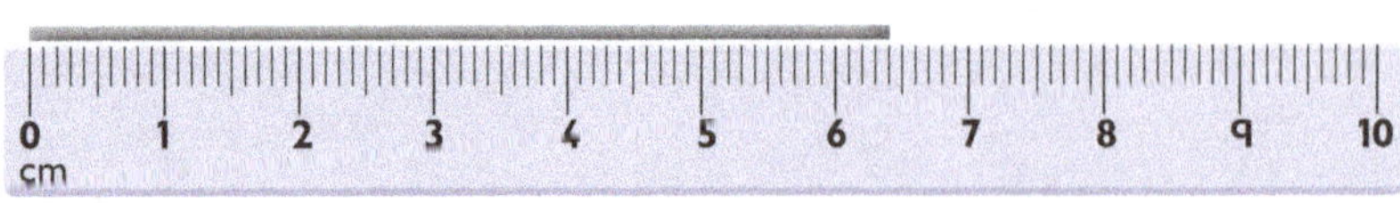

Practice 6: Measuring lines to the nearest centimetre and millimetre

1. Measure these lines to the nearest millimetre.

(a)

(b)

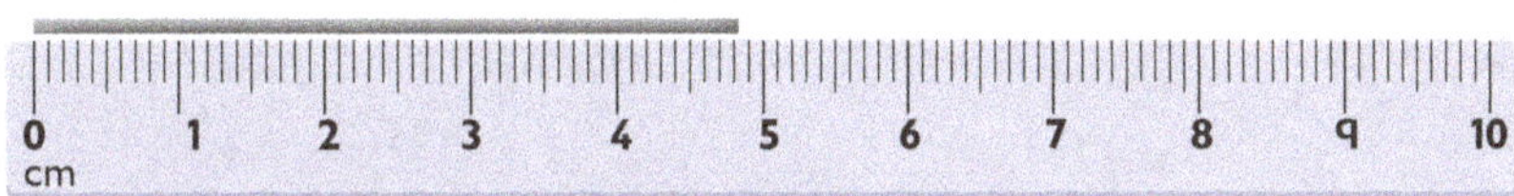

(c)

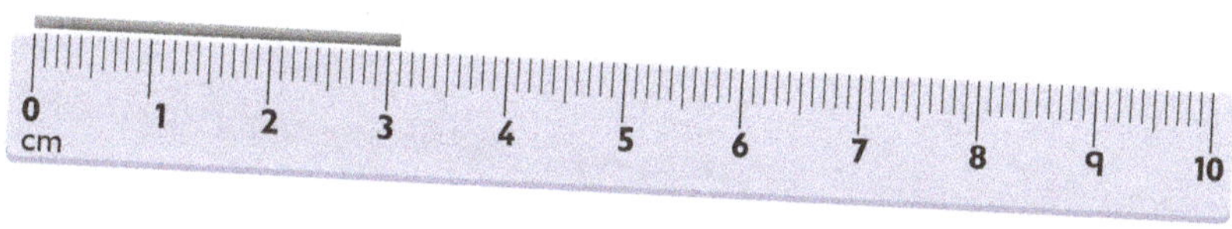

(d)

(e)

(f)

2 Measure these lines in centimetres with you own ruler.

(a) 6.4 cm

(b) cm

(c) cm

(d) cm

(e) cm

(f) cm

3 Draw lines of the length given.

(a) 3 cm 2 mm

(b) 7 cm 4 mm

(c) 8 cm 1 mm

(d) 4 cm 5 mm

(e) 9 mm

(f) 6 cm 7 mm

4. Which line is longer?

(a)

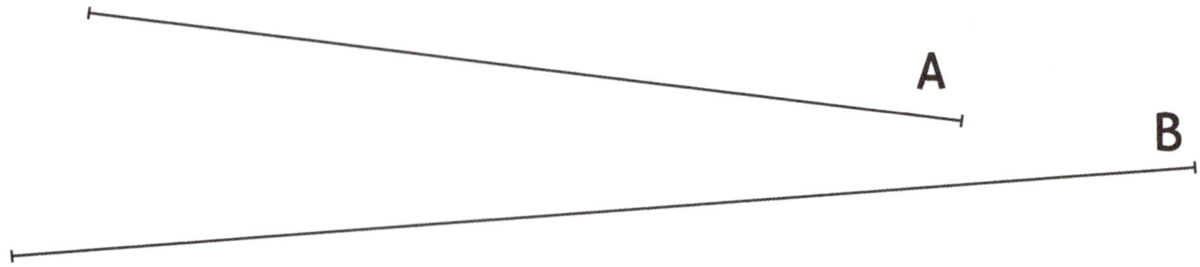

(b)

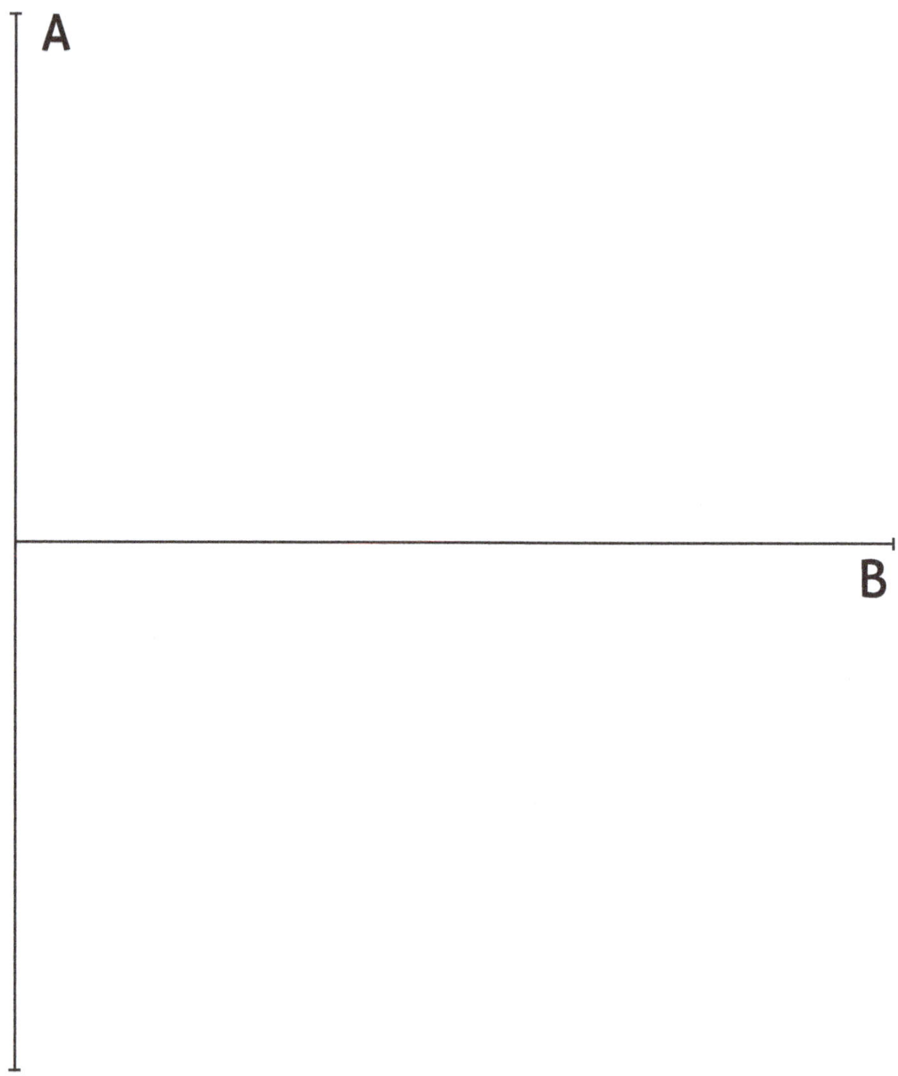

(c)

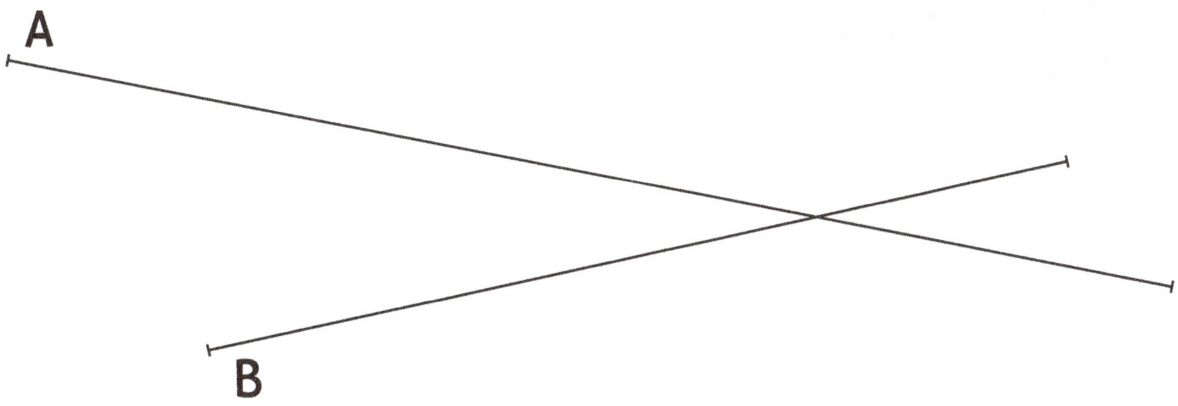

(d)

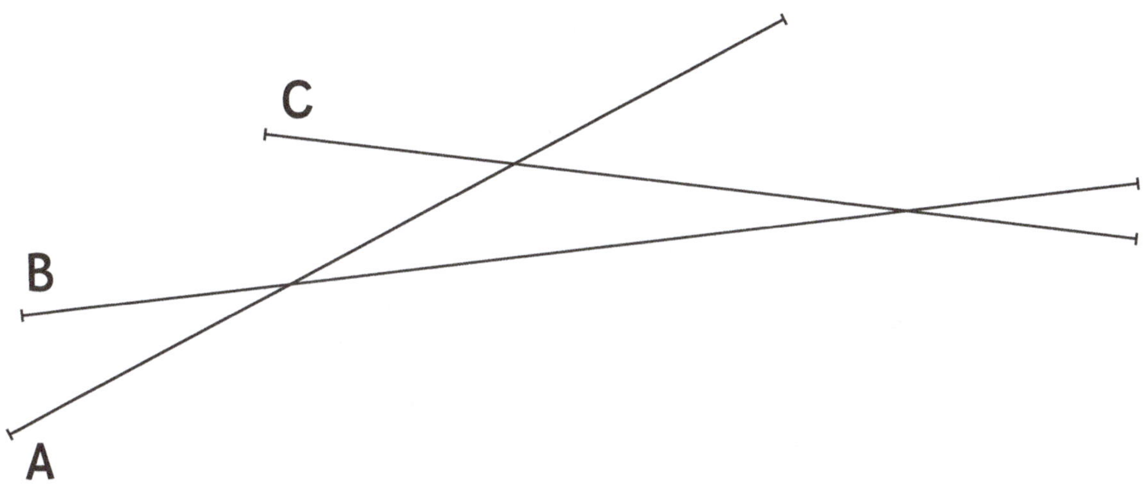

12 Data handling

Practice 1: Reading and constructing graphs

1. The line graph below shows the amount of money Jade has in her savings account with a bank at different times of the year.

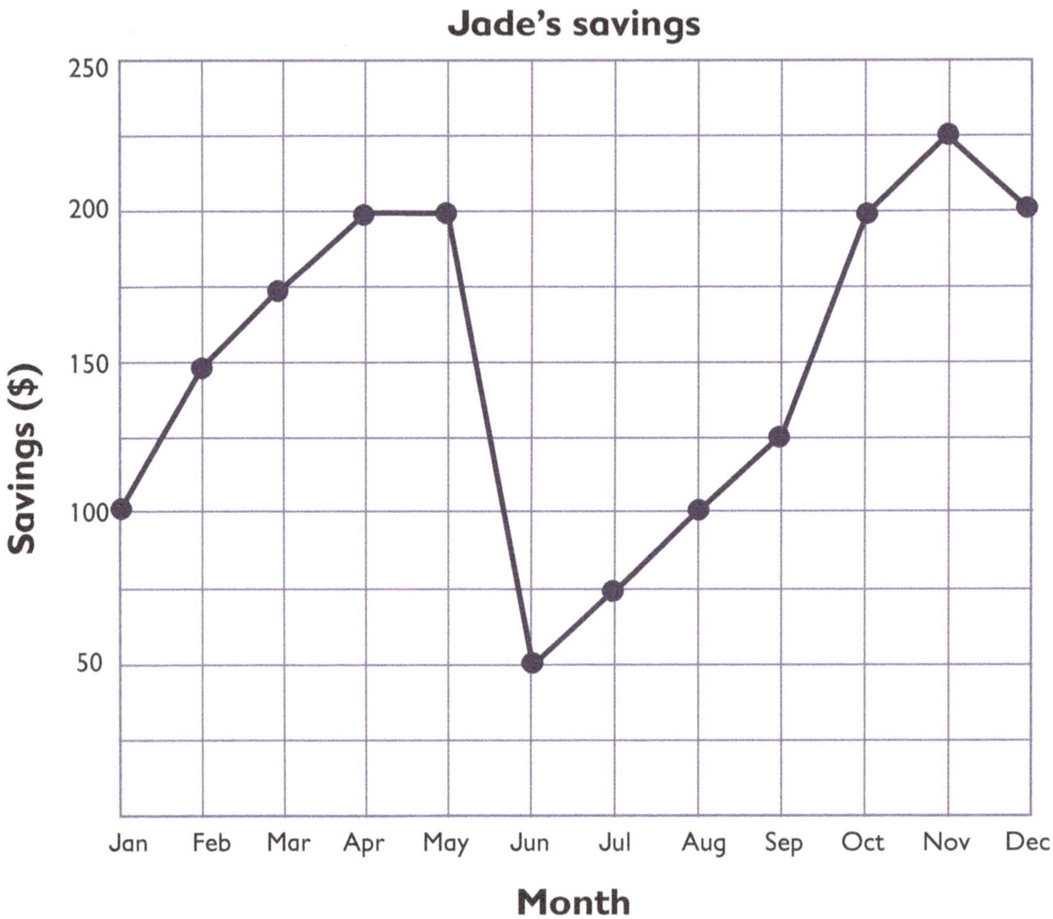

(a) In which month did Jade have only $50 in her savings account?

(b) How much money did Jade have in her savings account in March?

(c) In which month did Jade have the most money in her savings account?

[ ]

(d) How much savings did Jade have in September? [ ]

(e) How much more money did Jade have in her savings account in October than in January? [ ]

(f) Jade saved the most money between which 2 months?

[ ] and [ ]

(g) The mode of Jade's money is $200, which she has in four of the months. Which are the months?

[ ], [ ], [ ] and [ ].

(h) During the year, Jade bought a new mobile phone with her savings. The phone cost $150. In which month do you think Jade bought the mobile phone? Why did you choose this month?

[ ]

2 There was a sports carnival at a stadium. The line graph below shows the number of people in the stadium during that day.

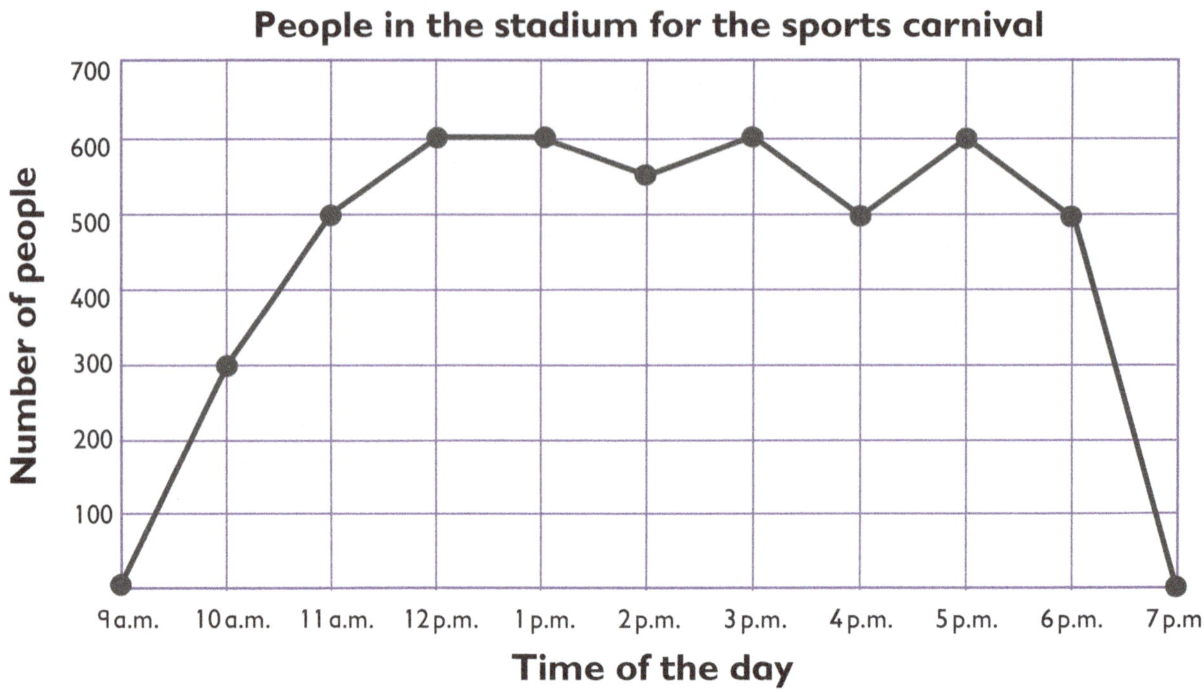

(a) How many people were in the stadium at 10 a.m.? ☐

(b) How many people were in the stadium at 4 p.m.? ☐

(c) There were 500 people in the stadium at ☐, ☐ and ☐.

(d) What time do you think the sports carnival finishes? Why?

☐

☐

(e) What was the mode number of people?

☐

3 Look at the line graph and complete the table.

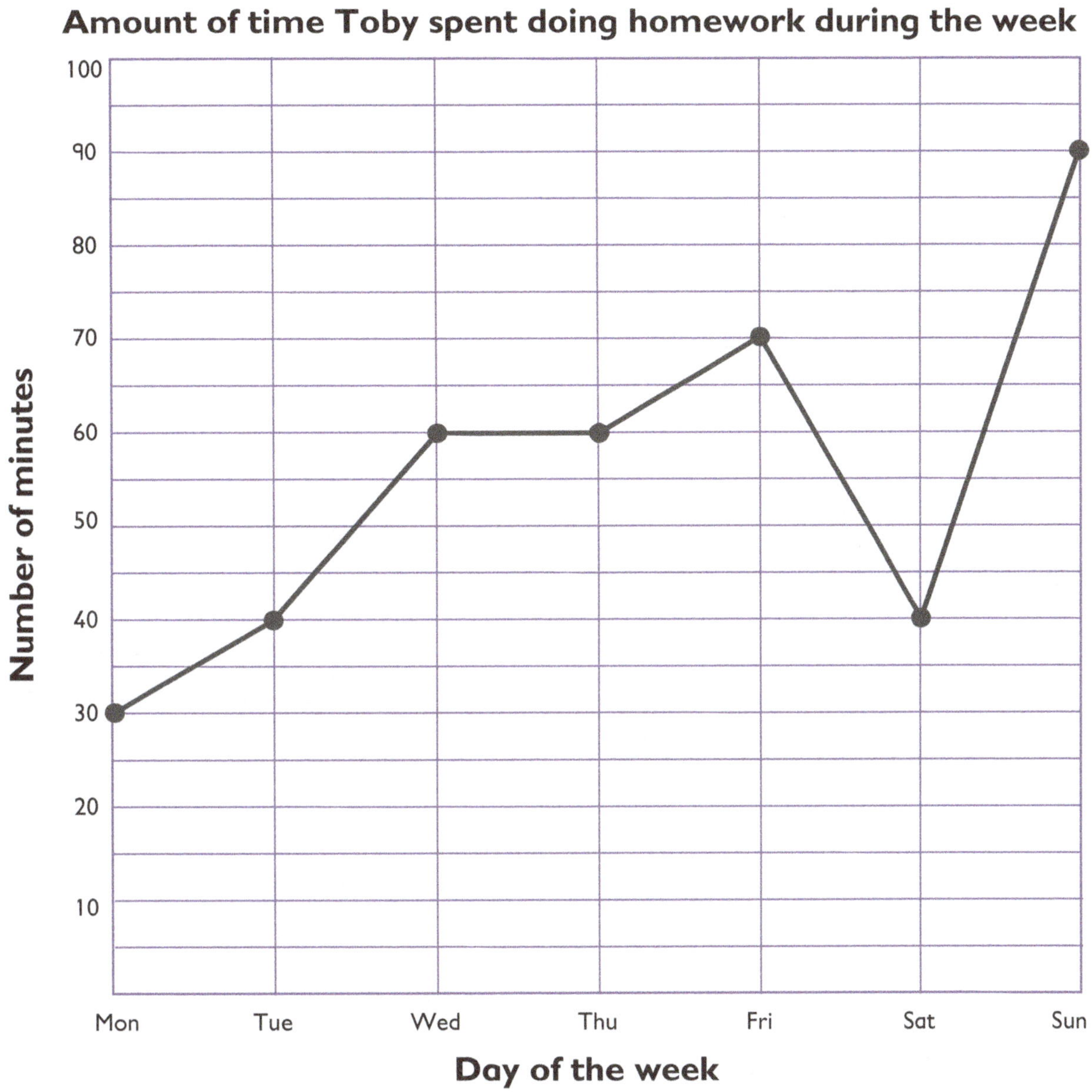

Day of the week							
Time spent doing homework (minutes)							

4 Samir placed some warm water into the freezer. He measured the temperature of the water for 45 minutes.

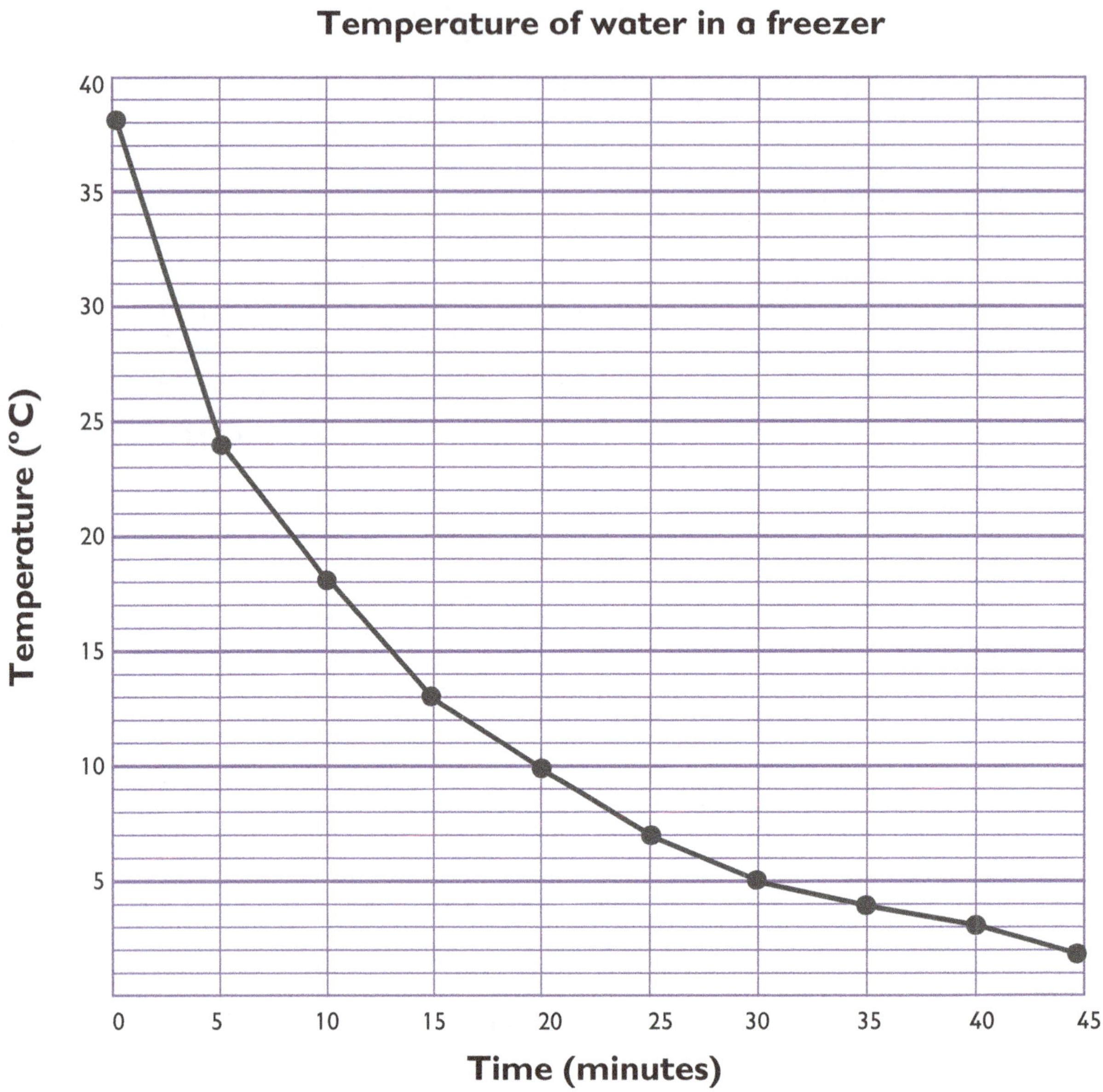

(a) What is the temperature of the water after 5 minutes? ☐ °C

(b) By how much does the temperature change in the first 5 minutes?

☐ °C ☐ ☐ °C = ☐ °C

The temperature changes by ☐ °C in the first 5 minutes.

(c) How long does it take for the temperature to drop to 10 °C ? ☐ min

(d) What is the temperature of the water after 25 minutes? ☐ °C

(e) By how much does the temperature change in the last 5 minutes?

☐ °C ☐ ☐ °C = ☐ °C

The temperature changes by ☐ °C in the last 5 minutes.

5 A noodle shop records the number of bowls of noodles it sold in 1 day.

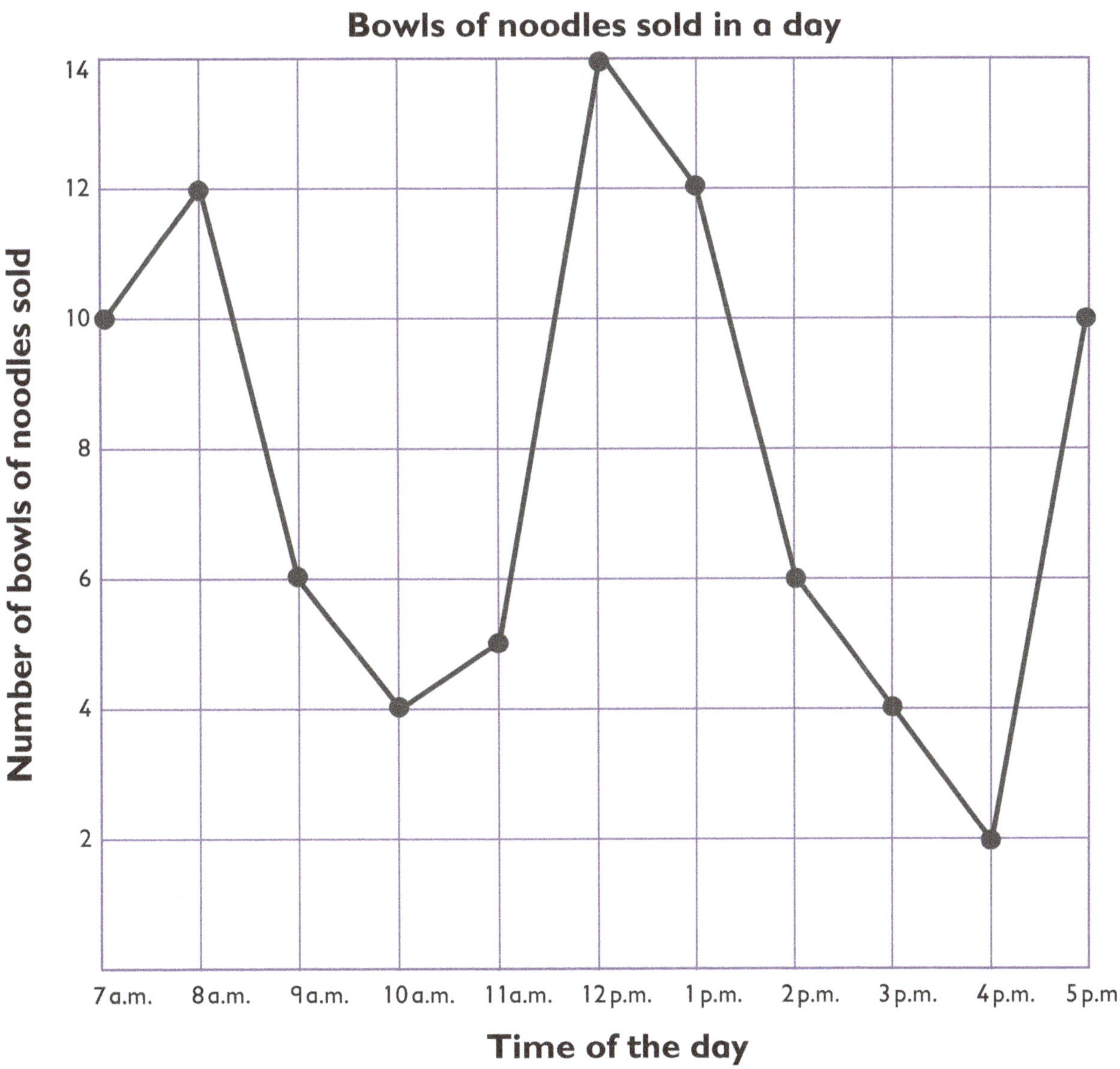

(a) How many bowls of noodles were sold at 7 a.m.? [ ]

(b) At what time were 2 bowls of noodles sold? [ ]

(c) How many bowls of noodles were sold at noon? [ ]

(d) At what times were 12 bowls of noodles sold? [ ] and [ ]

(e) At what times were 4 bowls of noodles sold? [ ] and [ ]

(f) How many bowls of noodles were sold between 11 a.m. and 12 p.m.?

[ ] □ [ ] = [ ]

[ ] bowls of noodles were sold between 11 a.m. and 12 p.m.

(g) The line graph has 3 high points at 8 a.m., 12 p.m. and 5 p.m.
Explain why more bowls of noodles were sold at these times.

6 The line graph below shows the number of visitors to the zoo on different days of the week.

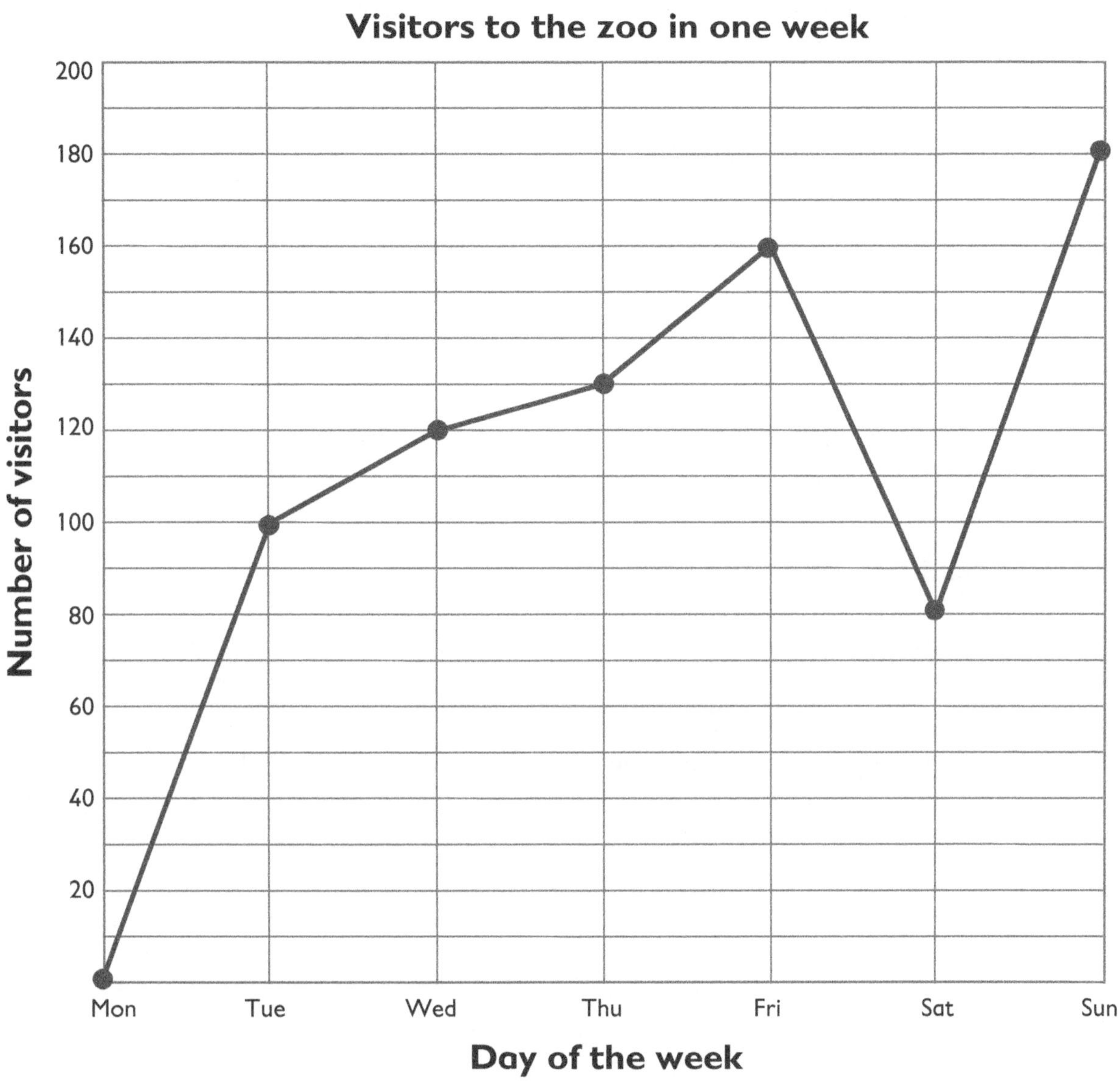

(a) How many people visited the zoo on Wednesday? ☐

(b) How many more people visited the zoo on Friday than on Thursday?

☐ ☐ ☐ = ☐

☐ more people visited the zoo on Friday than on Thursday.

(c) How many fewer people visited the zoo on Saturday than on Friday?

☐ ☐ ☐ = ☐

☐ fewer people visited the zoo on Saturday than on Friday.

(d) How many people visited the zoo on Tuesday and Wednesday altogether?

☐ ☐ ☐ = ☐

☐ people visited the zoo on Tuesday and Wednesday altogether.

(e) On which day do you think the zoo was closed?

Why do you think it is this day?

☐

☐

(f) How many people visited the zoo altogether during the week?

☐

☐ people visited the zoo altogether during the week.

7. Tya has a seedling. She measures its height every week for 10 weeks and records the information in a table. Help Tya show this information in a line graph.

Week	1	2	3	4	5	6	7	8	9	10
Height (cm)	1	2	4	10	13	15	17	18	19	20

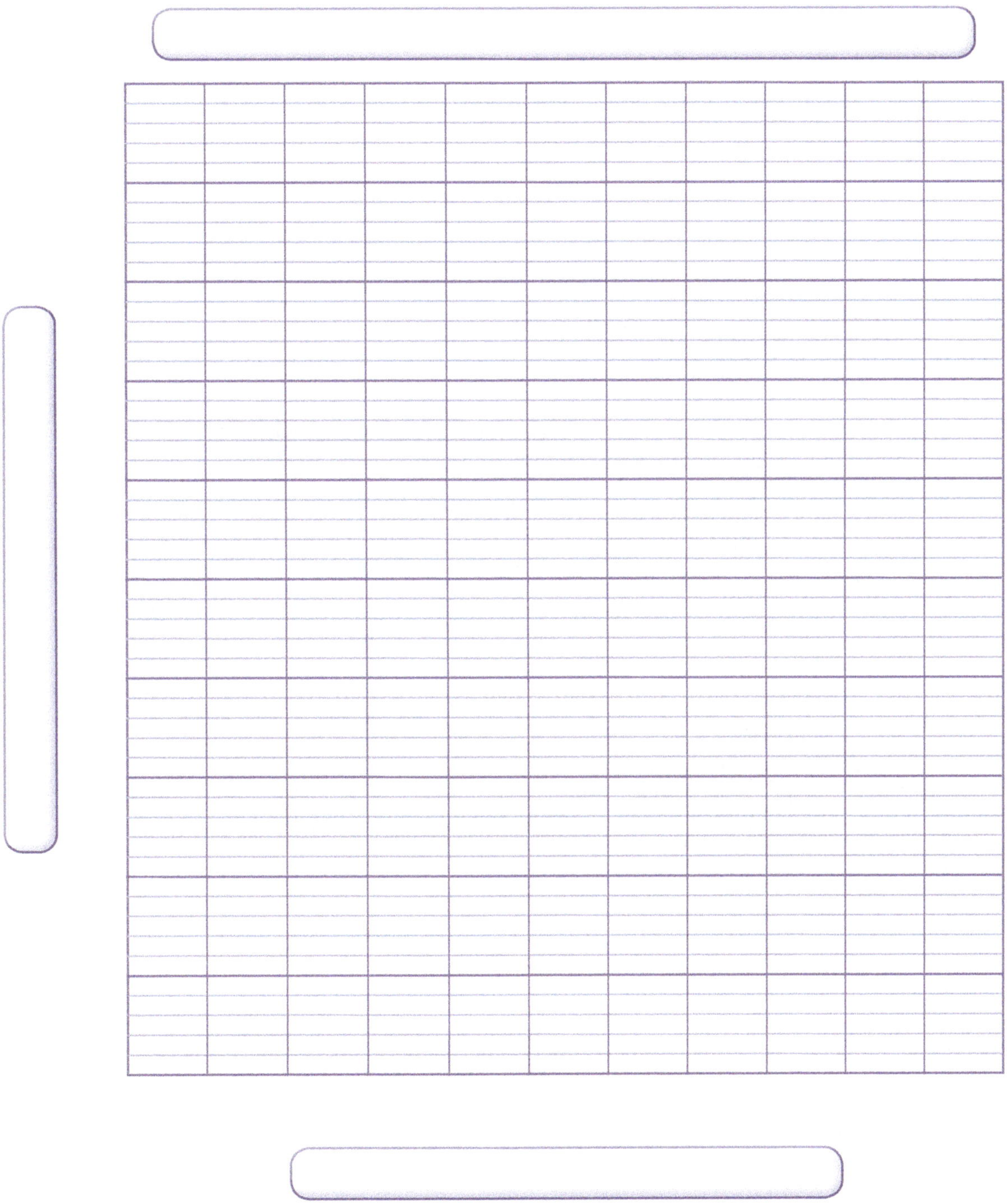

Practice 2: Describing the occurrence of familiar events

1. Look at the spinners. Write whether the likelihood of spinning the following numbers is impossible, unlikely, even, likely or certain.

(a)

The likelihood of spinning an odd number is ☐

(b)

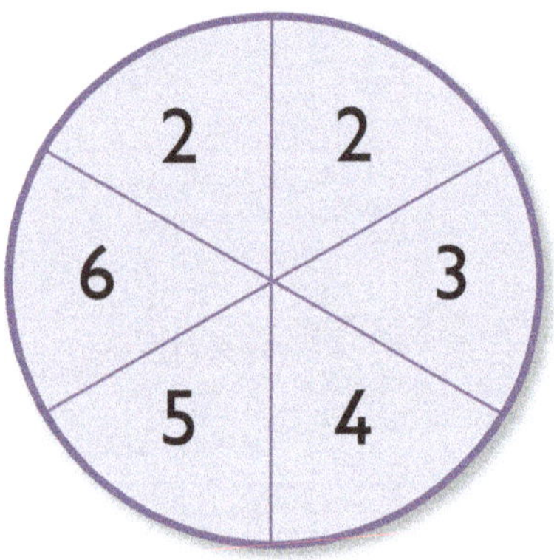

The likelihood of spinning 1 is ☐

(c)

The likelihood of spinning a prime number is ☐

(d)

The likelihood of spinning a multiple of 10 is [ ]

(e)

The likelihood of spinning a multiple of 3 is [ ]

(f)

The likelihood of spinning a multiple of 4 is [ ]

2. Decide whether the chance of these events is impossible, unlikely, even, likely or certain.

(a) The likelihood that you will draw a diamond from a pack of cards ______.

(b) The likelihood that the Sun will rise tomorrow ______.

(c) The likelihood that January will be the month before February ______.

(d) The likelihood that when you are 30, you will be taller than you are now ______.

(e) The likelihood that you will be the next person to walk on the Moon ______.

(f) The likelihood that you will shrink to two centimetres tall after school ______.

3. Write an event that would have a chance as stated.

Impossible ______

Unlikely ______

Even ______

Likely ______

Certain ______

13 Position and movement

Practice 1: Reading and plotting coordinates

1 Write the coordinates for each picture.

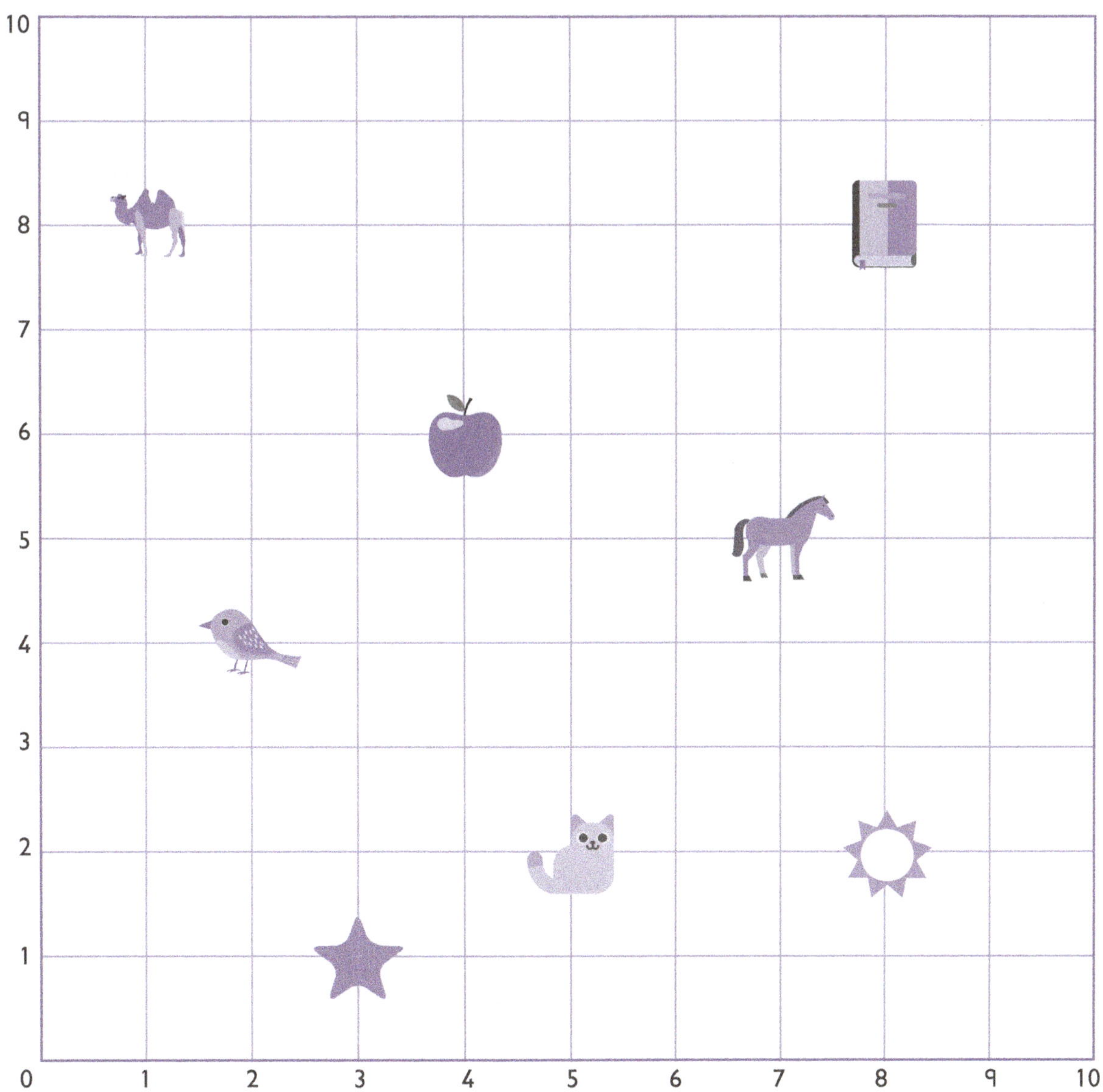

2. Plot these coordinates

(a) (3, 2), (8, 2), (8, 6), (3, 6)

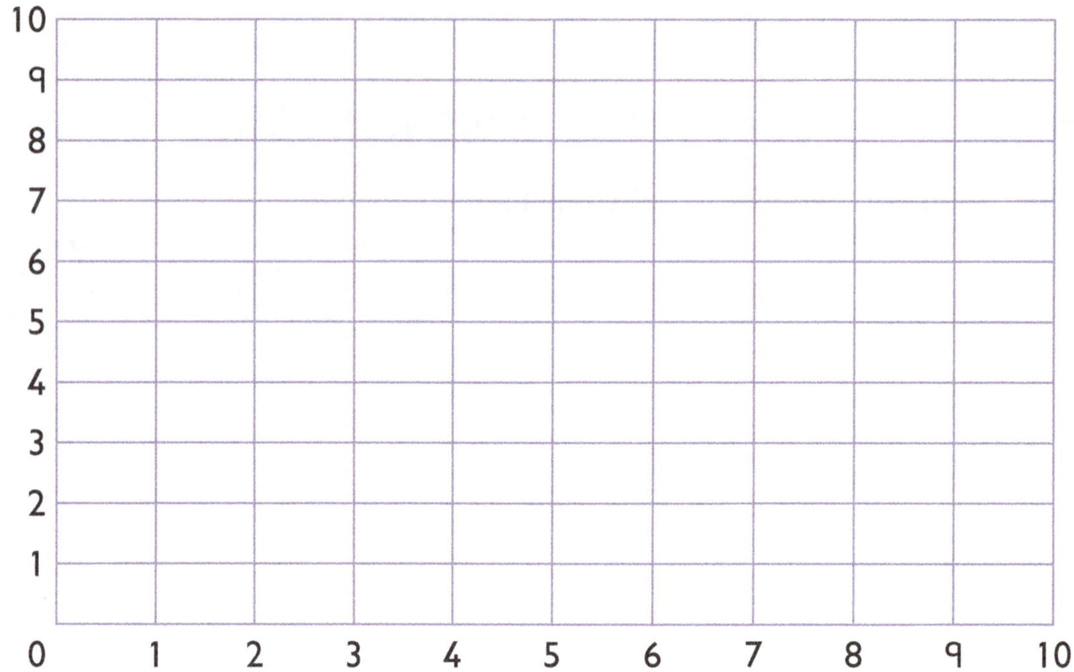

(b) (2, 6), (4, 6), (2, 4), (2, 2)

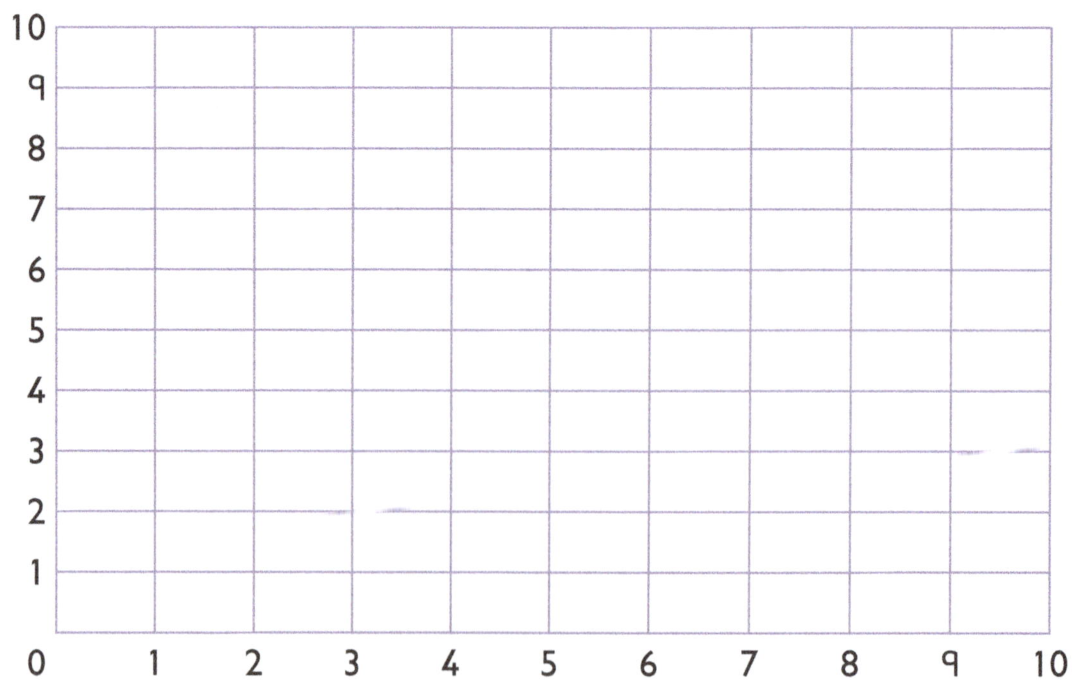

(c) (1, 6), (2, 3), (5, 4), (6, 7), (3, 8)

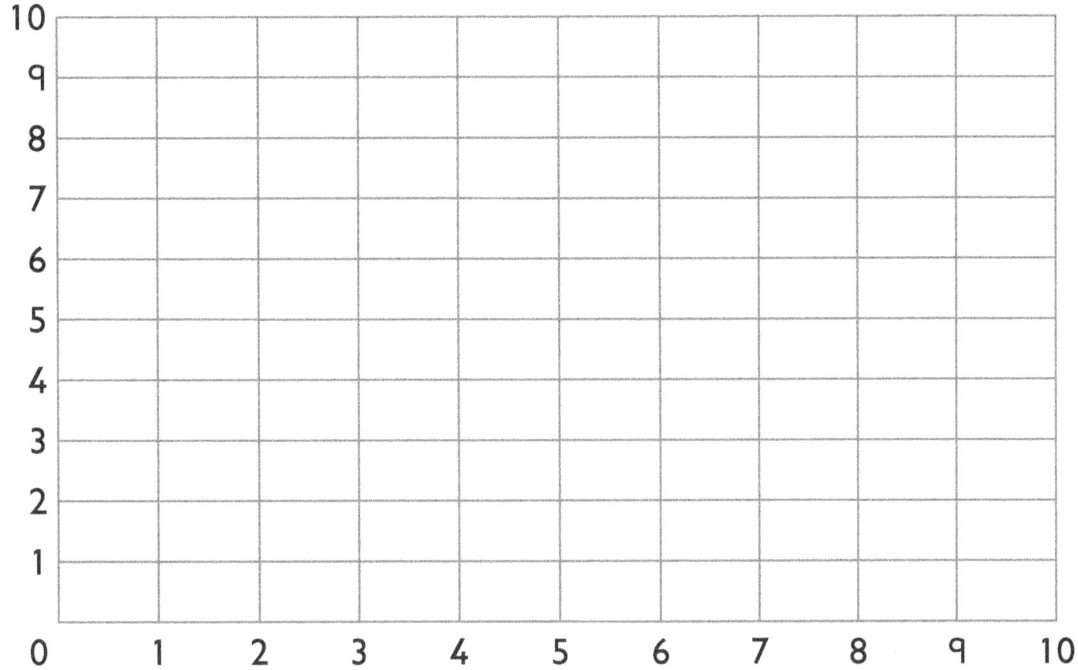

(d) (4, 7), (6, 5), (4, 1), (2, 5)

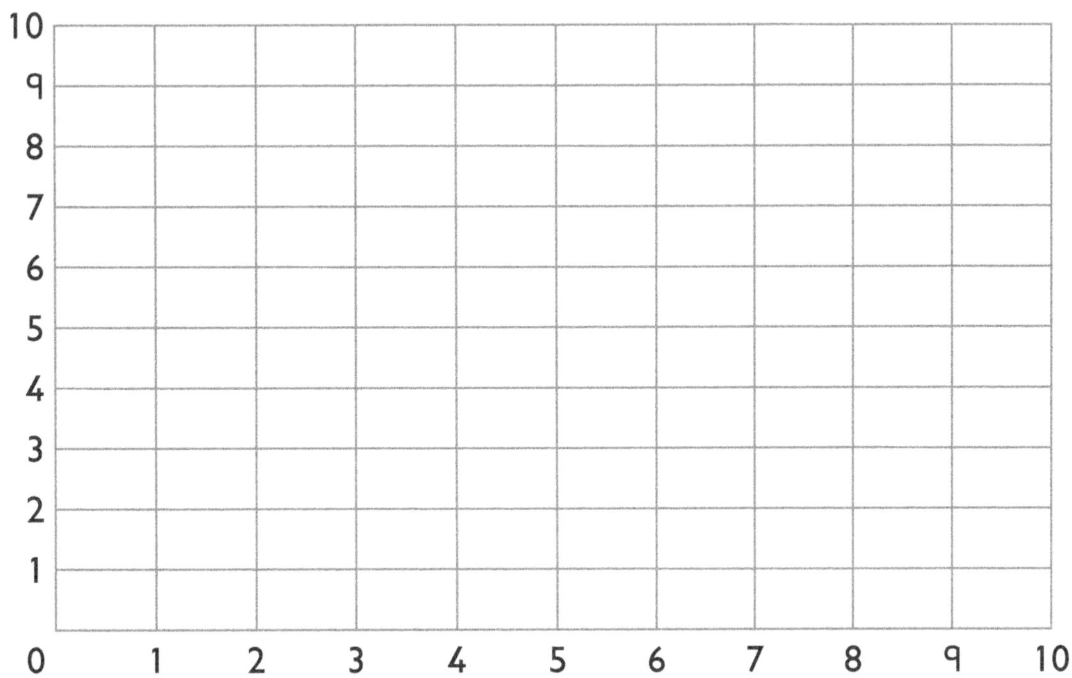

Practice 2: Reflection

Draw the reflection in the mirror line.

(a)

(b)

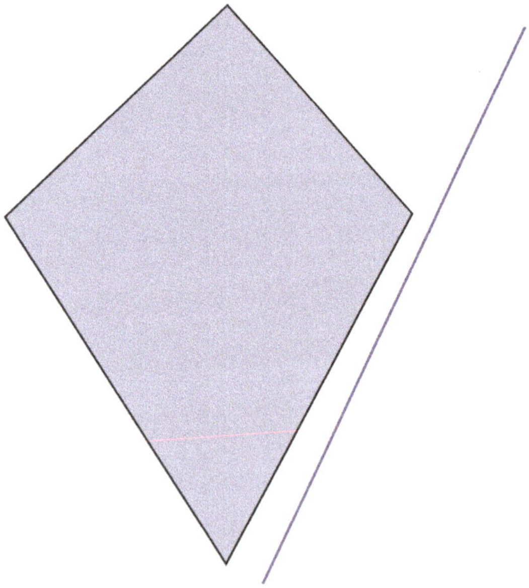

(c)

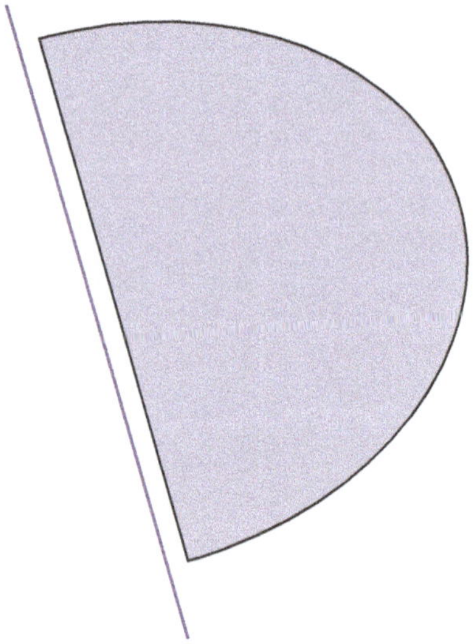

(d)

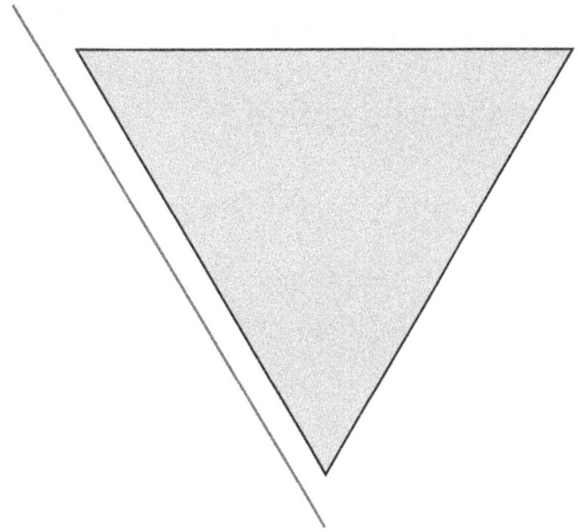

(e)

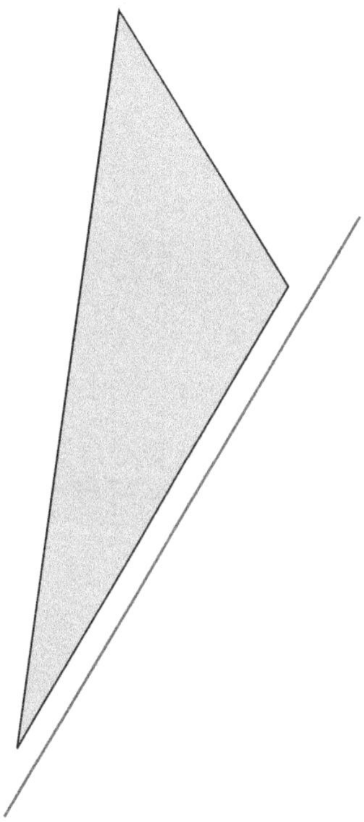

(f)

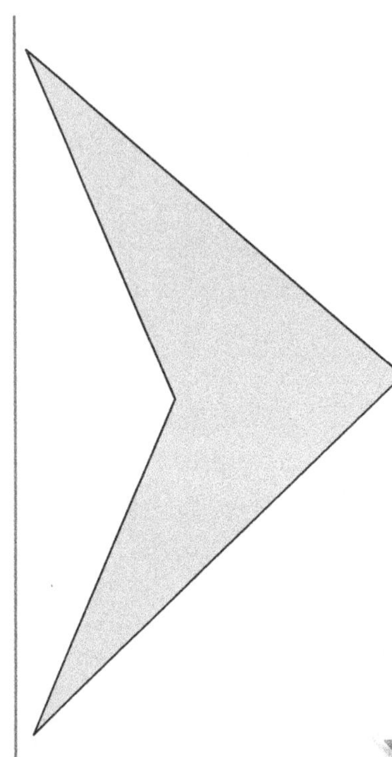

Practice 3: Translation

Draw the translated shape.

(a) Translate the square 3 squares to the right.

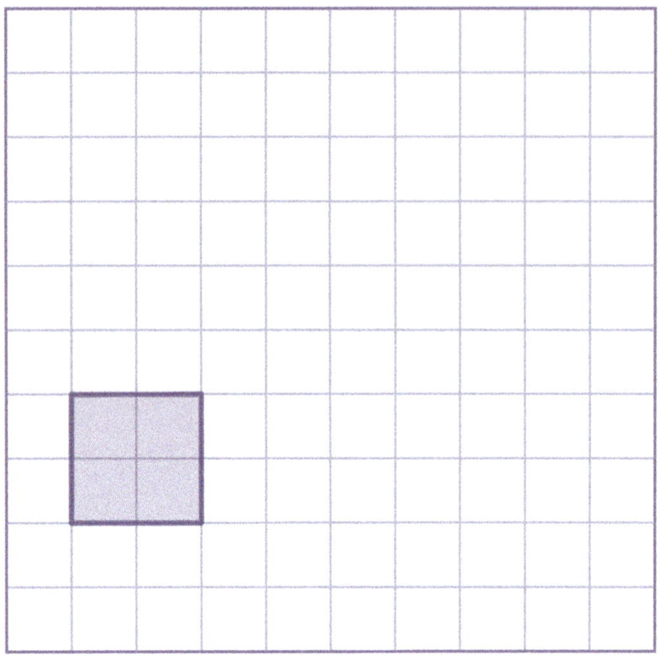

(b) Translate the triangle 2 squares up.

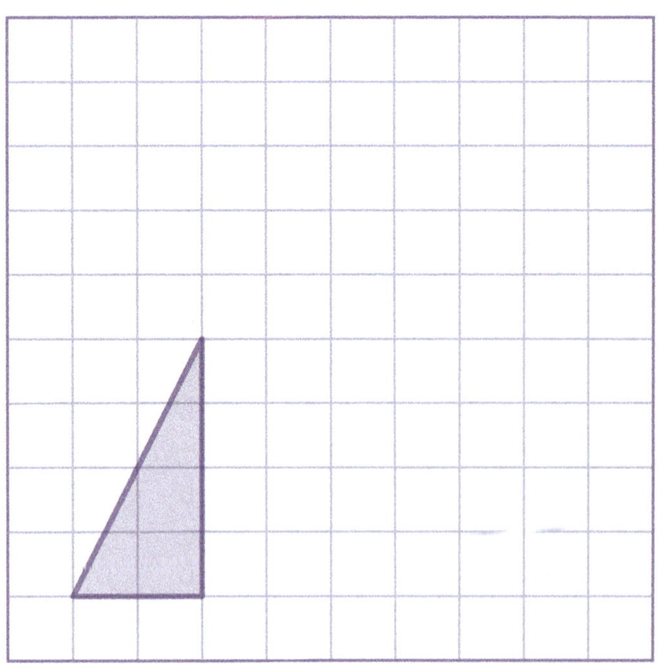

(c) Translate the rectangle 5 squares down.

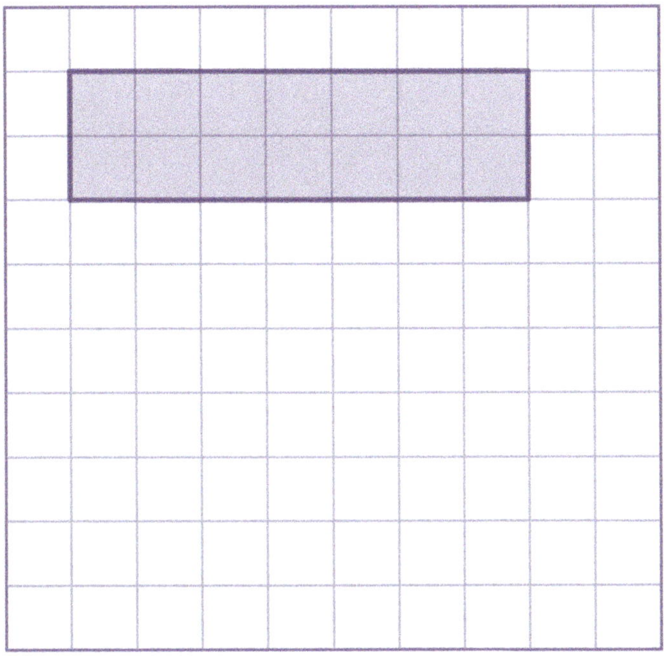

(d) Translate the triangle 2 squares to the left.

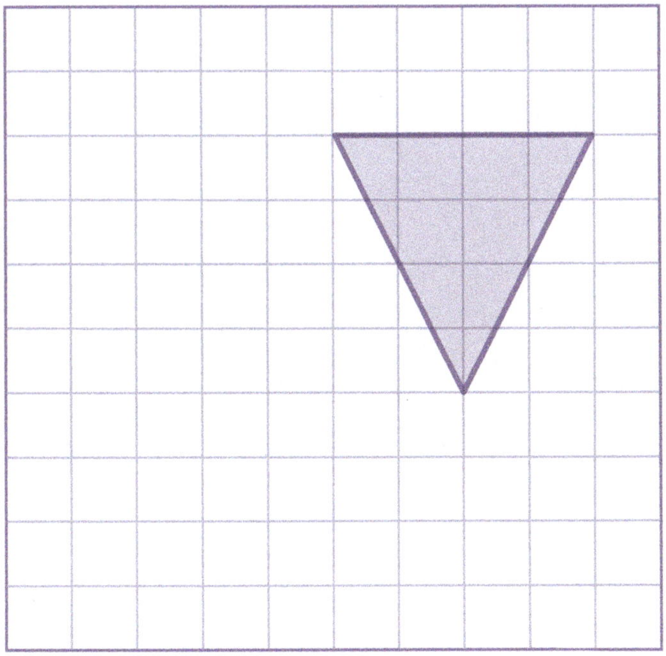